# More Praise for *I*

"This is the creative nonfiction guide we've been waiting for—as informed and thoughtful as a D'Agata or Lopate anthology, but with the practical and generous perspective of a writer who's done it all, from teaching to journalism to online curation, Julia Goldberg's new book, *Inside Story*, offers a uniquely ideal combination of personal perspective, practical examples, inspiring anecdotes from literary history, and a whole host of helpful challenges and prompts. I'd trust any writer and editor whose trunk was once filled to the brim with yellow notepads."

—**Nathan Deuel**, author of *Friday Was the Bomb: Five Years in the Middle East*

"*Inside Story* has at least two features no other craft book does. I love its section on reporting. And I am passionately enthusiastic about its generative discussion of the various shapes an essay or article might take. It rejects merely linear form as well as journalistic or academic prescriptions. This is the perfect book for beginning and advanced writers of creative nonfiction, and I will use it in my classroom."

—**Debra Monroe**, author of *My Unsentimental Education*

"Julia Goldberg's *Inside Story* is so much more than a genius book about craft, although it's the most accessible and enjoyable book about craft I've ever read. This book is for teachers, of course, but it's also for writers who are looking, in their own work, to unpack and better understand the increasingly popular but unwieldy, ever-evolving, and occasionally controversial genre of creative nonfiction. Goldberg blends her unique humor, practical insights from her many years as a journalist, and her own unique mastery of the craft in a book that will no doubt be a staple in college classrooms—and on the shelves of writers—for years to come."

—**Emily Rapp Black**, author of *The Still Point of the Turning World*

"With an approachable, engaging style, Goldberg delivers a ream of practical advice from working professionals and illustrative anecdotes from her own experience as a reporter and editor. *Inside Story* provides all of the essential information a beginning nonfiction writer needs without ever feeling like a textbook."

—**Gwyneth Doland**, correspondent, New Mexico PBS

"Creative nonfiction has a siren call for writers—it's a way to unflinchingly examine ourselves and our worlds. But it is a difficult pursuit. Julia Goldberg has made that pursuit easier, more productive, and more likely with her new book, *Inside Story*. Witty, incisive, and full of brilliance, she takes a clear and detailed look at the makings of both journalism and memoir. Goldberg's distinctive, intelligent voice makes reading *Inside Story* like having a personal writing teacher at your side."

—**Miriam Sagan**, author of *Map of the Lost* and *Tanka from the Edge*

"I don't know how I could like Julia Goldberg's *Inside Story* any more than I do. As a teacher, I will use this book as a primer for all my students who want to write for any form of journalism and media. As a writer, I will keep *Inside Story* nearby to remind myself of the vital issues of craft and technique as I compose and revise. To put it plainly: If you want to write creative nonfiction, this book is essential."

—**Robert Wilder**, author of *Daddy Needs a Drink*,
*Tales from the Teachers' Lounge*, and *Nickel*

"In the wise and thoroughly entertaining *Inside Story*, Julia Goldberg divulges the many truths of nonfiction writing, any one of which should be of immense help to writers embarking upon projects of most any genre. But beyond being a hands-on, practical guide to the craft of writing, it's also a smart, honest, and most deliciously irreverent dispatch from the real world of writing from a real-world writer."

—**T Cooper**, author of *Real Man Adventures* and *Changers*

"You have to love a how-to book that begins with the promise of a blow job. You have to love it even more when you realize that it's exactly the book you've been waiting to give to all your reporters, both beginning and advanced, to teach the former and remind the latter that while writing is indeed a noble art, it's also a craft that can, and should, be practiced and polished. Julia Goldberg's smart, funny book is the ideal guide. And that's no blow job."

—**Patricia Calhoun**, editor of *Westword*

"If you want real-world tools for becoming a standout nonfiction writer, look no further than this book. Instead of giving you platitudes from an ivory tower, Julia Goldberg dishes out the hard-earned wisdom she picked up from working fifteen years in the trenches of alternative journalism. If you're serious about a career as a writer, my advice is to take this book home, pour yourself a stiff drink, and prepare to get schooled by one of the most bad-ass editors to have worked in the alt-weekly industry."

—**Jason Zaragoza**, Executive Director, Association of Alternative Newsmedia

# INSIDE STORY

# INSIDE STORY

## EVERYONE'S GUIDE TO REPORTING
## AND WRITING CREATIVE NONFICTION

### JULIA GOLDBERG

Published by Leaf Storm Press
Post Office Box 4670
Santa Fe, NM 87502
U.S.A.
leafstormpress.com

Acquisitions Editor: Sarah Stark
Copy Editor: Maya Myers
Indexer: Diana Plattner

The following material is reprinted with permission:
"An Index for *Bi the Book: How to Become Bisexual in Less Than a Month*," by Chelsey
    Clammer, *The Drunken Odyssey*, November 2014. Copyright Chelsey Clammer.
"On Finding True Love and Deserving Happiness," by Emily Rapp Black, Feb. 11, 2015.
    This essay originally appeared on *Role Reboot*, an online magazine about living life
    off-script.
"Wrinkles and Time," by Julia Goldberg, Feb. 19, 2012, the *Rumpus*.
"On What Matters: An Interview with Noam Chomsky," by Julia Goldberg, *Santa Fe
    Reporter*, January 19, 2005.
"Daddy Needs a Drink: Eat, Drink, Man, Woman," by Robert Wilder, *Santa Fe Reporter*,
    May 7, 2008.
The Code of Ethics of the Society of Professional Journalists

Leaf Storm logos are trademarks of Leaf Storm Press LLC.

First edition
Book design by Alan Dino Hebel and Ian Shimkoviak, *The*BookDesigners

Printed in Canada

10  9  8  7  6  5  4  3  2

Library of Congress Control Number 2016944261
Publisher's Cataloging-in-Publication Data

Names: Goldberg, Julia R.
Title: Inside story : everyone's guide to reporting and writing creative nonfiction / Julia
    Goldberg.
Description: Santa Fe : Leaf Storm Press, 2017 | Includes bibliographical references and
    index.
Identifiers: LCCN 2016944261 | ISBN 978-0-9970207-7-9 (pbk.) | ISBN 978-0-9970207-6-2
    (Kindle ebook)
Subjects: LCSH: Creative nonfiction--Authorship. | Reportage literature--Authorship. |
    Journalism--Authorship. | Interviewing in journalism. | Narration (Rhetoric)--Study
    and teaching.| BISAC: LANGUAGE ARTS & DISCIPLINES / Journalism. | LAN-
    GUAGE ARTS & DISCIPLINES / Authorship. | REFERENCE / Writing Skills.
Classification: LCC PN145 .G63 2016 (print) | LCC PN145 (ebook) | DDC 808.066--dc23.

*for my family*

# CONTENTS

# INTRODUCTION

The courage to be a writer is, in a sense, the courage to be an individual, no matter what the consequences.

—**Erica Jong,** *The Devil at Large*

Successful writers are not the ones who write the best sentences. They are the ones who keep writing.

—**Bonnie Friedman,** *Writing Past Dark*

I
N SOME WAYS, this book began with a blow job.

Not an actual blow job.

Maybe this story works better with some context.

For close to eleven years, I was the editor of the *Santa Fe Reporter*, an alternative newsweekly in Santa Fe, New Mexico, founded in 1974. Like most alt weeklies around the country, *SFR* was created as an "alternative" to the "mainstream" press. I am using quotation marks because the industry has changed too much to take these terms for granted, but still, today, alt weeklies retain vestiges of that time period through their allegiance to long-form narrative journalism and their willingness to publish profanity (among other characteristics).

I learned journalism on the job. I began as an intern at the *Reporter*, and later became a staff writer there and at the community weekly, the *Rio Grande Sun*. I freelanced for a variety of local and national publications. I also attended and received a degree from the University of New Mexico's graduate creative writing program.

Shortly after I left the *Reporter* in April 2011, I began teaching writing at a variety of local colleges, and soon full-time at Santa Fe University of Art and Design. The school's Creative Writing and Literature Department was interested in creating more publishing opportunities, and so I helped design some journalism curriculum and the online student magazine, which I now team-teach each semester as a class.

Before that happened, I taught a feeder class to the magazine—and, yes, the blow job story is coming shortly.

One day, at the end of class, a student turned in to me a feature piece she had written. Picture a fresh-faced, very talented and earnest young college student who said to me (and I quote from memory):

"Will you let me know if this story is a blow job?"

At that point, it occurred to me that perhaps I needed to use some sort of textbook in my classes and not rely solely on my own newsroom vocabulary for instructional purposes.[1]

I perused numerous journalism textbooks, but in addition to being expensive, none seemed the right fit for my classes. I found several smaller books that provided some helpful ideas and guidance (*Telling True Stories* from the Nieman Foundation at Harvard University is a particular favorite). Portions of *Tell It Slant* (Brenda Miller and Suzanne Paola) were helpful, and I utilized the book in the introductory nonfiction course I teach in which the students also write memoirs and lyric essays. But what I couldn't find was the book that captured my own experiences, ideas, and influences. Because I am slow, it took me several years to realize I might actually need to write the book that

---

1    In journalism vernacular, a "blow job" is a piece of writing in which the author's critical judgment of his or her subject appears to have been replaced with a categorical desire to stroke the subject's ego.

said what I wanted it to say. This is that attempt.

Hybrids are popular now in both writing and media, and this book is itself a bit of a hybrid, incorporating memoir, craft lessons, interviews, and exercise suggestions I have found useful in my own classrooms. My hope is this book will be useful to anyone who is interested in learning or teaching aspects of creative non-fiction, be it reportage or otherwise. Writing nonfiction is not as complicated as, say, building a nuclear warhead (I assume this is complicated, at any rate), but its moving parts are many, and the lens through which its practice is viewed are myriad.

I have been lucky over the years to meet and work with many talented practitioners, and their insights, examples, and work have been paramount in my own ongoing education. I have called upon many of them to share their thoughts and expertise in this book. I have also included numerous examples and thoughts from other published works, and from writers I admire and have learned from on the page. Many of the chapters in this book also include writing and reporting prompts to practice and generate work, as well as resources for further reading.

Speaking of writers: In March 2016, I attended the annual Association of Writers & Writing Programs (AWP) Conference & Bookfair, held that year in Los Angeles. *Publishers Weekly* later reported twelve thousand people, writer-people, had attended. The book fair featured eight hundred exhibitors—magazines, presses, MFA programs—and the programming included hundreds and hundreds of sessions on everything from craft to publishing to teaching writing.

If this sounds exciting, I suppose it was. It also was exhausting, both physically and existentially. I found myself having a quiet sushi lunch with an old friend in a mostly deserted restaurant, talking about writing. Another friend had told me she had grown to dislike attending AWP because it made her feel insecure and depressed. I should say the friend who said that is extremely successful as a writer, not to mention talented. I was having a pretty good time, loading up my swag bag with books and notebooks, attending readings and book signings, and witnessing a thriving literary community.

I understood, though, my friend's comment about the insecurity-fostering quality of the environment. Writing is work, and even when it goes well, it has a Sisyphean quality to it. (The year before at AWP, I had sat in an auditorium for a panel on "rejection," packed to the rafters, in which one panelist had offered up, as an example of writerly rejection, *The Diary of Anne Frank*. I'm not entirely sure what the takeaway from that example was supposed to be, but, needless to say, there are worse things that can happen to a person than having one's work rejected.)

As I sat in the sushi bar with my friend, I confessed to her that I had never really liked the idea of identifying myself as a "writer." It seems elitist to me, as if a writer is some sort of "born that way" person, and a person either is one or isn't. For me, it also produces a fair amount of guilt. Writers write, so can one be a writer if one is having trouble writing? Is it writer's block or just laziness? Can't I just be a person who writes, sometimes for work, sometimes for pleasure, sometimes not at all?

I share this not particularly profound experience because I am fairly certain that many people who write, or who want to write, or who will decide at some point to write something, will struggle with the same questions I have regarding authenticity and inspiration. For any number of reasons, writing seems to be one of the creative pursuits about which people privilege notions of inspiration and talent over those of study and discipline. This is why, for all the training and writing experience I've had, I still think the best advice I ever received (as a teenager, from someone I can no longer name) was, "If you want to be a writer, keep writing." This is a variation of the advice quoted from the late *New York Times* writer David Carr at the opening of chapter 1.

Yes, there are certainly some writers, living and dead, who manage without study or editors to produce awe-inspiring works. But most of us have to work on our craft. By way of analogy, Yo-Yo Ma is obviously a born musical genius, but he is said to have days in which he practices for hours.[2]

Since I've brought up Yo-Yo Ma, I'll share his exact quote about practicing, which applies to writing as well:

"Mastering music is more than learning technical skills. Practicing is about quality, not quantity. Some days I practice for hours; other days it will be just a few minutes. Practicing is not only playing your instrument, either by yourself or rehearsing with others—it also includes imagining yourself practicing. Your brain forms the same neural connections and muscle memory whether you are imagining the task or actually doing it."[3]

Practicing writing also is about more than technical skills, although those technical skills can't be overrated or overlooked. Spending time thinking about writing, reading as much as possible, and courting inspiration are all part of the amalgam.

Part of courting inspiration is learning what makes you excited to write. Perhaps you are constantly excited to write. If so, lucky you! Perhaps you will never have one moment in which you don't feel like writing (if so, you should maybe ask for a refund on this book). Otherwise, chances are, you will experience times in which the writing comes slowly or not at all. You will have days of feeling guilty because you think you "should be writing." You will write something awful and wonder if you should have just gone to law school after all. I am inspired when I read books or articles or essays that have energy and wit. Reading great writing makes me want to write. Grief can catalyze creative energy; supposedly joy can as well. Ambition does

---

2    Anderman, Joan, "Yo-Yo Ma and the Mind Game of Music," *New York Times*, October 10, 2013, http://www.nytimes.com/2013/10/10/booming/yo-yo-ma-and-the-mind-game-of-music.html.

3    Ibid.

it for some folks; envy for others.

This, of course, is why people enjoy reading about writers' lives, habits, and techniques—because they are trying to find methods that will work for them. But there is not, of course, an actual formula. It's not as if "real writers" all wake at 5 a.m. and walk out to a stand-alone shed, work for exactly 4.3 hours each day and, thus, produce astonishing work. The only real trick is that to produce writing, one must write on a regular basis, seek feedback, and learn how to revise. Ideally, one also will be a capacious reader and become a generous critic.

Starting a new writing project and persevering through the writing process can be challenging, but perhaps the most diffi-cult task is to know when a piece of writing is finished.

My advice is to just go ahead and type a final sentence.

—Julia Goldberg, MARCH 2017

# CHAPTER ONE

# The Blank Page

There are zillions of ideas out there—they stream by like neutrons.

—**John McPhee,** *Paris Review*

Keep typing until it turns into writing.

—**David Carr**[4]

SOME OF MY students enter their first creative nonfiction class under the impression that there isn't much that's creative about nonfiction. As best I can tell, this is the result of writing research and term papers in high school and, perhaps, of having been assigned topics for these papers in which they had little if any interest. I have some sympathy. For a brief period, right after I stopped being a newspaper editor, I taught a few freshman composition classes wherein students were required to write papers arguing, for example, the pros and cons of topics

---

4    I think Carr said this often, but in the interest of sourcing the quote, here's a link to the Reddit thread where it's been sourced previously: https://www.reddit.com/r/IAmA/comments/16k598/iama_columnist_and_reporter_on_media_and_culture.

such as the US Social Security system. I am an active reader and an energetic editor, but even I didn't want to read much on this topic, nor would I want to sit around researching it.

Fortunately, very few publications are actively looking for such pieces. What they are often looking for, in the case of literary magazines, is creative nonfiction, whether rooted in memoir, reportage, or the more genre-bending creative nonfiction generally classified as the *lyric essay*. In the case of journalism, while this field certainly can include the standard, inverted pyramid, daily reporting story you might find on the front page of the *New York Times*, journalistic writing on the whole is far more expansive and creative than that, both in its long-form literary and non-narrative forms.

What all of these various categories and subcategories of writing have in common is their rooting, at various ends of the spectrum, in the real rather than imagined world. This doesn't mean, however, that nonfiction is antifiction, any more than it is antipoetry; creative nonfiction may, and often does, draw on the techniques from both of those genres, while still relying on the fact-finding, idea-pondering and reporting methodologies of classic nonfiction categories such as philosophy, journalism, and biography.

In John McPhee's *Paris Review* interview, from which this paragraph's opening epigraph is taken, the prolific writer[5] talks about how, as a new staff writer for the *New Yorker* in the 1960s, he would ask friends for story ideas. As he notes, ideas are everywhere, but part of finding story ideas is recognizing one's own interests and propensities. "What makes somebody pluck forth one thing—a thing you're going to be spending as much as three years with?" McPhee asks in the interview, answering that, for him, "If I went down a list of all the pieces I ever had in the *New Yorker*, upward of 90 percent would relate to things I did when I was a kid."

---

5    McPhee, currently in his eighties, has written approximately thirty books.

Journalists rely on a variety of methods for finding stories, but talking to people and developing sources, which I'll talk more about in the chapter on developing beats, is certainly a primary method. Creative nonfiction pieces can also come from exploring one's memories and ideas, writing in response to other works of art, such as literature, and, of course, from prompts. Creative nonfiction isn't the easiest term—and there are many who would rather use any other term to describe their work—but since it's the overall genre term I'm used to using, consider it a broad one to contain numerous subgenres of writing that are all based in the idea of writing that takes as its inspiration the real world.

## SOME APPROACHES

To list all potential types of creative nonfiction seems exhausting. Moreover, many of the subgenres overlap in various ways. For example, Emily Rapp Black's essay, "On Finding True Love and Deserving Happiness," included at the end of this chapter, is partially a work of memoir but also a meditation on grief that partakes in the tradition of the essay as an act of contemplation. My essay at the end of this chapter, "Wrinkles and Time," also has elements of memoir, while incorporating elements of cultural and academic criticism. With that said, the rest of this chapter considers those types of creative nonfiction under the brackets of

- Personal narrative
- Reportage
- Criticism and arts writing
- Hybrid forms, such as the lyric essay
- Idea-driven, opinion, and satirical writing

The chapter also provides an overview of some of the techniques that will be discussed at greater length throughout the book, as well as a few parting thoughts on writing habits.

····*Personal Narrative*

My first-year creative nonfiction students' initial assignment is
to write a short memoir. I start with memoir because it's possible (though not necessary) to write in the memoir tradition
simply by relying on one's own memory. This, too, is an exercise
in reporting, but in reporting on one's own recollections. I don't
want to promulgate false dichotomies, but one way to delineate
certain modes in creative nonfiction is to think of the internal
and the external. Memories, ideas, and associations come from
the way in which we internally remember, order, and value our
experiences and knowledge. External elements, then, are those
in writing that are more firmly documented in the outside world.

Most of my students seem to find it relatively easy to recall
the one story about their pasts they want to share. There is always
at least one student who feels uncomfortable writing about him
or herself. I rely, when talking about memoir, a great deal on the
advice of William Zinsser, whose book *Writing About Your Life*
remains a classic guide on how to approach memoir. Zinsser's
main message is to keep it small; don't try to write about everything at once. Pick one thing. When I was editor of the *Reporter*,
I used to annoy reporters a great deal by asking them to tell
me in one sentence what their stories were about. This is the
difference between a story and a topic: a story has a trajectory,
an arc; it's not a laundry list of everything known about a topic.
Similarly, with memoir pieces, keeping them tight and on point
is the main challenge writers face (although not, by any means,
the only challenge).

As the nonfiction editor of the *Nervous Breakdown*, I read
quite a lot of memoirs and memoir excerpts and remain awed by
the diversity of life stories out there. I am also very fond of the
"self-interviews" the writers conduct that are part of TNB's features, and run accompanying the excerpts. Memoirs do not necessarily have to be rooted in a story of trauma, although many

certainly are. Many of the memoirs I've read with pleasure over the last few years meld a personal narrative and a quest for understanding with reported information that supports both.

David Stuart MacLean's memoir, *The Answer to the Riddle Is Me*, details the amnesia MacLean suffered as the result of the anti-malaria medication he took when he went to India. It is a wonderful reported memoir that explores MacLean's terrifying experience of losing his memory along with the reported story of the drug Lariam and the wide impact it had on soldiers. I've assigned MacLean's book to my students for several semesters, and all were struck by the way in which MacLean was able to integrate his own harrowing personal journey with reportage of his own life (as necessitated by the amnesia) and of Lariam itself.

In *Harley and Me: Embracing Risk on the Road to a More Authentic Life*, Bernadette Murphy tells the story of embarking with a friend on a cross-country motorcycle trip in the wake of both their marriages ending. The book is a story of friendship as well as an examination of taking risks and confronting one's fears. As such, Murphy relied not only on her own experiences and impressions but also, she says in her self-interview, on a great deal of "research into the neuroscience and psychology of risk taking."

While the prospect of a book-length memoir may seem daunting, many authors I've spoken with found their way toward book length memoirs by working in pieces.

Nathan Deuel's *Friday Was the Bomb* recounts Deuel's five years living in the Middle East as the primary caretaker for his daughter, while his wife, an NPR correspondent, covered conflicts in the region as the Baghdad bureau chief. I interviewed Deuel twice when his book was published in 2014, and we discussed the propulsive nature of the story's arc, even though it was in fact a series of essays. "It kind of came out of nowhere that it might hold together as a book," he told me. "I knew a press was looking for essay collections; I started cutting and pasting and the aggregate looked like a book."

The three memoirs I've just mentioned primarily are set during the authors' adult lives; many memoirs also encompass biographical material beyond the author's scope of memory. Consider this excerpt from Emily Rapp Black's lauded first memoir, *Poster Child*:

> I believe that deep in my memory I hold this image of my mother behind the glass, sending me a kiss and looking at me as if I were the most precious and beautiful baby in the world. Although these circumstances of my birth are factual, it's difficult for me to imagine the scenes: being talked about in the maternity ward; being different, feared but pitied, classified as deformed. But this look, this look of love—this gift—I can easily imagine, because I would know it for the rest of my life.

In the scene quoted above, Rapp Black reimagines the scene of her mother blowing her a kiss through the glass windows of the newborns' room at the hospital shortly after learning that Rapp Black had been born with a congenital defect that eventually resulted in the amputation of her left foot. Rapp Black, in her writing, is transparent about what she can and can't remember, and actively distinguishes these memories for the reader.

Rapp Black's memoir also began as a series of essays she wrote when she was an MFA student and James A. Michener fellow at the University of Texas, Austin. Rapp Black had been writing fiction at the time when it was suggested to her that her material might work in a nonfiction piece.

"I was like, 'what's nonfiction?' I kind of knew what it was, but I didn't think much about it because I was writing fiction, so I took a class and I started writing it. It was the first time I had ever written about having a disability in any focused way, which I thought I was doing in fiction, but all the characters were really clichéd." Telling her story in nonfiction, Rapp Black says, "was a lesson to me if you have a story that's yours, telling it in nonfiction makes more sense than thinly veiling it as fiction." Black ended up writing three essays for that class, and two more in the next nonfiction class she took. "I had maybe 120 pages or something like that, and my teacher at the time was like, 'I think it's a book; I'd like to send it to my agent. Work on a synopsis.'" Rapp Black ended up selling the book and ultimately finishing the memoir.

Her second nonfiction book, *The Still Point of the Turning World*, is both memoir and meditation on the grief she experienced when her young son, Ronan, was diagnosed with the terminal and devastating Tay-Sachs disease. In that case, Rapp Black had no intention of writing a book, but had, at the urging of friends, begun a blog after his diagnosis.

"I didn't intend anyone to read it except for the people who were calling me on the phone, and I wasn't answering my phone," Rapp Black said. She began writing on the blog regularly. "At the time, I was doing a lot of writing anyway. I was really open and really sad and didn't know what to do with myself, so I started writing essays; they became a lifeline to my mind and I couldn't stop. I was writing these 5,000-word essays on my blog, and my friends were reading it and more people were reading it." Eventually, a friend suggested to Rapp Black that there was a book in what she had written and, indeed, from the hundreds of pages, a less narrative but more "thematically structured" book emerged. "My editor and agent helped me a lot with the structure because the material was so fresh it was difficult to organize. It's hard for everyone, but in this case I especially didn't know how to organize the material."

Rapp Black also has written extensively for a variety of magazines and anthologies, with much of her work focusing on grief and death. When I was talking to her for this book, she was exploring writing about the topic of resilience, as a concept, because of her own personal experiences and what she describes as her critical stance toward the standard "survivor narrative."

Ultimately, she says, much of what she has written comes from her own life, but more importantly, from considering its larger meaning. This, she says, is the challenge in personal nonfiction. "You have to be aware of what's going on in the world and how things strike you. Historically, crappy things have happened to me so I've written about them, but in terms of finding ideas, people have to go out and have experiences. They don't have to be traumatic, but they have to be in the world somehow and be interested in the world. Especially with nonfiction, inspiration is everywhere, but it's because you're thinking about the world as a writer and an observer; it's about attentiveness."

While many memoirs follow a linear structure, memoir can also be an element of other types of writing. Daniel Nester has described his recent book, *Shader: 99 Notes on Car Washes, Making Out in Church, Grief, and Other Unlearnable Subjects*, as "a memoir of linked essays." The book collects ninety-nine essays he wrote on his website for 99 days. In a self-interview for the *Nervous Breakdown*, Nester describes the project as one inspired by Susan Sontag's essay, "Notes on Camp," saying he "wanted to be as smart as Susan Sontag, so I used her title convention and format. I did not become the next Susan Sontag, but I did write ninety-nine essays, and it was fun to write in a segmented, numbered format."

To write memoir, one should, conceivably, have a story to tell, but also a firm grounding in other memoirs on similar topics. Rapp Black says she tells her students to "read memoirs about what you're writing about to see how you're going to do it differently."

#### ····*Reportage*

To some degree, drawing a line between types of creative nonfiction creates a false divide, as if some nonfiction writing is purely based on memory and other types of writing require research.

In reality, much of the most powerful writing blends the internal and external to some degree, whether it's the internal focus of the writer shaping a story about someone else or the external context the writer provides to his or her own personal story. In many ways, this blend is what people are thinking about when they reference the "literary journalists" of the late 1960s and 1970s, writers like John McPhee, Joan Didion, and Hunter S. Thompson. Although most of these writers are often admired for style and voice, they also broke new ground by blending those aspects of writing with their own observations and reportage of topics ranging from agriculture to California to politics. My own love of journalism was born from reading such writers, whose narrative abilities drew me into topics I might otherwise not have known or cared about.

Contemporary writers working in the genre most commonly described as memoir continue in this tradition. MacLean's book, though very much a personal narrative about a very specific individual experience, includes tremendous research on the drug Lariam; Rapp Black's story of her son's short life delves extensively into the harrowing world of Tay-Sachs disease. Each semester, I usually teach a classic example of blended memoir and reportage, Jo Ann Beard's famous essay "Fourth State of Matter." The essay is ostensibly about the mass shooting of Beard's colleagues—including a close friend—in the Physics Department at the University of Iowa in the early 1990s. The essay is usually (rightfully) praised for its associative qualities, as Beard weaves together the horror of the shooting with her own personal narratives (a dying dog, an estranged husband, a squirrel infestation). But the piece also artfully integrates reportage of the central event of the shooting—letters written by the shooter, for example. Leslie Jamison's essay collection, *The Empathy Exams*, similarly melds Jamison's reportage on a wide variety of topics (from Morgellons disease to reality television) with her reported and remembered observations and personal narratives.

Reported nonfiction may also include more straightforward journalistic endeavors such as investigative and breaking news writing. In chapter 3 on beat reporting, I speak with writers whose dedicated coverage of various fields feeds their work in these areas. If I could snap my fingers and make everyone do what I say,[6] I'd have every aspiring writer spend at least a year as a beat reporter at a small publication. Daily interviewing, writing on deadline, and turning out stories on a daily/weekly/monthly basis is a difficult experience to replicate on one's own, but invaluable. In his *Paris Review* interview, John McPhee, who is certainly a master practitioner of long-form literary journalism, characterizes his seven years at *Time*, which included five years reporting for the show business section, like this: "The sheer business of turning out five structured stories, however short they were, every week, was excellent training for me." From there, McPhee went on to become a staff writer at the *New Yorker*, where hundreds of his pieces have appeared since the early 1960s.

## ••••*Criticism and Other Arts Writing*

Ekphrasis is a poetry term used to describe writing that describes a work of art. It's a decent term to keep in mind when contemplating arts writing, as regardless of the type of art (visual, music, books), description is a foundational element. Arts writing can take many different forms—interviews, reviews, analysis, criticism—and it's an excellent go-to area when looking for subjects, as someone is always creating something worth writing about.

In his book *Criticizing Art: Understanding the Contemporary*, Professor Terry Barrett explains a "popular misconception" about arts writing is that it "is primarily judgmental and negative

---

6    a frequent fantasy in many realms

in tone; in actuality, most of the words written by critics are descriptive and interpretive rather than judgmental." Indeed, many of the art critics whose work I admire the most are less concerned with determining thumbs up or down, but in educating and determining a work's importance. I've been somewhat addicted for many years to NPR's *Pop Culture Happy Hour*, in large part because it's more interesting to me to think about why certain shows, books, or albums are interesting than it is to read a scathing movie review (although sometimes the latter can be fun, too).

Barrett's work informs a bit of how I ask students to critique each other's arts writing and revise their own, by providing four major elements within a piece of criticism: description of the work itself, analysis of how the piece works, reflection on its meaning and judgment about its success within the parameters already discussed.

Writing about the arts is an excellent entry point when searching for material, as movies, books, plays, and art are both plentiful and accessible to all. The best critics, though, work to not just pass judgment but to explicate the works for their audiences. My colleague novelist James Reich reviews books for the *Rumpus* and describes literary criticism as an act in which "The critic owes the writer a reading with depth and intensity, at least insofar as the writer has written with those qualities, but this is also something that the critic owes the broad audience." If "the work is done well," Reich says, "the critic suggests strategies for reading, and approaches that come from a particular engagement with literature and culture that might be distinct from the broader audience of the magazine. The critic should reveal subterranean qualities, not simply list the surface qualities of a work. I read as a writer, and believe in the proverb 'set a thief to catch a thief.' In other words, lazy reviews, platitudes, and orthodox reviewspeak don't serve us, so one should approach every work as we would want our own work approached."

Jon Frosch, reviews editor for the *Hollywood Reporter*, also served as film editor and critic at *France 24* and has written for the *New York Times*, the *Atlantic*, and numerous other publications (including the *Santa Fe Reporter*, back in the day). He describes a successful film critic as one who loves not just film, but writing as well. "There are plenty of folks with encyclopedic knowledge of film history and technique," Frosch says, "but if you can't compellingly express your opinion, you're only halfway there. So I think I've tried to keep this in mind throughout my career: yes, it's important to be a student, a scholar of film history, to keep watching movies, to try and go back and fill in gaps in my film knowledge (every critic has such gaps), to see as much as possible, including from genres and countries and periods that are less familiar or comfortable to me; but it's also important to continue to try to be the very best writer I can be—to push myself to craft each sentence, to find fresh ways to phrase things, to not fall back on clichés or overly convenient word choices, to edit myself (adjectives and adverbs are crucial tools for a critic, but we all overuse them), to try to convey my take on a movie with force, precision, humor (when it's appropriate) and sincerity. To have a voice."

Frosch was generous enough to describe for me, in writing, his process for film reviewing:

> Once I know what film I'm reviewing, I'll do some research. That consists of watching or rewatching (if my memory is too hazy) some of the director's other films and/or other recent or older films that are examples of the same genre or deal with similar themes. In other words, I want to be able to contextualize whatever film I'm writing about. Sometimes I don't end up even mentioning the other movies I watched for 'research,' but even if that's the case that research has inevitably enriched my perspective on the film I'm reviewing. Sometimes, research is minimal because of time constraints. Other times, it's

minimal because you know the director's work and the genre or type of film he/she is making sufficiently, or the director hasn't made any other films. When I see the film I'm reviewing, I take notes. My impressions, reactions, words that jump into my head while I'm watching, key plot points. Nothing super copious (I don't want to be scribbling away so much that I miss what's going on onscreen) but enough so that if I don't have time to write the review for a few days, I can still easily access my initial responses and thoughts.

Then I type out the notes. Next, I do a 'rough write,' in which I just type out my thoughts and map out the general structure of the review, but don't necessarily polish each sentence. Then I go back and rework the sentences.

## ····*Attack of the Hybrids: Lyric Essays*

Creative nonfiction generally means the use of techniques more commonly associated with fiction within stories that are fact-based. But creative nonfiction may also refer to the more overt blending of other different genres and forms. In creative nonfiction, "lyric essay" is the broad moniker used to describe such ambitious works that approach their subjects in these varied fashions.

Flash nonfiction and prose poetry experiment with compressed writing and an emphasis on lyric language, strong imagery and, in the case of flash, word limits. For many excellent examples of flash nonfiction, be sure to look at the online literary magazine *Brevity*, which accepts nonfiction up to 750 words. Micro-essays are even tinier. For example, *Creative Nonfiction* magazine has an ongoing call for micro-essays through Instagram, in which writers pair an image with text limited by Instagram's character count in the caption area. The magazine has a similar call through Twitter.

*Lyric essay* as a term was coined in 1997 by the *Seneca Review*, which surveyed a growing body of work it deemed "poetic essays" or "essayistic poems," noting that such hybrids "give primacy to artfulness over the conveying of information. They forsake narrative line, discursive logic, and the art of persuasion in favor of idiosyncratic meditation." Practically speaking, this genre can be and has been used to describe a wide variety of writings that vary in approach (and critical discourse on what constitutes a lyric essay also is plentiful).[7] In chapter 6 on structure, I'll delve a bit into some of lyric essay's more high-profile manifestations, such as received forms, collage, and braided essays.

Formal experiments with structure are certainly not limited to the literary realm. At the *Reporter*, we often experimented with various format-busting approaches to storytelling, whether that meant using a quiz format to discuss an environmental issue (this was, for what it's worth, prior to the ubiquitous online quiz culture in which we now reside), snarky lists to discuss the week's events, or maps to show how long it would take zombies to overrun Santa Fe (hypothetically speaking, of course).

····*Opinions, Ideas, Satire, Et Al.*

The personal essay has a long tradition of including not just personal experience as its subject in autobiographical writing, but also ideas and questions. In the introduction to the anthology *The Art of the Personal Essay*, essayist Phillip Lopate discusses the personal essay form as "mode of thinking and being," tracing that lineage to the Grandfather of the Essay, Michel de Montaigne, "and his endlessly suggestive use of the term *essai* for his writings. To essay is

---

7      In Fall 2015, I taught an upper-division class solely devoted to the lyric essay, which, if student evaluations and the work they produced are any indication, was successful. However, more than one student felt I had spent much too long delving into the critical debates about the genre itself, so I'll refrain from doing that here.

to attempt, to test, to make a run at something without knowing whether you are going to succeed." (Lopate and dozens of other contemporary writers contributed, in fact, to a 2015 University of Georgia anthology, *After Montaigne*, that features "covers" of Montaigne's essays; each writer undertook an essay with the same title and topic of a Montaigne essay.)

In *The Art of the Personal Essay*, Montaigne, as well as many other writers collected in the book, approach their topics both from a personal stance as well as a philosophical one. Seneca writes on the topic of noise, challenging the notion that noise is a legitimate reason for distraction (in a nutshell). Nineteenth-century writer William Hazlitt pondered such topics as "the pleasure of hating."

The contemporary news or magazine column might not seem, immediately, to follow in this tradition, but in fact is an example of contemporary writing that emphasizes the personal voice and view but is geared at topics or news rather than individual history (such topics are usually more time sensitive than "the pleasure of hating," which in journalism lingo might qualify as "evergreen").

Pure opinion writing in the form of editorials (or op-eds, also a regular crossword answer) is less exploratory and more focused and definitive. For example, newspaper endorsements in political races are a type of op-ed, written on behalf of the newspaper itself. I wrote gazillions of these as editor of the *Reporter* and, though frequently a tiresome undertaking, this type of focused public-service writing is a good exercise in crafting a supported argument.

More fun than political endorsements (although occasionally there is overlap): satirical and humor writing. Satire and other types of humor certainly don't belong solely to nonfiction, but as a mode of writing can be everywhere from *McSweeney's* "Open Letters" to the *New Yorker's* Shouts and Murmurs columns. For an older but still relevant example, consider Jonathan Swift's "A Modest Proposal."

## TECHNIQUES

Different types of nonfiction writing emphasize or use different techniques. The older form of the essay, as previously noted, was less concerned with the narrative storytelling structure that long-form contemporary memoir utilizes. Short-form flash writing disrupts, through compression, the chronological arc often applied to journalistic reportage. And so on and so forth. Throughout the book, you'll find various thoughts and discussions about craft techniques as they apply to the various types of nonfiction writing. These include strategies for structure, characterization, and voice.

## WRITING HABITS

I began this chapter with a quote from John McPhee's interview with the *Paris Review*. The magazine, since the 1950s, has regularly interviewed writers about their writing habits, techniques, and views on various aspects of literary craft and life. These make for fascinating reading and, as an added bonus, can suck away hours of your time!

Why do we find it interesting to hear writers' motivations for what they do and specifics for how they do it? Good question. Freud seemed to think writing was a way of recreating acts of fantasy from childhood, but he thought that about everything.

Rather than focus on *why*, a few words on *how* seem appropriate. I spent most of my adult life on deadline because I was either freelancing (after college) or working full-time for a newspaper. As one of my recent Facebook "memories" noted, from a post eight years ago or so, "Julia is on deadline forever." Deadlines are stressful, but have a built-in benefit: writing happens. Without deadlines, writing happens by creating habits. Some might, and do, argue that writing will happen when inspiration hits, but in surveying a rather large sampling of famous writers' thoughts on this topic, few cited inspiration as a substitute for a routine (a notable exception: Ray Bradbury, who said he writes all the time out of inspiration and could write anywhere at all).

For the rest of us mortals, establishing a routine, a mode of showing up every day to accomplish something, is the only way to actually produce the work. Joan Didion, in her *Paris Review* interview in the late 1960s, said she had a drink an hour before dinner to review what she'd written that day and started the next day by working on the notes she had made the night before (I have a similar process, except I just email myself little missives the night before).

Hemingway wrote first thing in the morning because, he said, "There is no one to disturb you and it is cool or cold and you come to your work and warm as you write." Jack Kerouac apparently went through a stage of writing at night by candlelight and only stopping when the candle went out (but, you know, the '60s). Less esoterically (and more helpfully), Zadie Smith advises to "work on a computer that is disconnected from the Internet."

In other words, audition and adopt habits that allow you to write on a regular basis. I am writing this chapter at seven a.m. with headphones on, listening to the ambient sound of a thunderstorm with the curtains drawn to block out a blazingly sunny day. (I find it easier to work when it's raining, but I live in New Mexico, so this is the work-around I've developed for that.) I've written a fair amount of this book sitting in coffee shops. I try to take at least an hour's walk each day to split the morning from the afternoon and consider what my next plan of attack should be.

Needless to say, my current routine has fallen by the wayside many days during the school year, since writing in the morning, walking, then editing and writing more in the afternoon doesn't actually work when I'm teaching three classes. This is more my holiday/weekend mode. Whatever your daily routine is, find a way to set aside some time to write.

#### •••• *Other Recommendations*

- Seek out deadline-writing opportunities. If writing isn't part of your job, and you're not ready/willing/able to start freelancing, volunteer to blog for an organization you support. Just the act of routine writing will bolster your skills and fluidity.

- Take a writing class or join a writing group. This will also help to create some structure, and possibly introduce you to other writers whose work and feedback you will value.

- Be open. By this I mean be willing to try out writing prompts, to stray from the work you think you should be doing and try new types of writing, to listen to feedback and editing. I believe in discipline, but rigidity and creativity aren't always compatible. "I am a big proponent of the process of writing," MacLean says. "It's through the process that you find the things that you didn't know you knew. If you write exactly what you expected to write, that's a failure. I like the idea of details that don't fit the story coming in, dilating, and veering the story off."

- Most—arguably all—writing improves from editing and feedback. If you're lucky to have teachers, editors, colleagues, and fellow writers who are genuinely interested in improving the work itself, listen to their feedback. But distinguish between feedback that helps you improve the work, and subjective judgments. Rejection—whether in the form of a rejection letter or an online insult—is a facet of writing in the world. Shake it off.

## PROMPTS AND PRACTICE

1. **Pay attention**. As Rapp Black noted earlier and other writers will mention in the pages ahead, attentiveness is a key element to observing, noting, generating and holding on to ideas for your writing. To this end, dedicate a notebook (and, hopefully, many notebooks to come[8]) to recording your ideas as they happen, and review them regularly. My colleague, novelist Anne Valente, says she has "carried a small notebook with me to help record fleeting observations, images, brief facts, and overhead dialogue" since she first began writing. Valente continues,

> I don't always know why they've caught my attention or how I'll use them, but I often end up going back to the things I've jotted down over time and am able to find connections between them (sometimes even by drawing lines between seemingly disparate notes that just happened to be taken down on the same page). I'd definitely advise new writers to carry a journal with them—something small that won't take up much space—and write down anything that sparks their interest in daily life, whether it's something someone says at a party or the unique color of the sky on a given afternoon. These can end up being the beginnings of new writing pieces, or even smaller things like the perfect title or the right image for a particular piece. I think they can also help a new writer determine over time what their passions are—what they notice and why, what was interesting enough to be recorded in the notebook, and what makes them want to write.

---

8    This seems as good a spot as any to confess that for many years I took all my notes on yellow legal pads and, when the pads filled, stored them in the trunk of my car until the entire trunk of the car was filled with legal pads and nothing else. I managed to eventually break myself of this habit.

2. **Blog it**. My first blog was titled, inauspiciously, "Julia Goldberg's Blog." I would describe the experience as "blogging under duress." It was early in the 2000s, and blogs were taking over the Internet. My bosses at the *Santa Fe Reporter* felt it was important that the paper also start having an online presence (we didn't have a website yet), which meant I needed to start blogging. I didn't know anything about blogging except that the idea of writing straight to the world without several rounds of copyediting sounded like a bad idea all around. Nonetheless, I began and soon found that even though my blog posts ranged from the personal to the political (in other words, the blog didn't have much focus other than being about whatever was on my mind), it helped create a regular daily writing practice and, occasionally, essays would emerge from the blog that I later reshaped into larger (edited) pieces. Many authors have gone from blog to book; perhaps you will too.

3. **Dig deep**. Emily Rapp Black suggests asking yourself to describe "your most profound experience of love," or "the most grief-stricken you've ever been" and exploring "why" for both questions as an entryway for a personal essay on love and grief. Read Rapp Black's essay "On Finding True Love and Deserving Happiness" at the end of this chapter for inspiration.

4. **Head out**. Make a list of 10 activities you've always wanted to try. Now pick one. If you've got some real time on your hands, embark on a significant experience you wouldn't normally undertake. (See David Foster Wallace's "Shipping Out," available online through *Harper's* magazine, in which he chronicles his experience on a luxury cruise ship, for an inspired example.) If you're more pressed for time, pick an event in your community, attend and write an "on the scene" story about the experience.

5. **Consider your environs**. Take a photo each day for a week, and write a few hundred words either describing what you've captured

or responding to the scene. At the end of the week, look at all the vignettes. Do you have a unified essay here? Or a few shorter photo essays, perhaps? You may want to consider posting these on Instagram. In fact, as of this writing, *Creative Nonfiction* has an open call for #microstories such as these. *Virginia Quarterly Review* also launched in 2015 its #VQRtruestory series, in which writers use VQR's Instagram feed to post photos and stories that are later presented as essays in the magazine.

6. **Ask a question**. Find a top story for the day—that headline flooding your newsfeeds, the issue your friends won't stop posting about, the event you can't stop mulling. Ask five people to respond to the issue and write down everything they say verbatim. Now, review what you've learned about other people's views on the issue/scandal/question. What do you think about it? Write a short personal essay incorporating (or not) the views of others.

7. **List it.** Although occasionally maligned for its role in our sound-bite culture, lists can be a fun and relatively pain-free way to generate a list-form story, a.k.a. a listicle, or even just ideas for a story. The List App is a fun way to find ideas for lists, or just start simple: Ten Books That Changed Your Life. Go! For inspiration, check out OneGrandBooks.com—curated lists of noted authors' and celebrities' top ten books.

8. **Soundtrack.** *Brevity Magazine*, known for its—yes—brevity, published the essay "Soundtrack" by Sally Ashton in September 2015, in which the narrator uses the Yes song "Owner of a Lonely Heart" as a through line for an observational piece at a train spot. Pick a song that has meaning to you, and listen to it as you go for a walk, drive to work, or wait for the bus. Can you juxtapose the song and your environment? For another soundtrack essay idea, read Lisa Groen Braner's essay of the same title from

*Creative Nonfiction* magazine, in which she creates a chronology of her life and relationships through songs.

9. **Interview yourself**. I first encountered the "self-interview" through the literary website the *Nervous Breakdown*, and began incorporating it as an exercise in the classroom. What I love about this prompt is that often we really do just need to ask ourselves questions to find material. One student interviewed himself about his obsession with *The Walking Dead* and, while the original interview format fell away during revision, much of what he generated in response to his own questions to himself created the bed of an interesting and provocative essay.

10. **Be prompted**. Use published columns as prompts. Many publications have regular columns open for submissions from the public. You may not end up sending your work to them, or you may send a submission and not be accepted, but these columns—along with thematic-based contest guidelines— serve as prompts when you're looking for a story or idea for your own writing. Consider the *New York Times'* Modern Love column, for example, or *Creative Nonfiction's* regular call for essays on particular topics (from Waiting to Siblings to Joy in recent months).

## ESSAYS

# The Sunday Essay: Wrinkles and Time
Julia Goldberg

Two roads really did diverge in a wood near the townhouse complex where I spent my 'tween years. On one side of the road was suburbia: bland and uniform, dozens of doors with numbers and letters and little else to distinguish them. We were 14-B for many years—a ground-floor two-bedroom apartment—until a fire caused us to relocate into an identical townhouse closer to the complex's main entrance.

Across the street I could enter the woods: overgrown and mysterious, tracts of land settled hundreds of years ago by Pennsylvania Quakers. There, my best friend Falle and I took our dogs Kimba and Emma on daily walks, constructing an alternative universe with magical stumps and malevolent wells; a majestic castle and an invisible spaceship; and—because we were girls—unicorns, unicorns, unicorns.

My mother, sister, and I had moved to this particular outpost of suburban Philadelphia in the wake of my parents' divorce, downsizing from a multi-storied house with two staircases and separate bedrooms for my sister and me. My acclimation of the following few years coincided with my first reading of Madeleine L'Engle's *A Wrinkle in Time*, which celebrates its 50th birthday this year. I read the book and suddenly recognized my new environment—identical townhouses with identical squares of green in front and identical walled-in porches in the back—for what it was: Camazotz. I had been unwittingly resettled on a black planet ruled by IT, where everyone was expected to look and act the same. I was the misunderstood heroine of this story: Meg Murray, minus the math skills and Aspergianesque little brother.

I was certain the mysteries of the universe were about to be revealed, even though childhood had already yielded disappointments of the mystical variety. I had spent countless hours in various closets (my sister's walk-in closet in our old house had been my favorite), waiting for Narnia to appear. I attributed its lack of manifestation in part to the concurrent lack of fur coats in most of the closets to which I had access (I was strangely literal in my thinking for someone convinced an alternative reality was just a closet away).

The teleportation and telepathy of *A Wrinkle in Time* gave me more with which to work. I practiced reading Falle's mind (kything) as often as she would let me by commanding her to think of numbers so I could guess them (it only took guessing right once every now and then to convince me I was making psychic progress). In the room I shared with my sister, my bed was positioned next to the window. I sometimes opened it and popped out into the night in case any strangers from other worlds were hanging about waiting to take me to another planet where my services were needed. As a back-up plan, I considered the possibilities presented in *Goldenrod*, a YA book written by Mary Towne in the '70s. In this book, a babysitter is hired to care for the five Madder kids, whose newly single mother needs child-care help. Goldenrod's special gift is the ability to teleport anywhere that starts with the letter "G." She is able to share this gift with her charges, and they travel to places corresponding to the names of the kids: Venice (Val); Laramie (Laurel); St. Martin (Susan); the Himalayas (Heath); Danbury (Daisy's choice, because that's where her Daddy lived). Domestic and international travel didn't seem quite as exciting to me as inter-dimensional tessering, but worth a shot. Unfortunately, I didn't know that many places that started with the letter "J." There was New Jersey, minus the "new" part, but the three of us drove there regularly when we went to visit my grand-parents in New York, all of us rolling up the windows to block the smell of landfills and refineries as we passed through Newark. I focused instead on Jamaica, but fuzzily since I didn't know where it was or what it looked like. That my two favorite books featured fatherless children who could beam in and out of their lives at will escaped my notice at the time. I was not actively unhappy—diary entries from the period indicate a whirlwind of activities ranging from museum visits to tennis lessons—but displaced and disoriented.

Then came Lois Duncan's 1982 *Stranger With My Face*, introducing the concept of astral projection. This I practiced nightly in bed, trying desper-ately to leave my body before concluding that perhaps this only worked if one was: Native American, a twin, and in a coma.

When I wasn't actively trying to transport myself to another world, I wrote stories about short misunderstood girls who had more success. I typed up descriptions of these stories onto index cards that I kept in a small orange file box. I assiduously noted the stories' progress at the top of the card (the vast majority were "unfinished"). For example:

SUSAN, MISSY AND SPACE: TWO GIRLS BY ACCIDENT GO TO ANOTHER PLANET . . . AFTER A SERIES OF ADVENTURES SUSAN GETS HOMESICK. TEAREFULLY [sic] THEY LEAVE UNAWARE THEY WILL COME BACK.

What I lacked in spelling and story arc I made up for with single-minded focus: I wanted to be somewhere else, but I wanted to be able to come home when I was ready.

*

I read Margaret Atwood's *The Handmaid's Tale* my senior year of high school, an all-girls boarding school planted in Amish Country, Pennsylvania, where the breeze blew either the scent of chocolate from the factory down the street or pig manure from God knows where. As I always had with every book I liked, I read *The Handmaid's Tale* 10 times in a row. The '80s were drawing to a close along with my adolescence, but not fast enough for me. I fancied myself politically knowledgeable, and nursed an antipathy toward Ronald Reagan and the decade's culture wars that was short on details and long on emotional angst. I took Atwood's dystopic reality seriously and thought I had one or two years tops before I was rounded up and forced to procreate and wear a red cloak. (When I interviewed Atwood three years ago following the publication of *The Year of the Flood*, I tried to broach this incident by telling her that some people think she's prophetic; "I know," she said, "but I'm not.")

My shift from fantasy to speculative fiction coincided with my exit from childhood and adolescence to adult-in-training. I was no longer interested in leaving my body or my planet, but had honed in on the alternative possibilities of the future. Marge Piercy's 1993 *He, She and It* depicts a North American post-environmental disaster, in which corporations rule the world, technology has advanced to cyborgs and full "Net" immersion, and in which no one can breathe the air. I had just purchased my first Apple computer and stared at it warily when it talked to me. Jean Hegland's 1998 *Into the Forest* chronicles two sisters' struggle to survive as the world collapses into decay. I read this in the midst of the pre-Y2K hype and immediately began stockpiling water and panicking over my lack of useful survival skills (a willingness to discuss *New Yorker* articles did not strike me as a bargainable commodity in the future I envisioned). There were several power outages in my neighborhood the winter I read *Into the Forest*, one of the same early warning signs in the book that society is crumbling. As I had done when reading *The Handmaid's Tale*, I became convinced it was not a matter of if, but when. I spent much more time imagining the grim future than focused on my recent marriage, which was, unlike the world, actually imminently doomed.

*

Just a few years ago, I was struck with the desire to re-read *A Wrinkle in Time*, but was unable to find it on any of the dozen poorly organized bookshelves in my house. So I paid a visit to a local bookstore and broached, with slight embarrassment, the Young Adult section. I was fuzzily aware of the boom in YA spec fiction, but this was the first time I'd come face-to-face with the were-wolves and vampires and...more vampires. But there, among the bloodsucker romances, was *The Adoration of Jenna Fox*, Mary Pearson's 2008 story of a 17-year-old girl who eventually learns that her parents cloned 90 percent of her after a car crash left her facing certain death (an operation illegal but doable in the bioethically uncertain future). Scott Westerfeld's *Uglies* constructs a world in which everyone is "ugly" until the 16th year when extensive plastic surgery strips individuality and makes them beautiful (or "pretties," as the second in the four-book series is called). I was re-hooked, but also embarrassed. Wasn't I a slightly serious person? Why was I reading books that took less than an hour to finish? Was my brain rotting? Was I regressing? Was I having yet another mid-life crisis? Also: was I actually pretending to buy these books for an imaginary teenage girl? Reminding myself that I had a graduate degree and had read many other books that were not written for teenagers was momentarily comforting until I realized that my one major academic paper—published and delivered to a room of very old men—had been on *Gulliver's Travels*. Sure, I had gussied it up with an analysis of linguistic manipulation, but underneath all that was just a 12-year-old girl saying: "Look! A world where horses talk!"

*

In her 2011 book *In Other Worlds, SF and the Human Imagination*, Margaret Atwood delineates science and speculative fiction respectively as literature that is concerned with things that can't happen versus things that could happen but have not yet. Her demarcation reminded me of my own shift away from L'Engle's centaurs and cherubim toward the inchoate dangers of technocracy and environmental devastation. Both genres privilege human tenacity against the unknown, but science fiction and fantasy always provide the extra boost of magical elements. We root for Harry Potter because he's good, but vicariously enjoy the possibilities of winning the supernatural lottery through which we can read minds, disappear, and have a tactical advantage over dark forces. In spec fiction, the darkness is a direct consequence of humanity's greed and blindness. Spec fiction does not provide magical spectacles to fight off evil, only bravery and perseverance.

The book helped me recast my ongoing love affair with speculative fiction—regardless of intended audience. I was not, it turned out, a stunted geek, but actually a highly imaginative and empathetic human being. And only slightly stunted. Subsequently, I read on a recent 10-hour flight all 900-and-something pages of Suzanne Collins' *The Hunger Games* trilogy. The books—coming to a theater soon—concern a dystopic future in which the country has been divided into districts, and teenagers compete annually in a reality-TV style live-or-die competition. The heroine, Katniss, wins against all odds and ends up leading a rebellion in a war against a government that has sacrificed the well-being of most of its citizens in favor of the few who live lives of wealth and privilege. The books are clever and poignant and dark. They conclude with the harrowing deaths of innocent characters; the heroine's victories are shadowed by permanent sorrow and a determination to never forget those who were sacrificed to make a better world.

As I finished the final book, *Mockingjay*, I tried to imagine reading it as a teenager and accepting its grim realities. The book failed to provide the vicarious escape valve I had come to expect; the line it drew between now and maybe later was too thin. Perhaps I have not changed as much as I think I have in the last 30-odd years but, clearly, the world—real and imaginary—has.

# On Finding True Love and Deserving Happiness
## Emily Rapp Black

*Every day as I love this baby in my lap, I think of my other baby. Poor older brother, poor missing one . . . The love for the first magnifies the love for the second, and vice versa.*
  —Elizabeth McCracken, *An Exact Replica of a Figment of My Imagination*

February is a month of panic for me, a month of hurt. Everything feels like a trigger—a suggestion, an imagined slight, anticipated encounters that cannot be controlled. On their surface, many of these triggers have nothing to do with the death of my son, but they point to a vibrating anxiety that his death two years ago on Valentine's Day created.

During this cold, bright month, snow falling in foot-high drifts in some parts of the country, the sky clear and blue where I live in New Mexico, this shaky, volcanic uncertainty governs my emotions, my life. "Grief is frustrating," a friend of mine wisely notes. It's troubling to be aware of being ungrounded and not be able to think one's way out of it.

All I can think about is things coming apart, or things that might. I'm an expert at rolling out any imagined scenario to the worst possible outcome: loneliness, despair, betrayal, confirmation of the worst fears about myself that years of therapy have failed to completely eradicate. "I'd like to be less broken," I tell my therapist. "Maybe you should start with changing your self-description," she suggests, and she's right, and yet that's the word that comes to mind.

I was on a metaphorical ground, a rock bottom, during the two long years of Ronan's illness—locked in terror, bullied by his father—and I'm not sure I've ever gotten up. Part of me is still in that room with Ronan after he died, staring at the circus poster on the wall, the smell of rancid diapers lingering in the air, the sense of a spirit having just been crushed. How can you absorb seeing your child for the last time?

My baby, my boy.

Elizabeth McCracken, in her memoir about having a stillborn baby, written while her second, living child was a baby himself, loses the ability to speak French after her first son's death (she and her husband lived in France at the time). Now, she writes, she must look words up, the "blunt-force" trauma of losing a child having knocked that ability away from her, a ball kicked far off the field, never to be retrieved. The game goes on, as of course it must.

Everyone loses someone they love, and then loses something else. What I lost was trust. Trust in the goodness of the world, in luck, in sure things. Truthfully, I knew these concepts were capricious long before Ronan was diagnosed with a terminal disease that took his life before his third birthday, but it has worsened since, even with a happy (finally) marriage, even with a healthy daughter who crawls and babbles and reaches for me and sleeps tucked into my side each night, snoring and sighing.

I feel an increasing need for reassurance, a need for life and emotions to be locked, immovable, steady. I feel protective of the details of my intimate life, circumscribed by my domestic space, wanting to ward off any force that might puncture it. "People can't be trusted," I tell my therapist. "Stop acting insane," she says. "OK," I agree, but then dream about our house surrounded by an electrified fence that will stun anyone who doesn't have the appropriate password, anyone who isn't welcome. I'm feeling wildly uncharitable. I imagine bodies being knocked back into the arroyo, access denied.

Alongside this feeling of being unsettled bustles the business of Valentine's Day: chocolates, cards, elaborate or not so elaborate gifts for the beloved, champagne brunches, spray-tanned women who look desperate for a sandwich slinking across the television screen in red lingerie, wings affixed to their skinny backs while votive candles twinkle seductively on bedside tables. What I want is to be left alone in a room with only the people I trust. No more friends, no more commitments, no more struggle. A big circus tent full of affection and laughter and beauty and art and talent and brainpower. Nobody would ever want to leave.

*It would be easy*, I think, but of course this is an illusion, and a close cousin of nostalgia, that dangerous and disastrous longing that is built on lies, on projections, on controllable fantasies that never align with the truth of what has passed between people. The ultimate act of navel-gazing. The memory likes to distort, the imagination likes to wander and spin, master of its own elaborate outcomes.

This, I know, is a way of staying safe. And of course I know that in order to live, one must sacrifice safety. One must trust. "Why do you think you're bad and wrong?" my therapist asks. "Why don't you think you deserve to be happy?" I consider this. "I am happy," I say. "But trust is a trickster." She sighs. "Why are you so stubborn?"

This Valentine's Day, I'm going to remember all of the people I love and have loved, all the ways in which we are undone and then re-membered, re-assembled by love, and try to actively trust. I will resist this, I know, but I will work through this resistance, if only as an experiment, perhaps as a tribute to Ronan, to my husband and daughter.

Here's what I trust, a list of statements that are true about my life right now, in this moment: I live with the love of my life. I have a beautiful girl. I had a beautiful boy. The love for what I've lost magnifies the love for what is now. I deserve to be happy.

# READING AND RESOURCES
# FROM THIS CHAPTER

Ashton, Sally. "Soundtrack." *Brevity* 50, Fall 2015. http://brevitymag.com/nonfiction/soundtrack.

Barrett, Terry. *Criticizing Art: Understanding the Contemporary*. Mountain View, CA: Mayfield, 2000.

Beard, Jo Ann. "The Fourth State of Matter." *New Yorker*, June 24, 1996. http://www.newyorker.com/magazine/1996/06/24/the-fourth-state-of-matter.

Braner, Lisa Groen. "Soundtrack." *Brevity* 25. https://www.creativenonfiction.org/brevity/past%20issues/brev25/braner_sound.htm.

Deuel, Nathan. *Friday Was the Bomb: Five Years in the Middle East*. Ann Arbor, MI: Dzanc Books/Disquiet, 2014.

Didion, Joan. "Why I Write," *New York Times Book Review*, December 5, 1976.

Franklin, Joey. "The Beautiful Untrue Things of the Lyric Essay." *TriQuarterly*, September 17, 2014. https://www.triquarterly.org/craft-essays/beautiful-untrue-things-lyric-essay.

Hessler, Peter. "John McPhee, The Art of Nonfiction No. 3." *Paris Review*, 2010. http://www.theparisreview.org/interviews/5997/the-art-of-nonfiction-no-3-john-mcphee.

Jamison, Leslie. *The Empathy Exams: Essays*. Minneapolis: Graywolf, 2014.

Jamison, Leslie. "The Devil's Bait." *Harper's*, September 2013. https://harpers.org/archive/2013/09/the-devils-bait/.

Lopate, Phillip. *The Art of the Personal Essay: An Anthology from the Classical Era to the Present*. New York: Anchor, 1994.

MacLean, David Stuart. *The Answer to the Riddle Is Me: A Memoir of Amnesia*. Boston: Houghton Mifflin Harcourt, 2014.

Marcus, Ben. "On the Lyric Essay." *Believer*, July 2013. http://benmarcus.com/writing/on-the-lyric-essay.

Murphy, Bernadette. *Harley and Me: Embracing Risk on the Road to a More Authentic Life*. Berkeley: Counterpoint, 2016.

Nester, Daniel. *Shader: 99 Notes on Car Washes, Making Out in Church, Grief, and Other Unlearnable Subjects*. San Francisco: 99: The Press, 2015.

Rapp Black, Emily. *Poster Child: A Memoir*. New York: Bloomsbury, 2007.

Rapp Black, Emily. *The Still Point of the Turning World*. New York: Penguin, 2013.

Shepherd, Reginald. "Why I Write." *Poets.org*, September 12, 2008. https://www.poets.org/poetsorg/text/why-i-write.

Smith, Zadie. "Zadie Smith's Rules for Writers." *Guardian*, February 22, 2010. http://www.theguardian.com/books/2010/feb/22/zadie-smith-rules-for-writers.

Tall, Deborah, and John D'Agata. "The Lyric Essay." *Seneca Review*, Fall 1997. http://www.hws.edu/senecareview/lyricessay.aspx.

"The Square Root of True: A Roundtable Discussion." *Creative Nonfiction*, Fall 2013. https://www.creativenonfiction.org/online-reading/square-root-true.

"#VQRTrueStory: A Social-Media Experiment in Nonfiction." *Virginia Quarterly Review*, December 7, 2015. http://www.vqronline.org/articles/2015/12/vqrtruestory.

Wallace, David Foster. "Shipping Out: On the (Nearly Lethal) Comforts of a Luxury Cruise." *Harper's*, January 1996. https://harpers.org/wpcontent/uploads/2008/09/HarpersMagazine-1996-01-0007859.pdf.

"Wanted: Instagram Micro Essays." *Creative Nonfiction.* https://www.creativenonfiction.org/news/ wanted-instagram-micro-essays.

Zinsser, William. *Writing About Your Life: A Journey into the Past.* New York: Marlowe, 2004.

# CHAPTER TWO

# Interview with a Vampire ... or a Politician

Journalism is kind of like dating. You have to be yourself but less ... Intention is important too, because your intentions come through.

—**Mike Sager,** *Esquire* contributing editor

The disparity between what seems to be the intention of an interview as it is taking place and what it actually turns out to have been in aid of always comes as a shock to the subject.

—**Janet Malcolm,** *The Journalist and the Murderer*

MANY YEARS BEFORE I knew there was such a thing as a "journalist," my life's ambition was to be a detective. I blame *Harriet the Spy,* and possibly *Charlie's Angels,* but mostly what appears to be a possibly cellular disposition toward nosiness about other people. To that end, I owned, by the time I was in grade school, a private eye kit, which included a magnifying glass and fingerprinting materials; a lie detector, which required assembling and never seemed to work to my satisfaction (I was nosy but not mechanically inclined);

and business cards, courtesy of my father, which read: Julia R. Goldberg, Private Eye.

In addition to skulking around my apartment complex dusting for fingerprints on neighbors' front doors, compulsively eavesdropping, and searching for people to interrogate, I also kept close tabs on my classmates. I have on my desk at home still a small orange index card box filled, mostly, with cards identifying my peers from elementary school. When I was in grade school, students would exchange the smallest class portrait photos with one another (maybe they still do this . . . despite Facebook). I don't know what anyone else did with their photos of classmates, but I stapled mine to index cards that included pertinent information about each person: which reading group someone was in, for example; which boy (or girl) they liked, popularity rank, best friends, the marital status of their parents.

*I'm not making this up. I kept tabs on my classmates.*

This box no longer serves any purpose (except, perhaps, potentially as the pièce de résistance should I ever undergo extensive psychotherapy), but I could no more throw it away than I could any of my multiple Rolodexes (google twentieth-century form of record keeping, if you're unfamiliar with the term). Although it sometimes feels as though everyone we need to find or talk to is just a click away, this is far from true. In fact, I observed, during my time as editor of the *Reporter*, a dramatic shift in reporters' abilities to track down people as folks dumped their landlines (this also was why I refused to let anyone throw away any of the old phone books at the *Reporter* while I was there). Beyond practical reasons for storing (in one way or another) contact information, there is a writerly impulse to hold on to our records, notes, and documents because one never knows what information will be needed in the future (and if this all sounds like a giant rationale for paper-hoarding, I promise that my boxes of old newspaper clippings and notes have been crucial in working on this book).

By high school, my career goals had shifted from detective to journalist. This was almost entirely due to Hunter S. Thompson's *Fear and Loathing: On the Campaign Trail of '72*. To be clear, 1972 was long gone by the time I read the book, and much of the inside baseball of politics Thompson discusses was over my head at the time (and possibly still is; I am writing right now in the midst of the various presidential caucuses and just had to reread the byzantine background for the Iowa caucuses three times to understand what was going on). But Thompson's truth-to-power approach to covering that race—along with his first-person unreliable narrative writing style—hit me hard. I worked on my high school newspaper, and then on my college newspaper. For reasons that are no longer clear (if they ever were), I went to a college without a journalism program and, then, went to graduate school to study creative writing. Everything I learned about journalism, I learned from doing it. And the bedrock of it all returned me to my roots of extreme nosiness about other people: interviewing.

When I first started teaching a variety of journalism courses and overseeing the student online magazine at Santa Fe University of Art and Design, it became quickly clear to me that interviewing was one of the main barriers to my students' interest in the field. They were also suspicious in general of journalism, and in some cases expressed startling abhorrence of it, but it was the idea of interviewing that really got them. By the time I was teaching, I had interviewed so many people I had forgotten what it was like when I started out—the actual nervousness involved with calling up people you don't know and asking them questions. And it's true, even if you're preternaturally inclined to ask a lot of questions, journalism requires both asking hard questions to people and asking questions to hard people.

For many years, I had thought of interviewing simply as a mechanism serving the larger purpose of the story. My viewpoint has changed and evolved over the years as I've come to realize that interviews serve different purposes at different times, and that context is a large driving force when it comes to the interviewing process.

Additionally, I believe in the power of interviewing as not just a mode of obtaining information, but also as a form of conversation, of dialogue. In 2014, I participated in a local festival in Santa Fe, the After Hours Alliance Festival of Progressive Arts, setting up an all-day interview tent. Along with a few colleagues, I provided the chance for anyone who was interested in being interviewed to participate in the experience.

When I first began as a reporter, interviewing was more often the means to securing a quote that worked with a story or information that I needed for the story. When I became editor of the *Reporter*, I also took the lead in conducting endorsement interviews in which the staff and I interviewed political candidates. These were often less for quotes and more  to understand each candidate's position on issues.

For Q&A-style interviews, the emphasis is often on trying to construct a print version of a series of questions and answers in an edited piece that reads more like an organic conversation. The print version of an interview is not a raw transcript but a construction, and much of the work takes place in the editing process: eliminating redundant exchanges and looking for the moments that stand out in the larger conversation.

For a long-form profile, interviewing can take hours in order to be able to write an in-depth story that captures and characterizes the person about whom one is writing. This means that some of the interview is used for descriptive elements rather than dialogue.

From 2013 through the early part of 2016, I hosted a radio program. For the first year, this was a daily show, and then it became a weekly show when I began teaching full-time. But for that first year, I often found myself interviewing, on average, 20 to 25 people a week, live on air. This was a startling shift from the interviewing practice to which I had grown accustomed. In an interview that will eventually be used in print form, the interviewer often becomes invisible in the final product, and the process of the interview is itself camouflaged as only the answers, most often the quotes, are part of a story. Even in a Q&A, the questions themselves are often condensed and edited in a final story.

But a live interview is a different experience; in many ways, it felt to me when I began as though I was proverbially showing how the sausage got made. On the bright side, radio interviews didn't require me, as the interviewer, to take copious notes on everything my subjects were saying in order to transform them to print. It also allowed, I began to see, for more organic conversations.

When I started teaching, I began to try to articulate more fully my own view of interviewing techniques, and to devise ways for students to practice interviewing. This was particularly true during several international journalism workshops I taught for schools that were at the time part of the larger network for the university where I teach. In the classroom with students for a few hours at a time, all interviewing occurred under false pretenses: the students had only one another to interview, and barely time to begin to write the shortest of profiles on one another.

Nonetheless, I watched them engage with the process and actually ask one another questions that, even though they had

had daily contact and, in some cases, had known one another for years, they had never felt comfortable discussing before. In a classroom in Mexico City, I saw two students, both in tears, toward the end of the exercise. When I asked them what was wrong, they told me they had learned things about each other that, despite a long friendship, they hadn't known.

Many creative nonfiction publications expect and require a level of research integrated into the essays they solicit. For example, at *Creative Nonfiction*, a literary magazine that in many ways has pioneered the genre, it's expected that even personal essays will rely to some degree on research and reporting. That magazine's editor, Lee Gutkind, has an oft-cited essay, "The 5 Rs of Creative Nonfiction," in which he outlines five tenets of successful creative nonfiction: real life, reflection, research, reading and (w)riting. Two of these five principles: real world and research, often rely on interviewing other people. Interviews don't just allow a writer access to information; they also put the writer in the real world, interacting with others and hearing their stories.

Although some writers may be primarily interested in telling their own stories, many of the essays that have played a role in defining the genre due to their craft and artistry also rely on a bedrock of research and discussions with other people to add depth and texture. Interviewing other people and allowing their voices and stories in one's own writing does not mean that the story becomes less your own, or that your own voice disappears. If anything, the most successful creative nonfiction has more impact because of its integration of information and points of view.

"For Paul, it started with a fishing trip. For Lenny, it was an addict whose knuckles were covered in sores. Dawn found pimples clustered around her swimming goggles. Kendra noticed ingrown hairs. Patricia was attacked by sand flies on a Gulf Coast beach."

—Leslie Jamison, "Devil's Bait"

I assign this essay by Jamison each semester, partly because it serves so many instructional purposes for writing and partly to introduce my students to the entire essay collection. "Devil's Bait" has a lot to teach any writer about language, structure, and voice, but it also very quietly highlights the importance of interviewing. As the introductory paragraph quoted above demonstrates, Jamison's reportage on the phenomenon of Morgellons disease (an uncommon, unexplained skin disorder with both physical and psychological components) included not just research of documents (although that was part of it), but a great number of conversations with people who attended a Morgellons conference Jamison uses as part of the ongoing narrative in the essay.

What Jamison pulls off in this essay is much trickier than, say, a straight journalistic report or immersive essay on a Morgellons conference. As she writes toward the essay's midpoint, the essay isn't about whether or not the disease itself is real but, rather, "about what kinds of reality are considered prerequisites for compassion" and whether or not it's "wrong to call it empathy when you trust the fact of the suffering but not the source."

The "characters" or people with whom Jamison begins her essay were not just people she interviewed to gather quotes, nor are they people she interviewed in search of anecdotal stories for the piece. Her responses to their stories and what they have to say are just as important as the information the reader learns about Morgellons in the essay. Jamison's collection on empathy requires other people in the equation—what is empathy without interaction? Although empathy is the unifying and intellectual subject of Jamison's work, I would argue that it's also the unifying element of the interview practice itself. We learn about the world from our interactions with other people, from trying to listen and understand their lives.

"Bill Bradley is what college students nowadays call a superstar, and the thing that distinguishes him from other such paragons is not so much that he has happened into the Ivy League as that he is a superstar at all. For one thing, he has overcome the disadvantage of wealth."

—John McPhee, "A Sense of Where You Are"

I'm not generally that interested in basketball, or roadkill, or Atlantic City, but I became interested in all of these topics, and many more, as a result of John McPhee's essays. Although "A Sense of Where You Are" only quotes lightly from Bradley (and mostly on the topics of basketball), the profile itself is filled with the narrative arc of Bradley's life—a profile of a man McPhee describes as singularly disciplined—built on the information and stories McPhee garnered from his subject. A master journalist and practitioner of creative nonfiction, McPhee noted in an April 2010 interview with the *Paris Review* that he is "interested in people who are expert at something, because they're going to lead me into some field, teach it to me, and then in turn I'm going to tell others about it." To a degree, both McPhee's and Jamison's work are a reminder to reconsider the old adage of "write what you know." Writing what other people know means learning what they know and, thus, knowing it yourself—their stories then become a part of your own storytelling.

"In short order, Roseanne and I were alone. She seemed happy and expansive; there was a sparkle in her smallish, dark-brown eyes. She was considerably less brassy than her well-known public persona, the loudmouthed Domestic Goddess, queen of tabloids and tattoo parlors, desecrater of our national anthem and most of our notions of good taste."

—Mike Sager, "The Multitudes of Roseanne Barr"

I've had many opportunities to hear Mike Sager talk about the art of interviewing, as he was a repeat and popular presenter at several conferences for the Association of Alternative Newsweeklies during my time on its board of directors as editorial chairwoman.

A journalist with roots in the altweekly business, Sager also wrote the introduction for a book I helped edit, *Best Altweekly Writing 2009-2010*, published by Northwestern University Press. Sager writes both fiction and nonfiction, and has spent a fair amount of his career interviewing celebrities, an undertaking that can often require the full arsenal of a journalist's skill set.

As mentioned in the quote that begins this chapter, Sager has a theory "of reporting like old fashioned dating, where there's a set of decorum and ways of dealing with people and looking at them and paying attention to them." Sager says over the years he's also added "a bit of ministering. I feel like when you listen to them and listen well and listen without judgment in the moment, in a way you're providing sort of ministerial function."

Sager's approach isn't solely based on its being the best way of "getting" a story or quote; he says it's also "as close as I can come to finding something that we're actually giving back to the people that we take our stories from." Valuing his subjects is important, Sager says, "because without our subjects we don't have a story, and I'm deeply cognizant of that at all times." Sager also points out that unlike public information in document form—where the material is legally accessible—people "don't have the obligation to tell you what's inside of them. We have to go the extra mile to get it, because ultimately that's what we want to know."

While Sager's approach is usually in the service of long-form journalism, it bears a similarity to *Wall Street Journal* reporter Dan Frosch's approach to interviewing, which he sees as more of a "listening" experience. "You're just simply acting as a guide for them to impart this information to you. Obviously, there's some questions you're going to need them to address in the course of your conversation, but there's ways to do that without it becoming sort of a disruptive encounter."

## LOGISTICS

Standard advice for preparing for an interview includes the obvious: read up on the person and have questions. This is certainly the case with a story on a particular topic for which you actually have questions. But for longer interviews, particularly those leading toward a profile of a person, questions can sometimes get in the way of actually finding the story. Sager says for celebrity interviews, of which he's done many, he will often have questions prepared given that there is usually a time limit on the interview and a pending deadline. But for other stories, he tries to simply be there and let the subject lead the conversation.

Of course, there is no cookie-cutter approach to interviewing. For Sager, a celebrity interview, such as the one he conducted with J. J. Abrams for his December 2015 *Vanity Fair* profile, was rescheduled repeatedly and, when finally conducted, was limited to an hour. For that story, Sager interviewed numerous members of Abrams's family, weaving together a profile that grew out of a portrait of the filmmaker as a young boy. In the case of his profile of Barr, quoted earlier, he was able to spend a fair amount of time with her and capture her natural way of speaking in a way that extended beyond what can usually be found in a limited interview setting.

Non-journalists may be finding this depiction of interviewers as warm-hearted listeners surprising and possibly even delusional. It certainly doesn't jibe with the contemporary depiction of journalists: a scrum of shouting, insensitive interrogators knocking each other over to get the scoop.

Indeed, some interview subjects require a less gentle approach. For example: most politicians. In search of less-gentle advice, I spoke with Mark Zusman, one of the owners of the *Santa Fe Reporter*, as well as co-owner and editor of the Portland, Oregon, *Willamette Week,* which won the Pulitzer Prize for investigative journalism in 2005. I have a very distinct memory of Zusman sitting in on an interview I conducted years ago with a political candidate and almost bringing the man (who, as I recall, did not win his race) to tears. I called Zusman with a slight bit of trepidation, hoping that he would not bring me to tears in the course of the conversation.

By the time I interviewed Zusman for this book, I was in what felt like an interview groove. I'd had a series of fun, open-ended conversations—some over lunch, some over dinner, some by phone—with a variety of writers I'd known for years and perhaps had been lulled into a false sense of comfort. Zusman was less inclined to shoot the shit with me and instead pointed out whenever my questions seemed vague or meandering. I like to think my interview style is vague and meandering by intention—it's intended to make people feel comfortable, as if they are having a meandering conversation rather than being interrogated. Obviously, this doesn't work with everyone. In Zusman's case, my interview reminded me that if interviewing someone who likes to get to the point, then one should get to the point. This was one of his points as well.

"In the same way that there's a recognition that a manager has to handle people differently based on their strengths and weaknesses, the reporter has to ask questions differently depending on the people they're talking to," Zusman said. There are times, he continued, "when asking pointed questions that are aggressive is completely appropriate; there are times when asking questions that are more open-ended yields better results; there are times when making your subject comfortable and relaxed is the most important role of the interview; and there are some times when it's not that at all. Being able to understand that and have a strategy when you walk into an interview is very important."

Additional advice, Zusman notes, is to make sure the questions asked are actually answered.

"I do find that oftentimes reporters who are less skilled

than others will ask a good question, and if they're asking it of someone who's fairly skilled with dealing with the media and the individual doesn't answer the question but answers another question—which is what politicians are skilled to do—I'm often-times amazed at how seldom the reporter will say, 'with all due respect, you didn't answer the question.'"

## ····*The Joys of Transcription*

For many of my early years as a reporter, I took all my notes by hand. I no longer have any idea how that was effective and can only conclude that my handwriting, eyesight, or mental fortitude was significantly better than it is today. My current practice is to both take notes and record. Some writers, such as Sager, just record, preferring not to have his attention diverted from his subject by note taking. I use my recordings as a backup for my notes, so that when I encounter illegible portions of an interview, or a fast-talking subject, I can review sections of the taped interview. As with questions, the methodology choices can vary from interview to interview. A face-to-face interview provides more opportunities for connection and observation. A telephone interview means I can easily type answers while listening (I am a very fast, albeit sloppy, typist) and cuts down on transcription later. I don't type when interviewing someone in person as I think it's distracting (for all involved), although some writers do. It probably goes without saying, but always make sure you have more than one pen, since pens have been known to dry out in the middle of an interview (I've learned this one the hard way).

Transcription simply means writing out a verbatim record of the interview, and is the first step prior to then editing and extracting from the raw transcript. The process can be a long haul, but it also has its rewards, allowing the writer to revisit the interview, hear important moments that might have passed by quickly and unnoticed. For Sager, the "secondary" work of transcription is where he figures out what the story is about.

"I don't skimp on reviewing my material," he says. "If I'm writing while I'm gathering, I'm missing stuff . . . do the perspiration and then the inspiration comes when you go through all of your notes. You can't scrimp on your secondary work. You have to spend time steeping in the material." Regardless of how much time Sager has for the story, he says—three weeks or one week—he spends hours listening to the recordings, transcribing and "fixing up" the transcripts. By the time he's finished, "I know what the story is."

#### ····*Interview Clean Up*

An inevitable question when it comes to interviewing is how much a writer should "clean up" a subject's quotes. Most of us do not speak with perfect grammar or even in complete sentences (if you know anyone who does, you might want to ascertain if he or she is a cyborg). So do you fix people's quotes so that they make sense? Can you trim them to make them more concise? Can you leave out the inevitable interjections that are a part of regular speech? The answers are yes, usually you can, but, as with all choices to modify direct quotes, these decisions should be made thoughtfully and consistently.

Much of this will depend on the editorial policy of your publication but, generally speaking, interviewing people for nonfiction is not the same as being a court reporter; the goal is not a perfect transcription that includes every throat clearing, stutter, or misplaced modifier. Rather, it's a rendered version of what has been said.

Right about now, there are likely some die-hard purists' heads exploding, or perhaps some newcomers to interviewing who are wondering where to draw the line between faithfulness and fabrication. I draw that line here: Never add to quoted material without an editorial note. Modify or reduce quoted material to avoid redundancy, confusion, or tedium.

## ···· Redundancy

If someone says essentially the same sentiment or information three times in a row, is it necessary to include the entire quotation? No. Unless you are doing so to emphasize a particular personality trait of the person (such as a tendency to repeat oneself), repetitious quotes do not aid the larger narrative.

## ···· Direct Quotation, Partial Quotation, and Paraphrasing

Once the interviews are transcribed, it's time to make decisions about which quotes should be used directly, which should be picked at for partial quotation, and what information would be better used in paraphrase. This is crucial work, unless you decide it's best to provide an edited version of a Q&A (more on this later). I've manufactured (that's fancy talk for "made up") some quotes for people no longer living to illustrate how this works:

### Exact Quote (albeit fabricated)

**Anaïs Nin**: "I am definitely meeting Henry Miller for coffee today. I'm going to meet him at 10 a.m. Paris time at Shakespeare and Company and from there we'll walk along the Seine until we find a coffee shop. Then we'll have coffee. I love meeting Henry for coffee because we have such amazing talks about love and life and sex and stuff. I guess what it comes down to, I guess, is if I'm being totally honest in what I'm telling you is that nothing is as important as friendship, except coffee and maybe sex.

## Edited Direct Quote with Paraphrase and Partial Quotation

Anaïs Nin said she had plans to meet Henry Miller in the morning at Shakespeare and Company, take a walk along the Seine, and then have coffee. "I love meeting Henry for coffee because we have such amazing talks about love and life and sex and stuff," Nin said, noting that friendship and coffee were among the most important things to her in life—in addition, she added, to "maybe sex."

In the slightly odd example I've manufactured above, I paraphrased the specifics of where Nin would be meeting Miller and only used in direct quotation her emotive response to the prospect of her coffee date. Because her manufactured quote about friendship, coffee, and sex was not particularly succinct, I paraphrased part of it and used a partial quotation, "maybe sex," to end with. In general, quotes work better when they express an opinion or feeling. Quotes that are purely expository ("The meeting will be held at 6 p.m. in Council Chambers") normally are better paraphrased into the exposition of the piece.

## Bracketing Change

Sometimes, however, a direct quote does require amending. This may be simply to clarify information contained within the interviewee's speech, or to modify the tense of a verb so that it reads as grammatically correct in the sentence. In these cases, brackets tell the reader that the words inside have been altered. For example:

**Joe R Smith:** "After the election, I spent five hours throwing up in the waiting room at St. Vincent's [Regional Medical Center]."

In this case, the brackets let the reader know that the text has been edited to include the proper name of the hospital.

Had Mr. Smith's original quote read, "After the election, I spend five hours throwing up in the waiting room," then substituting the proper past-tense verb "spent" would correct the grammar of the quote without sacrificing its meaning.

## Let 'Em Hang

Purists say let folks speak for themselves and don't correct minor grammatical mistakes. I tend to fix minor grammatical mistakes in speech since they translate into grammatical mistakes in writing. Want to split the difference? You can leave in the grammatical mistakes but include the notation "sic" to let readers know that you are aware of the error and it was left in intentionally. For example:

**School Board Member:** "Can you believe we're on the school board when we never even read no books [sic]?"

Sadly, the above example was taken from real life.

#### ···· *Ten Rules for Interviewing*

1. **Ask good questions.** What is a good question? Presumably a good question is one to which you and/or your readers would like to hear an answer. A good question does not have to be exquisitely phrased or designed to show off your own knowledge. One of my favorite examples of a deceptively good question happened during the Association of Alternative Newsweeklies 2006 annual convention in Little Rock, Arkansas, at which former President Bill Clinton was the keynote luncheon speaker. He took a few questions at the end, and Mark Zusman asked him something along the lines of "Can you offer your thoughts on George W. Bush?" Clinton declined—for about two seconds—before launching into some thoughts on Bush. Perhaps a secondary rule here is: Never hurts to ask.

At a very basic, Communications 101 level, questions fall into two categories. A closed question is generally designed to pull specific information, and can often be a question requiring a simple yes or no response. Closed questions can't be avoided, as you will usually need basic information from an interview subject, such as his or her age, but closed questions—particularly from tight-lipped subjects—are unlikely to elicit more emotional responses.

Open-ended questions, on the other hand, are more flexible and exploratory and will, hopefully, lead to more quotable responses. For me, a great interview is as much a conversation as it is a back-and-forth of questions and answers, but when in doubt, open-ended questions are more likely to garner interesting answers.

Here is a comparison of some simple topics posed as closed versus open questions:

| Open | Closed |
|---|---|
| What is it like to be 18 in this political climate? | How old are you? |
| What's an alternative career you could imagine for yourself and why? | What are you studying? |
| Describe your relationship with your family. | How many siblings do you have? |
| When did you realize you wanted to . . . ? | Where did you grow up? |

2. **Be interested.** Perhaps in an ideal world, we would only talk to fascinating people with interesting stories who articulated them in captivating ways. In reality, sometimes interviewing requires cultivating an interest in subjects and people whom you might not seek out otherwise. But as *Wall Street Journal*

reporter Dan Frosch points out, an interview is less about talking and more about listening. Although there are, for sure, some people who have no desire to talk about themselves or their subjects, most people are willing to open up if they feel they have an audience with a stake in hearing what they have to say. Being interested is a skill you can cultivate by listening.

The best example I have, personally, is a story I worked on in the late 1990s for the *Santa Fe Reporter* on the subject of electricity deregulation. I don't remember exactly how or why I came to work on this story, but as I recall it, I was approached by sources who believed there was a story and, after talking with them at length, I agreed with them—the potential deregulation issue about which they were concerned was indeed, a story worth telling. The challenge for me, as a reporter, was both my complete lack of knowledge about the topic and, frankly, an almost narcoleptic response to hearing about it. One of the rewarding aspects of reporting, though, isn't simply staying in one's wheelhouse but actually diving into subjects that seemed, previously, both uninteresting and opaque. With that said, don't ask me today anything about electric deregulation.

3. **Interview face-to-face.** Whenever possible, conduct an interview in person so that you, the writer, also have access to the elements of characterization: appearance, nuance, environment.

Avoid email interviews, except for factual information. Interviews by email do happen, but writing is different from talking, and an interview subject who responds to questions in writing has the chance to edit his or her responses. The goal of an interview is in large part to allow for organic discussion and surprises.

A telephone interview, like an email interview, may provide information and even quotes you can use, but it deprives you of any visual information or cues about the subject.

**Arranging an Interview**

Don't hesitate to ask: you will be surprised how many people are willing to talk to you—particularly about themselves.

Send a clear (typo-free) email requesting an interview that states your needs.

> Dear Councilor X,
>
> I am writing a story on the City Council's decision to ban nude bicyclists. You spoke against this decision based on your history as a nude bicyclist. I'd love to hear more about this. Is there a convenient time this week for an interview?

4. **Be yourself—or at least some version of yourself.** I have had, over the last few years, several shy students for whom the prospect of interviewing was daunting. I'm not without sympathy. I'm not the kind of person who walks into a party and starts introducing myself to strangers either. In fact, journalism can have a special appeal for The Shy because it provides a legitimate excuse to talk to people. Acts of journalism can require an element of performance that varies from your day-to-day comportment in the same way that writing a job application cover letter differs from sending a text to a friend. This doesn't mean that your demeanor during an interview needs to be formal necessarily; it means that you need to foster flexibility within your personality in order to make the interview subject as comfortable as possible.

My favorite example of this is that many years ago I was scheduled to interview Jane Fonda on the phone regarding a book she had written. One of the drawbacks of the phone interview is that it makes it very difficult to gauge the attitude of the person and to try to meet that attitude appropriately. As a result, I opened with a joke. Jane Fonda did not think my joke was funny, and the interview devolved and ended rapidly.

5. **Prepare—but not too much.** Sager tells me he doesn't enter interviews with prepared questions but, rather, uses the interview to discover what questions he wants to ask. This runs a bit counter to the standard advice about preparing for interviews, but the truth is it really depends on the type of interview and, of course, how long the interview will be. While I was talking to Sager, I was remembering a blatant case of overpreparation on my part when I interviewed author Margaret Atwood in 2009.

By the time this interview happened, I had worked myself into a lunatic frenzy of overpreparation. I deeply admire Atwood's writing, had read (at the time) all of her work, and had written a somewhat exhaustive paper on her in graduate school. In advance of the interview, I reread my exhaustive paper, and then began rereading its source material, and then went down a truly crazed rabbit hole of reading the scholarship I had read to write the paper. Atwood did not sound particularly jazzed to have to do the interview in the first place, and she became even less enthusiastic when I started asking her about statements she had made in the 1970s. She even at one point asked me with a tone of frustrated desperation how many more questions I was going to ask her (and the answer, had I been truthful, would have been "a million more questions, Margaret Atwood!"). Fortunately for me, she humored me and let me ask a fair number of my questions, but the truth is, I had too many and was so frazzled and determined to keep her talking that I bummed out my literary hero. When I finally finished transcribing that interview and putting it into a Q&A form, it became clear to me that while the finished product was OK (in my humble opinion), my questions had turned into statements, and it was Atwood who had ended up asking me questions. For example:

> **SFR**: In a 1970s interview with Graeme Gibson, he asked you about a scene in *The Edible Women*, and you responded that any time one acts, one is exercising power; that if there are

only killers and victims, from a survival point of view, it's preferable to be a killer, even if it's morally preferable to be a victim. I was thinking about that as I was reading *The Year of the Flood*, those were the choices. Although I guess Ren survives almost by luck.

**MA**: You could be a lucky person. You can be a killer, a victim or a lucky person, so I've expanded my categories. But when push comes to shove, what does Toby do?

**SFR**: Kill. . . . You've drawn parallels in the past between gender and national politics. You wrote an essay in 1987 opposing the Canada-US Free Trade Agreement.

**MA**: And was I right?

**Pro tip:** Should you ever have the chance to interview Margaret Atwood, she's always right. Although the interview didn't live up to my ideal scenario (ideal scenarios rarely include annoying one's literary hero), my willingness to be a tedious pest paid off because despite obviously finding me annoying, Atwood did answer my questions.

6. **Be willing to go off script.** In 2005, I had the opportunity to interview Noam Chomsky in advance of a lecture he was set to give in Santa Fe, primarily on the topic of international politics. Here's an excerpt from that interview, which I've included in its entirety at the end of the chapter:

**SFR**: CNN pointed out that Bush wants Mahmoud Abbas to visit the White House, but he never invited Arafat because Bush viewed Arafat as standing in the way of peace. Does this seem like a legitimate characterization to you?

**NC**: We're watching an interesting illustration of how doctrinal systems work. The main principle of a doctrinal system is you have to turn attention from yourself and onto the
misdeeds of others. Here's a perfect example of it. Whatever
you think about Arafat, he was not the obstacle to peace.
The obstacle to peace was the U.S. The U.S. has been refusing to accept a political settlement that has overwhelming
international support, but the U.S. refuses and the Bush
administration is extreme in refusing . . . so therefore, take
a look at the framework for media coverage or commentary. What you have to focus on are the alleged differences
between Arafat and Abbas because that, you know, blames
it on the Palestinians . . . if it doesn't work the way the U.S.
wants, they can blame it on Abbas.

Sounds OK, right? What you don't know from that excerpt (or the
rest of the interview) was that I had stayed up the entire night
before attempting to read half a dozen of Chomsky's books ranging from his views of hegemony to linguistic theory. It's unclear
what I thought would be accomplished by this futile effort, but
as the sun rose that morning I had assembled a list of questions I barely understood myself. Chomsky was very nice and
attempted to answer my first few convoluted questions, but I
could tell the interview was failing. I quickly gave up on my quest
to prove to Chomsky how smart I was or was not and instead,
asked Chomsky questions about issues I actually understood
and knew at least something about. The interview picked up, and
I even managed to make a few jokes here and there.

7. **Have backup questions.** This is the flip side to overpreparation: underpreparation. Backup questions are important, particularly for live interviews, since the worst-case scenario in any
interview is deafening silence. Backup questions can simply be
"go-to" questions that are less about the specifics of the person

and his or her work and more general human questions that, in theory, anyone can answer. Some people might refer to these as "softball" questions (easy questions that don't create much tension), but I would argue that the occasional easy question can help put the subject at ease and, sometimes, help you understand who they are. For example:

- If you weren't a (fill in the blank), what career would you have pursued?

- What's the last book you read?[9]

- Tell me a story about the most challenging time you've had with (fill in the blank).

- Who do you admire in your field and why?

- What have you done in your life that you're most ashamed of?

OK, that last question doesn't really qualify as softball, but when posed to politicians it can prompt some interesting responses. One time, a political candidate actually responded by telling me about the time she had stepped over a passed-out drunk man in her hometown.

8. **Follow up.** Sometimes people say things that are confusing—either because the subject is complicated (see electric deregulation) or because the person talking is inarticulate. It can be easy to simply write down what a person says and regurgitate it with no real understanding, but that's not the goal of interviewing. If you don't understand what's being said, ask for it to be explained again. Ninety-nine percent of people would rather repeat themselves than be misunderstood (that's a made-up statistic, but I stand by it). Similarly, if

---

9   When I conducted interviews with politicians for the *Reporter's* endorsements, I almost always asked candidates either what book they were reading or for the title of a book that had been influential. And if their answer was either the Bible or *The Seven Habits of Highly Effective People*, I was not impressed.

you're going through your notes from an interview and come across a confusing quote, don't be afraid to follow up via email or phone call with a subject and ask for clarification. Again, no one wants to be misquoted, taken out of context, or sound confusing in print. Unless there is a good reason to include a confusing quote (like you're writing a story on the Most Confusing Person Alive), go back for elucidation. The ultimate goal in any published piece is to serve the reader, and no one is served by confusion. To this end:

- Don't be afraid to ask people to slow down if they're talking too fast.

- Make them spell everything! Never assume you know how to spell their name. And don't rely on the Internet; if you haven't noticed, it's not the most reliable source of information.

- Ask for a business card and file it for future reference. This small act has saved me untold hours of frustration.

Every interview also is a chance to further your story by asking the subject for more ideas and more sources. If you're working on a story with multiple voices, ask everyone you interview, "Who else do you think I should talk to?"


9. **Quote hunt.** A common trend I see with new interviewers is a tendency to quote every word said, even when the words are not particularly interesting. As already noted, some interview material is better paraphrased or summarized. As you're reading through your interview notes, identify those places in which your subject was eloquent, passionate, funny, or interesting. As with fiction dialogue, choose quotations that help move the story, those that reveal the person speaking or that reveal elements of the story itself. Compare the following (fabricated) examples.

**Boring:** "We will vote on the nude bicyclist amendment on Thursday."

**Less boring:** "I'm planning to stand up for every nude bicyclist in the city—naked is beautiful, and I'll vote naked if I have to."

10. **Be willing to admit failure.** I like to think that anyone can be interviewed by anyone, but my own experience tells me this isn't true. I haven't had to scrap too many interviews, but I have had to throw away a few. If you've planned a Q&A with someone who simply won't respond with any sort of content, you'll be hard-pressed to let their words speak for themselves.

## PROMPTS AND PRACTICE

1. **Reverse interview.** Behind every great story or quote lies a question. Read a reported essay or article and highlight all the quotes. Now, try to see if you can derive the questions that led to the highlighted responses.

2. **Follow up.** Read an interview or a profile of someone unfamiliar. Write out a list of questions that weren't asked but should have been.

3. **Crowdsource.** Social media, though often a mind-numbing, soul-sucking waste of time, can also be a fertile spot for finding both questions and answers. Post an open-ended question on your social media channel of choice and see what types of responses you get. This is a chance to test out the vibrancy of your question and also may give you some ideas for a future interview. Along the same lines, if you have an interview or interview idea, use social media to ask your networks to help you come up with questions for your interview.

4. **Use your friends and family.** If you're really new to interviewing, practice on a friend or relative. I often begin new classes by having students interview one another. Interviewing someone you already know isn't the same as interviewing a stranger, but the mere act of creating an interview framework can create interesting and sometimes unexpected shifts in dynamics. The point here is to get you comfortable with asking questions—an acquired skill, but one that is accessible to everyone.

5. **Turn the tables.** I've been interviewed several times and have learned from the experience that (a) I'm a terrible interview subject, and (b) much can be learned from being on the receiving end of the experience. Find a fellow writer, reporter-friend, or just someone who is game, and ask that person to interview you.

6. **Practice note taking.** Listen to one of the so-called great speeches in US history and take notes as quickly as you can. Clean up your notes and compare what you ended up with to a transcript of the speech (both speeches and transcripts are available on the *American Rhetoric* website).

7. **Rewrite.** Speaking of speeches, at the end of this chapter you'll find the complete speech President Barack Obama delivered on April 29, 2016, at the White House Jazz Festival. Read this speech, and then write a short story in which you use direct quotation, indirect quotation, partial quotation, and narrative.

8. **Go public.** Events offer an opportunity to practice honing your questioning skills as many events—such as author readings and lectures—include a Q&A segment for the audience. Attend an event of interest, steel up your nerve, and ask a question. See if you get a satisfying response.

9. **Practice prep.** OK, maybe you're not going to get an interview with your idol (yet). But what if you could? Read up and become an expert on your subject. Now write out questions that show your knowledge and curiosity (but don't stay up all night!). Make sure a few of them are tough ones.

10. **Pick up the phone.** Are you ready to actually interview someone? Go for it. Not quite? Many radio programs—particularly public radio shows—allow listeners to call in and ask questions of special guests.

# ADDITIONAL READING

## On What Matters
Noam Chomsky interviewed by Julia Goldberg
*Santa Fe Reporter,* January 19, 2005

**SFR: What was your take on the criticisms that the U.S. didn't react quickly enough to the tsunami?**
**NC**: The initial response was really scandalous. It was virtually nothing and then, after criticism—international criticism and domestic criticism—the U.S. involvement was increased, funding was increased, but it's still a tiny fraction if you compare it to the scale of the economy. It's a tiny percentage and, in fact, that's true of foreign aid generally, it's not unique to the United States. The percentage of total foreign aid is tiny, but in fact the U.S. has the worst record among the industrialized countries in percentage of the economy, the gross domestic product. The public's attitude toward this is interesting. The public thinks we give way too much money for public aid but when asked how much we should be giving thinks we should be giving far more than we're actually giving. There's just gross illusion about the amount.

**It's been said the U.S. is improving its international image by helping the tsunami victims.**
Yes, there's that total cynicism. You don't give aid because you hope it's going to improve your image. The PR aspect of it is overwhelming, which is disgraceful, and the actual amount given is far below what it should be, but in a way we're kind of missing the point. The tsunami disaster was horrible, the latest figures are 150,000 killed . . . in eastern Congo, that many people are killed every five months. Are we doing anything about that? There are about 1,000 people being killed a day there, or if you take a look at easily preventable deaths in southern Africa alone, just among children, the number dying from easily preventable deaths is probably on the order of 1,000 a day or something. It's Rwanda-level killing every day, and that can be prevented by providing medicine or infrastructure.

**Will your Santa Fe appearance with Tariq Ali focus on Palestine and the Middle East?**

Precisely for that reason it won't. I'll talk about other issues, obviously I'll have to bring up Iraq. I'll try to focus on other issues assuming that in the conversation with Tariq we'll discuss the Middle East.

**CNN pointed out that Bush wants Mahmoud Abbas to visit the White House, but he never invited Arafat because Bush viewed Arafat as standing in the way of peace. Does this seem like a legitimate characterization to you?**

We're watching an interesting illustration of how doctrinal systems work. The main principle of a doctrinal system is you have to turn attention from yourself and onto the misdeeds of others. Here's a perfect example of it. Whatever you think about Arafat, he was not the obstacle to peace. The obstacle to peace was the U.S. The U.S. has been refusing to accept a political settlement that has overwhelming international support, but the U.S. refuses and the Bush administration is extreme in refusing . . . so therefore, take a look at the framework for media coverage or commentary. What you have to focus on are the alleged differences between Arafat and Abbas because that, you know, blames it on the Palestinians . . . if it doesn't work the way the U.S. wants, they can blame it on Abbas.

**You wrote an article, I think on Znet, that said the November 2 elections told us very little about the state of the country. Can you elaborate?**

For a very simple reason. The elections very self-consciously evaded issues of political significance and were focused almost entirely on projecting images in an effort to delude the public into purchasing the candidate who was being sold by the imagery creation. That's not very surprising. The elections are run by the PR industry and that's what they do in their everyday lives. What they're doing is trying to delude you into purchasing this commodity rather than that identical one. When the same industry is given the task of selling candidates, they do it the same way. That's not a democratic election. It's as much of an election as when you can delude someone into buying a Chevy instead of a Ford by deceit and, in fact, it's much worse than that because right before the election the major institutions in the country that monitor public attitude . . . released important studies of the public's opinion on major issues that were almost completely suppressed in the media and what they showed was the two political parties are way to the right of the public on issue after issue.

**So the subsequent discussions of blue states and red states and moral values, you don't see that as legitimate?**
First of all, what do people mean by "values"? Suppose people say "I'm voting because of values." That tells you right off they're not voting on issues, and in a democratic society people should be voting on issues. The second issue is what are people's values? That's rarely been investigated, and the few times it's been looked at it turns out the values are the country is too materialistic and should be more fair and egalitarian or their values are that they are opposed to the war in Iraq. The red-blue state business, yeah there are differences and, in fact, look at the factors that differentiate them. Probably the most striking one, statistically, has to do with rising inequality. The states where inequality has been rising, and it's rising very fast—especially under Bush, but for some years—the states where it's risen the most rapidly are the blues states, which suggests people are voting on economic issues even though the economic issues aren't coming up in the election.

**What are the domestic issues in this country that interest you right now?**
One major issue in the country is the collapse of the democratic system as illustrated, for example, in the last election. Another crucial issue is healthcare costs. These are really significant. This could well bankrupt the economy. They are going up very fast; they are out of control. A lot of it has to do with the fact it's privatized and the enormous power of the pharmaceutical industry. And it's being evaded in favor of a non-issue, mainly Social Security. The huge fuss about the Social Security crisis, which first of all doesn't exist. It's all a fraud. Everyone in the press is talking about it and there's no crisis, and to the extent that there's any problem at all it's tiny when compared with medical care. But the point is the ideological reason behind it. Social Security is a democratic system based on the principle that people care about each other, that we have a community responsibility to make sure vulnerable people are taken care of, so therefore there's a huge attack on Social Security to try to dismantle it, even though there's no issue. The transformation of the military to an extremely aggressive posture which is leading to the ultimate doom that mainstream strategists are correct in predicting, that's another major problem. It's kind of interesting. When you read the mainstream analysts, they barely even hope that it could be dealt with by the American population. Their faith in American democracy is so slight they barely bring that up. What they hope is a coalition of peace-loving states will counter U.S. aggressiveness. They don't think we can. That's a very serious problem domestically.

**Do you disagree with the analysis there's little to be hopeful about in American democracy?**

I think there's a tremendous amount to be hopeful about. Look at public opinion polls. What they show is that the large majority of public opinion probably agrees with you and the position of your paper. I don't know the position of your paper but I'm just guessing. . . . Take the activist positions. That's a hopeful sign. The point is the activists happen to be in the mainstream of opinion. That's hopeful because it means there are ways to overcome what's going on now by creating a more democratic society.

# Remarks by the President
# at White House Jazz Festival
President Barack Obama
April 29, 2016

Good evening, everybody! Welcome to the White House! Good-looking crowd. For five years, International Jazz Day's main event has been celebrated around the world, from Istanbul, to Osaka, to Paris. So we couldn't be prouder that, this year, jazz comes back home to America. (Applause.) I want to thank UNESCO, its Director General Irina Bokova, and the Thelonious Monk Institute for helping us to put on this unbelievable event. (Applause.) I also want to thank someone who has been a great friend to me and Michelle—UNESCO ambassador, legendary jazz musician, and all-around cool cat Herbie Hancock. (Applause.) And our emcee for the evening, who some people say has a pretty good voice, Morgan Freeman. (Applause.)

In 1964, Dizzy Gillespie ran for President—this is a true story—and he said, "When I am elected President of the United States, my first executive order will be to change the name of the White House to the Blues House." (Laughter.) So tonight, we're going to do right by Dizzy. We are turning this place into the Blues House. (Applause.) And before anybody calls this executive overreach—(laughter)—or some sort of power-grab, I want to clarify that I did not issue a new executive order. I just invited all my favorite jazz musicians to play in my backyard, which is one of the great perks of the job.

I don't need to tell this crowd the story of jazz. From humble origins as the music of the black working class—largely invisible to the mainstream—it went on to become America's most significant artistic contribution to the world. Jazz took shape in that most American of cities, New Orleans, where the rich blend of Spanish, and French, and Creole, and other influences sparked an innovative new sound. By the early 20th century, you could walk down the street of the infamous Storyville district and—maybe as you tried to stay out of trouble—hear the likes of Jelly Roll Morton and King Oliver and, of course, Louis Armstrong.

Over the years, the sound traveled and changed—hot jazz, swing, bebop, Latin, fusion, and experiments that defied labels. But its essence has always remained the same.

Most jazz lovers probably remember the first time this music got into our bones. Maybe it was Miles teaching us to make room for silence, to hear life in the notes that he didn't play. Or how Herbie could hang our hearts on a suspended chord. Or how Billie's voice, shimmering and shattered, seemed to bend time itself.

For me, that happened as a child, when my father, who I barely knew, came to visit me for about a month. And in the few weeks that I spent with him, one of the things that he did was take me to my first jazz concert—to see Dave Brubeck in Honolulu, Hawaii, in 1971. And I didn't realize at the time that it had, but the world that that concert opened up for a 10-year-old boy was spectacular. And I was hooked.

Many have said that they've been hooked as well. And perhaps more than any other form of art, jazz is driven by an unmistakably American spirit—it is, in so many ways, the story of our nation's progress. Born out of the struggle of African Americans yearning for freedom. Forged in a crucible of cultures—a product of the diversity that would forever define our nation's greatness. Rooted in a common language from which to depart to places unknown. It's both "the ultimate in rugged individualism"—to get out on stage with nothing but your instrument and improvise, spontaneously create; and the truest expression of community—the unspoken bond of musicians who take that leap of faith together. There is something fearless and true about jazz. This is truth-telling music.

Jazz is perhaps the most honest reflection of who we are as a nation. Because after all, has there ever been any greater improvisation than America itself? We do it in our own way. We move forward even when the road ahead is uncertain, stubbornly insistent that we'll get to somewhere better, and confident that we've got all the right notes up our sleeve.

And that's what's attracted a global audience to this music. It speaks to something universal about our humanity—the restlessness that stirs in every soul, the desire to create with no boundaries.

"Jazz is a good barometer of freedom," Duke Ellington once said. No wonder it has such an outsized imprint on the DNA of global music. It has spread like wildfire across the world, from Africa to Asia. And jazz blended with the bossa nova of Brazil or the tango of Argentina—which, from here on out, I will endeavor to appreciate as a listener and observer, rather than as a dancer. (Laughter and applause.) It can be heard on the Scottish bagpipe, on the Indian sitar. It opened up new exchanges with classical music, and with Eastern music—and it can make the oldest folk songs sound new.

Jazz. It's always been where people come together, across seemingly unbridgeable divides. And here at home, before schools and sports, it was jazz that desegregated—because for so many players, the only thing that mattered was the music.

The same was true around the world. I was recently in Cuba, the first American President to make that trip in 88 years. (Applause.) And in Havana, you can hear the beautiful sounds of Afro-Cuban jazz, and that unlikely marriage of cultures that, a century later, still captivates us. We hope this music will lead to new avenues for dialogue, and new collaborations across borders. And if we can keep faith with that spirit, there's no doubt that jazz will live on for generations to come.

So let me stop talking. We've got an all-star lineup of artists from around the country and around the world. Is everybody ready? (Applause.) Let's do this thing.  Jazz at the Blues House. (Applause.)

# READING AND RESOURCES FROM THIS CHAPTER

"American Rhetoric Top 100 Speeches Archive." *American Rhetoric.* http:// www.americanrhetoric.com/ top100speechesall.html.

Goldberg, Julia. "On What Matters: An Interview with Noam Chomsky." *Santa Fe Reporter,* August 2005. https:// chomsky.info/20050119/.

——. "Present Tense: An Interview with Margaret Atwood." *Santa Fe Reporter,* November 2009. http://www.sfreporter. com/santafe/article -5017-present-tense.html.

Gutkind, Lee. "The Five R's of Creative Nonfiction." *Creative Nonfiction,* 1996. https://www.creativenonfiction.org/ online-reading/whats-story-6.

Jamison, Leslie. "The Devil's Bait." *Harper's,* September 2013. http://harpers.org/archive/2013/09/the-devils-bait/.

McPhee, John. "A Sense of Where You Are." *The New Yorker,* January 23, 1965. http://www.newyorker.com/ magazine/1965/01/23/a-sense-of-where-you-are.

Nankani, Sandhya, and Holly Epstein Ojalvo. "Beyond Question: Learning the Art of the Interview." *New York Times Learning Network,* September 20, 2010. http:// learning.blogs.nytimes.com/2010/09/20/ beyond-question-learning-the-art-of-the-interview.

"Nonfiction Self-Interview Archive." *Nervous Breakdown.* http://www.thenervousbreakdown.com/category/ nonfiction/self-interview--nonfiction/.

Obama, Barack. "Remarks by the President at White House Jazz Festival." Speech, Washington, DC, April 29, 2016. The White House, https://www.whitehouse.gov/the-press-office/2016/04/30/remarks-president-white-house-jazz-festival.

Sager, Mike. "The Multitudes of Roseanne Barr." *Esquire*, August 2001. http://longform.org/stories/the-multitudes-of-roseanne.

CHAPTER THREE

# Story Hunting or
# Beat Reporting for Everyone

Thursday was not a good day for McGovern. By noon there was not much left of Wednesday night's Triumphant Warrior smile. He spent most of Thursday afternoon grappling with a long list of vice-presidential possibilities and by two, the Doral lobby was foaming with reporters and TV cameras. The name had to be formally submitted by 3:59 PM, but it was 4:05 when Mankiewicz finally appeared to say McGovern had decided on Senator Thomas Eagleton of Missouri.

There is a very tangled story behind that choice, but I don't feel like writing it now. My immediate reaction was not enthusiastic, and the staff people I talked to seemed vaguely depressed—if only because it was a concession to "the Old Politics," a nice-looking Catholic boy from Missouri with friends in the Labor Movement. His acceptance speech that night was not memorable—perhaps because it was followed by the long-awaited appearance of Ted Kennedy, who had turned the job down.

—**Hunter S. Thompson,** *Fear and Loathing
on the Campaign Trail '72*

ERHAPS YOU'RE WONDERING why, of all the inflam-
matory, funny, or gonzo sentences written by the late
Hunter S. Thompson, I chose the quote above (from the
chapter "July," with a larger excerpt available on *Rolling Stone*'s
website) as an epigraph to this chapter.

Although it was Thompson's voice and fearlessness that
drew me to *Fear and Loathing* as a teenager, later I realized
that I had been equally drawn to his immersive knowledge of
politics. Thompson understood politics, he knew the players,
he talked to the sources. The result was an ability to translate the jargon and minutiae of a political campaign (and just
about any sector that intersects with government is laden
with jargon and minutiae) into a human drama, unreliable
narrator notwithstanding. Hunter S. Thompson—and his
legion of fans—probably would take issue with me describing
him as a beat reporter, but any journalist who hones in on a
particular topic and makes knowing its every crevice his or
her job is a beat reporter.

In Thompson's case, the beat was a specific political campaign, and his knowledge of the importance of that campaign and the electoral process—the nuts and bolts as well as
the political gestalt—forms the book's backbone just as much
as Thompson's binges, digressions, and personal voice. Beat
reporting is about developing sources to find stories, a process that leads to other stories. It's about knowing the people
who maneuver behind a particular topic or sector and learning
their stories (and secrets). It's also about knowing the names,
dates, places, and numbers—the crucial specificity—required for
all good writing. The 1970s were long gone by the time I read
Thompson, and I had the sense that I had missed out on the
seminal time in journalism (yes, this was during the 1990s and
before the Internet, but I still felt that way).

Fifteen years or so after first encountering *Fear and Loathing*,
I was hired as a beat reporter for the weekly *Rio Grande Sun* in

Española, New Mexico, a 10,000-circulation community weekly that covers Rio Arriba County. My first week on the job, I was tasked with covering and writing about the Española School Board meeting. If this scene were a movie, the opening shots would show a not-tall woman in her late twenties driving a small, beat-up Hyundai down a desolate New Mexico highway, making a series of wrong turns and illegal U-turns. Close-ups might show the anxiety on her face as the car's clock ticks forward and the evening grows later. Voice-over might reflect an inner monologue of profanity-laden panic.

Finally, an expression of relief crosses her face as she pulls, shakily, into the parking lot of San Juan Elementary School at the Ohkay Owingeh Pueblo, grabs her notebook, and runs into the building.

I had just finished up my graduate degree in Creative Writing at the University of New Mexico and was slightly at loose ends. I'd written a novel for my thesis, secured an agent, and was waiting for it to sell (it never did). I had been freelancing for numerous local newspapers and magazines, writing a variety of arts stories and features. I had applied, half on a whim but mostly out of desperation, to be employed in some form or another as a writer, for a reporter position at the *Sun*. I had also been intrigued and amused by the *Sun*'s ad for the job:

> The Worst Hometown Newspaper that ever existed has an immediate opening for a general assignment reporter covering exciting Rio Arriba County.

Despite my growing pile of clips at that point, my news chops were fairly untested. The *Sun*'s owner, the late great Bob Trapp, had given me a chance, though—it seemed to me the turning point in my interview had come when he asked me why I wanted to be a reporter and I told him that it seemed to be the only profession where my incessant nosiness was an asset.

Bravado aside, I had no idea what I was doing. Becoming a freelance writer had taken persistence, but writing regular previews of arts events and evergreen features for special issues was a fairly easy gig (I think of those days as the "How to Have a Perfect Picnic" era, as I'm pretty sure I wrote at least two stories with that headline). I had no idea how to be a beat reporter and had just been assigned the Rio Arriba County School District and County Commission as my first beats. I knew nothing about either entity. I had told the paper's news editor I hoped to cover politics, and when he told me, "Everything is political in Española," I had no idea what he was talking about. My mind was still full of politics as understood in an academic setting, which is to say, as an abstraction. Now I was about to cover my first school board meeting, and I was going to be late because I couldn't actually find the school.

When I finally entered the gymnasium, sweaty and panicked, the meeting was underway. The school board members sat at a long table, with the district superintendent, facing the meeting attendees, who sat on bleachers. Everyone stopped talking when I entered and the superintendent introduced me, saying in an unexpressive tone, "This is our new school's reporter, Mrs. Goldberg."

"Sorry, I'm late," I said. "I got lost."

"Welcome to Española," he intoned as a packed gymnasium of onlookers stared at me.

The time I spent at the *Sun* was a reporting boot camp. This was pre-Internet, and the pressure to fill the paper with column inches was considerable. Stories were found solely through the basic tenets of beat reporting: attending meetings, making rounds, developing sources, digging. The vast majority of all the interviews I conducted took place face-to-face. Española is a small town, but Rio Arriba County is large, with wildly divergent communities around every corner. The people I met were storytellers; the shenanigans of public officials were nonstop.

I soon learned what the news editor had meant when he told me I'd be covering politics one way or another. He didn't mean electoral politics, he meant politics like the school board deciding to fire the middle school principal and replace her with a crony. He meant the state attorney general deciding to convene a grand jury to build voter fraud cases against county officials. He meant following the money.

The *Sun* has earned, over the decades, a symbiotic relationship with the community. Everyone reads it. Traffic backs up Wednesday evenings as people stop to buy it from street vendors. Public officials know a *Sun* reporter is always coming, whether to a meeting or to seek comment; no shortage of people steadily fed me story ideas, tips, and leaked documents throughout my tenure at the paper.

How do you go from knowing next to nothing about a subject to reporting and writing about it? Through beat reporting. My job at the *Sun* was to attend every school board and county meeting, to get to know the people associated with each beat, to cover the important events and issues for each area, and to (ideally) find stories therein—preferably ones that followed the money and uncovered misuse.

Beat reporting can sound daunting and overwhelming, but in truth it's about putting in the hours and time in order to deeply know a subject. The *Sun* has such a cemented relationship with the surrounding communities that it wasn't long before everyone knew me and began either contacting me with stories or avoiding my calls. Within a year, I had sat through countless late-night meetings; I had prowled around government offices shamelessly eavesdropping; I had caused a small uproar at the high school by spending an unsupervised day on campus; and I had been called as a witness to a grand jury in an election fraud case.

I met a lot of people I dropped in on just to chat and see what was up. If Bob Trapp had hired me because I was nosy, the *Sun* provided endless fodder for this particular personality flaw. In small towns, everyone has a story; in northern New Mexico, where government is one of the leading employers, looking for grift at worst and waste at best was investigative reporting boot camp.[10]

The *Sun* was a small town newspaper with a traditional model of covering the city and county government, the cops and the courts, and the schools. We also all were tasked with general assignment reporting, which meant that if I needed a break from writing about education, I could always go rustle up a story about ongoing litigation over logging, or write a quick feature on a local man's rehabilitation of an old Cessna (pro tip: if you decide to undertake the latter, you may find yourself with very little warning strapped into a tiny and terrifying plane). Working at the *Sun* taught me that I could always find stories just by keeping my eyes and ears open.

A paper of record functions somewhat differently than a paper like the *Santa Fe Reporter*. Although also a weekly, the *Reporter*—and other papers that follow either the altweekly model or are niche publications—is less tied to traditional beat reporting models. When I became editor of the *Reporter* in 2000, the reporters' beats included government, but the writers also had a rotating list of areas they covered. We weren't the paper of record, and this gave us a little more freedom from attending every single public meeting. And we quasi-regularly reviewed what we were focusing on in order to mix things up. At one point, "weird people" was a beat because . . . well, it was Santa Fe.

Beat reporting has been the topic of a great deal of conversation in the age of new media. The common narrative goes that with the decline of newspapers has come the decline of the beat, leading to a lack of accountability of government and a decline in the investigative journalism that often grows out of a reporter's

---

10      The *Sun* has received numerous awards and recognition for its doggedness, which is the subject of the 2012 documentary film *The Sun Never Sets*—highly recommended.

daily scrutiny of one particular area. A parallel narrative suggests that beat reporting no longer fits the needs of today's news culture. Former *Economist* writer Gideon Lichfield suggested in a 2012 blog that "beats aren't so much an objective taxonomy as a convenient management tool, devised for an old technology," pointing to the newspaper "sections" of yore (yore being roughly the early 1800s through now) as the raison d'être for dividing editors and reporters into beats in the first place. Lichfield suggested in his post that "obsessions" are a more fitting taxonomy for today's global online reader, such as those cultivated by the online site he became editor for (*Quartz*: qz.com), where "we structure our newsroom around an ever-evolving collection of phenomena . . . ."

While it is possibly true that the average media consumer doesn't pick up his or her daily paper to flip, first thing, to the police notes (except in Santa Fe, New Mexico, where people most certainly did this back when our daily paper still had the police notes), it seems clear to me from reading *Quartz*'s staff list that most of its impressive staff grew their credentials through following, closely, a particular beat (the global financial one). Regardless of what you call it—beat reporting, obsessive stalking, story hunting—reporters find stories by drilling down into a particular area, meeting the players, and reporting on its big and small twists and turns. This isn't to suggest that you should pick only one topic and never look back. Perhaps you will have several topics that become your area of expertise; maybe these will change over time. But digging into a topic in a sustained way will yield better stories and more narrative authority in the long run than writing perpetually as a generalist.

"The owners of Gringo's Mexican Kitchen are old hands at confronting the typical challenges of a burgeoning restaurant business—hiring, competition, even developing a 'gluten guide.' But recently the Tex-Mex chain has been facing an unusual dilemma: whether to allow customers to openly display their guns while munching fajitas."

—Dan Frosch, "Texas Gears Up for New Open-Carry Handgun Law"

Dan Frosch, a reporter for the *Wall Street Journal* and formerly the *New York Times*, practices beat reporting at the national level. He is one of several reporters whose "beat" is essentially the western states. For Frosch, this means keeping an eye out daily for any important stories that may be happening in an entire region. Frosch spends at least an hour each morning scanning daily papers from across these states, looking to see if there are any news events happening or emerging that he'll need to cover.

With so much terrain as his beat, Frosch frequently has to jump into action to cover multiple stories breaking on his beat at a moment's notice. For example, in the last week of December 2015, Frosch covered stories on the aftermath of a fatal shooting by police in Chicago, the more than forty deaths from the tornadoes that swept Texas, and the story quoted above that examined Texas's new open-carry law for handguns. The story relies on a variety of sources and perspectives—the lawyers of the restaurant chain mentioned in the opening of the story, a gun-rights group, law enforcement officials.

All of these stories followed what had already been an intensive week or so for Frosch of covering the shooting rampage that took place in San Bernardino, California, earlier in December. The San Bernardino shooting had not only fallen under Frosch's beat of western state reporting, but also overlapped with beat reporting work he does at the *WSJ* as part of a group of reporters who cover ISIS in America.

"The reason [*WSJ*] brought me into [covering ISIS in America] was because I started to develop federal law enforcement sources who could help confirm information when there were breaking news stories," Frosch said, "or guide us in the right direction on certain stories."

Frosch, who worked as a staff writer at the *Reporter* during my tenure as editor, had developed those sources in the same way any reporter would develop new sources: "I just started out by building relationships, just having a cup of coffee, then a cup of coffee turns into beer, you start meeting with a couple of people, maybe one or two people periodically, and developing a sense of trust. They learn to trust you; you learn to trust them."

Source development serves Frosch well in one of his roles at *WSJ*, which involves contacting law-enforcement officials for background confirmation on breaking and ongoing stories.

Julie Ann Grimm spent a decade covering the city beat for the daily *Santa Fe New Mexican* before becoming the editor of the weekly *Santa Fe Reporter* in 2013. She describes her decade covering city hall in Santa Fe as one of complete immersion into the ins and outs of municipal government.

She emphasizes the importance as a beat reporter of developing an organizational system and, particularly for reporters covering government, availing oneself of all the public documents that are accessible. Grimm worked for the Associated Press's New Mexico bureau out of Albuquerque for approximately three years before becoming the city reporter for the *Santa Fe New Mexican*.

"When your beat is government, it's easy to immerse yourself," she says. "You're there every time the gavel bangs, you know who has which jobs and . . . here are these processes you can follow for long periods of time . . . maybe you're not writing about the processes themselves, but as you follow them, you're finding interesting things to write about." Grimm also emphasizes how important it was to read everything about her beat, whether it meant stories from the competing daily paper, stories written by her predecessors on the beat, or public documents, such as meeting minutes, coming out of city hall.

"I would often sit at home on my couch while I was watching junk TV and read the minutes of meetings I had attended," she said. "There's always something that jumps out at you that you can follow up on . . . I would just circle stuff out of the minutes and stick it on my bulletin board and have a story later on."

Grimm also continues to keep a "phone log" of everyone she talks to, often with notes, as a place she can look to when she needs to find a source for a story. She does this in spite— or maybe because—of all the electronic resources available to today's reporters. "Everyone has their own organizational strategy and some people are more successful than others," she says, but the bottom line as a beat reporter is it's important to have a "structure for retaining source information so you can access it in a hurry." Relying on typing a name into Google may not always be the most efficient—or even reliable—process.

The result of putting in the legwork and hours on a beat, Grimm says, is the ability to write with authority, always have a well of stories from which to draw, and to have the context for important stories on one's beat. For example, she talks about covering the City of Santa Fe's "living wage" law and realizing—before anyone else—that the city had actually neglected to adjust it to the federal consumer price index. Her story on that oversight, which ran in the *Santa Fe New Mexican* in November 2011, begins, "Santa Fe city workers who are struggling away at minimum-wage jobs could have earned a few cents more per hour this year if officials had paid attention to their own rules."

Grimm "found" that story because she was looking into reporting a story about the following year's increase as part of her beat. After her story was published, she remembers the mayor acknowledging her at a public meeting saying, "'Julie Ann Grimm figured this out, and we owe her a round of applause or a gold star or something intangible like that.' But I wasn't going to find that story just by doing the press releases, and sometimes it really matters. Sometimes the beat reporter figures out something that was overlooked because you're an extra set of eyes on the problem."

Ultimately, Grimm says, beat reporting serves multiple purposes. "You really get the context of what you're writing about.

You're able to write with authority and figure out what the motivations are or what the consequences will be, and it's more of a service to your readers maybe than if your editor says 'go to that press conference' as a general assignment reporter. And, if you're doing your beat right, stories are falling out of your pocket."

Laura Paskus came to investigative and environmental journalism as a second career. She had worked as an archaeologist and tribal consultant in several states across the south western United States. "Once I was out here doing archaeology, I became more interested in western land and water issues, and so I was kind of learning some of that stuff on the job, but I felt really frustrated that the coolest stuff I was learning, whether it was archaeology or these broader issues on land and water or cultural issues too, everything ended up written up in these reports that went to government officials and the public never got to read. I was like, 'wow, but there are so many interesting things happening that the public should really know about.'"

Since becoming a journalist in 2002, Paskus's work has appeared in *Al Jazeera America*, *Ms.* magazine, *Columbia Journalism Review*, and many other state, regional, and national publications. She focuses on long-form narrative stories from a position of advocacy, whether the topic is continuing coverage of climate change or a two-year investigative series on youth suicide. These ongoing, often multi-year projects require deep beat and source development. Paskus writes about environmental issues regularly, and from an environmentalist perspective. Nonetheless, she also reports on those issues, meaning many of her sources are people or agencies whose practices may be criticized or investigated in her stories.

Although Paskus entered the field with some knowledge of her subject, "There was a total shift . . . as far as understanding the different agencies and what they did and who would talk and who wouldn't; that was something that I started learning as a reporter and am still learning."

"There are currently some agencies in New Mexico . . . that deliberately ignore me and won't talk to me, and they seem completely comfortable with that," Paskus admits, but federal agencies and "some of the more professional officials" respond, regardless of the story's topic or stance. "I have always tried to be really fair to my sources, even if the story is kind of showing something they are doing that is pretty anti-environmental or having some sort of negative impact. There's one source in particular I'm thinking of who I've interviewed I don't even know how many times over the past probably ten or twelve years. He knows that his perspective is going to be among—not the bad-guy perspective—but anti-environment perspective and you know, that's just his representation and his idea and his place in . . . the issue."

For Paskus, one of the rewards of beat reporting is being able to cover an issue about which she's passionate, and "see some impact in really small ways for the work that I do." For example, she says, her first news story was about the plight of the Rio Grande and the silvery minnow. Fourteen years later, she's still writing about both. "I had someone say to me a few years ago, 'If you hadn't been covering this the whole time, I feel like our agency might not have paid as close attention.'"

Beat reporting is not just a useful model to know or use for journalists. For any writer who feels drawn to a particular topic, the precepts of beat reporting are a means toward learning the topic and creating a regular routine of following stories and developing sources to find stories versus having ideas on broad topics related to a particular subject. Reporting is not just a specific occupation; it's a mode of learning about the world. Writer Dave Eggers, who is both a novelist and a nonfiction writer, began as a journalist. In a 2009 *Time* magazine interview, Eggers was asked to respond to the notion that journalism wasn't "real writing," and that only fiction and creative nonfiction constituted "art." Eggers replied:

Well, my background is journalism. I don't have any creative-writing experience except for one class I took as a sophomore in college. I worked at magazines for over ten years before I even thought of writing a book. When I teach kids at [my tutoring center] 826 Valencia, the first thing I do is I send them out to report. They sign up for a class that they think is going to be creative writing, and I send them out to interview people. I think it's very important to know how to engage the world. If you want to write about people, you can make it up. But if you spend time talking to someone and examining what it is you want to write about, you discover a level of detail that you wouldn't have noticed otherwise.

## SOURCES

Beat reporting—all reporting—requires a variety of sourcing material. Source material is another way of saying "information." Information can come from reports and data, but mostly when journalists refer to sources they are talking about people. Developing sources is arguably the most important facet of successful nonfiction writing. A source is essentially a person who can provide you with a story, information for a story, a quote, or a tip.

If I were to open my email inbox right now (which I am not going to do as then I will become distracted and not finish this chapter), I would find any number of emails pitching me story and interview ideas. When I was hosting a regular radio show, part of my beat reporting was putting myself on the press release distribution lists for local government, politicians, non-profits and the like. When I was editor of a weekly newspaper, these emails came at such alarming frequency I maintained a disciplined regime of only checking them twice a day. Before email and cell phones, people used to just call me on the phone or send me anonymous tips in the mail. I kind of preferred that, but those days appear to be gone forever. As the 2000s unfolded, journalists also began using social media as part of beat development—following people and stories central to various areas of interest.

Many of the emails I've received over the years have been from public relations people essentially pitching stories for their clients; these were largely stories geared toward generating positive exposure. Sometimes these yield stories: an author with a book event, an expert on a key news story, an advance on a specific event that might be of interest to readers and listeners. Because I have mostly worked in local markets, I tend to pass on national trend stories (experts on pet communication, dating, and work-related topics, for example). But in general, the best sources are the ones a reporter personally cultivates. PR folks have a job to do, and many do it well, but that job is to present a pre-packaged story in a way that makes their constituencies look good.

#### ····Background Sources

There is a woman in Santa Fe with a deep knowledge of city politics and the history of this town. She is not someone I would necessarily interview for every topic or include in every story (although she has been widely and often quoted on a variety of topics). She is, however, someone I can call if I need explanations or background on topics. I have found her, over many years, to be on point and factually correct, and she has a shockingly good memory. It's important, for all beats, to have people who simply understand the field and can explain it. This doesn't mean they are providing stories; it doesn't even mean they are providing quotes in the stories. It means they are resources for your own understanding and contextualization of your stories.

···· *Quotable Sources*

Sometimes the people who help with background may also be good choices for quotes in a story. For example, if I call the head of the water utility for help in understanding billing changes, I may find that he is not only helpful in explaining how the system works, but is an appropriate source to provide a useful quote that will enhance my story. A quotable source is anyone willing to be interviewed, quoted, and have his or her name used in a story either with direct quotation or attributable information.

···· *Anonymous Sources*

On the other end of the spectrum, anonymous sources are people who are willing to be quoted or provide information for a story but are not willing to be identified. As a general rule, publications try to avoid anonymous sources since part of the credibility of a story comes from the attribution. Anonymous sources also have been widely criticized by readers given that anonymous sources have been connected to some of the more disheartening events in contemporary journalism. Some recent examples discussed in a *New York Times* December 2015 article include erroneous reporting that government officials missed open social media declarations by one of the shooters in the San Bernardino killings, as well as an inaccurate story from the previous summer regarding a potential Department of Justice investigation of Hillary Clinton. Both stories relied on anonymous sourcing, a topic the *Times*'s former public editor, Margaret Sullivan, addressed repeatedly in her columns.[11] Most major publications now have their

---

11    Margaret Sullivan, "Systemic Change Needed After Faulty Times Article," *New York Times*, December 18, 2015, http://publiceditor.blogs.nytimes.com/2015/12/18/new-york-times-san-bernardino-correction-margaret-sullivan-public-editor/.

ethics policies—which include policies on using anonymous
sources—online. Although they vary in scope and specificity,
the bottom line is that anonymous sources should be considered a last resort. In other words, the information they offer is
vital and can't be obtained in any other way.

#### ····*Off-the-Record Tipsters*

Some sources, however, don't provide background understanding or quotes. They provide stories, on the down low. "Off the
record" means that the information can't be used, even anonymously. Off-the-record information functions as a tip, a lead for
the reporter to find other ways to follow up.

Sometimes these sources are citizens who have become
aware of a financial problem or a flaw in government and want it
investigated. Sometimes, these sources are disgruntled employees or political adversaries of someone in power and they are
hoping to cause trouble. People who are behind the scenes,
regardless of motives, are—in my experience—the best resource
for learning about an institution and finding the stories behind
the public facades often presented by those on the front lines.
The key is to understand an off-the-record source's motivations.
Sometimes people need to stay off the record to protect their
jobs or other aspects of their lives. Other times, however, it's
because they want to stir up trouble anonymously. Motivation
is not necessarily the only measure by which to value an off-the-
record source (people with bad motivations can still have good
information), but it should be taken into consideration.

#### ····*Do Sources Know What Kind of Sources They Are?*

No one is required to talk to a journalist, although, arguably, elected officials should feel some compunction to respond to them. Officials who deal with the media on a regular basis should be expected to understand that "off the record" means a reporter can't use what is said in print. A reporter can negotiate with an off-the-record source to use the information but keep the source anonymous. A reporter can also look for other ways to verify the information if the source won't grant use of the information, even anonymously.

Granting someone the privilege of complete anonymity and using that person's information in a story means the reporter is taking on the responsibility of protecting that person's identity. Shield laws protect the reporter's right to do so, and these vary from state to state, ranging from no protection to complete protection, with numerous states somewhere in the middle.[12] You can read more on this issue in chapter 8 on ethics.

When a source agrees to be an anonymous source, this means the information provided can be used but not attributed, and that, unless it's specified, all discussions with a reporter are "on the record." Not everyone understands the distinctions between on and off the record and, certainly, people who aren't used to being interviewed may not be clear on their rights. When in doubt, reporters should always clarify a source's understanding of the discussion. Providing clear definitions at the start of a conversation can help avoid misunderstandings later:

- On-the-record: anything said can be used in print for attribution

---

12    Reporters Committee for the Freedom of the Press state-by-state shield laws, https://www.rcfp.org/browse-media-law-resources/guides/reporters privilege/shield-laws.

- Off-the-record: the discussion is only for background and can't be quoted or used

- Anonymous source: the information can be used and the source quoted, but not identified

•••• *Document Sources*

For many reporters, meeting agendas, budgets, public reports, and minutes are part of the day-to-day work of beat reporting. Meeting agendas help a reporter take an advance look at what may make a story tomorrow. Understanding budgets is a part of understanding how government works (or doesn't work) and where the money is being spent. In New Mexico, reporters have spent a great deal of time (and their lawyers' billable hours) trying to get a look at public officials' emails, as these are—at least in theory—part of a public record. As Wikileaks has shown, a fairly large amount of information is generated in document form, and no matter what type of nonfiction you are writing, chances are you'll need more than people to tell your story. You can read more on chasing paper in chapter 7.

## BEAT DEVELOPMENT

Covering a brand-new topic or entity, possibly in a brand-new city, can be daunting—in the same way that approaching any new task can be intimidating. On the front end, it seems impossible to get to know and learn about all the people, problems, and sometimes jargon associated with a topic. Beat work, though, essentially encompasses the same challenges as reporting an individual story, writ on a larger, ongoing scale. Every story requires jumping into a topic, finding sources, and becoming, if only temporarily, an expert on the subject. With beat reporting, the reporting is continuous. This means that through beat reporting, eventually the issues and stories will become more comfortable. For general assignment, a writer is often thrust into reporting and writing from scratch on topics hitherto unknown. Early on as a reporter, I was assigned stories on topics as varied as rural development, water rights, and homeless teens. None of these topics were part of a beat I covered, so I had to start from scratch, finding experts to explain (and sometimes re-explain) the issues to me.

In my classes, the students writing for the online magazine course are also required to pick and follow a beat for a portion of the semester, as a way of jumping in to the work of finding, reporting, and writing stories. Although in the world of reporting sometimes journalists will be asked to cover topics about which their interest is minimal, it's always better—of course—to seek out areas that are of some natural interest and grow that interest into expertise. I have one student who, for several semesters, staked out the area of LGBTQ as her beat. At times, this beat expanded to cover issues of diversity on campus. Her stories included everything from interviews with the campus feminist group to writing about the creation of gender-neutral bathrooms. She interviewed students for their reactions to the American Dialect Society's designation of "they" as a gender-neutral pronoun for 2015. Although the student began with a fair degree of knowledge and passion about her beat, her reporting expanded her own expertise. She wrote from a clear point of view—as an activist for equal rights—and her passion bolstered by her reporting helped inform and galvanize other students. One of the most exciting aspects of reported creative nonfiction, whether it's journalism or another type of writing, is finding stories that allow you, as a writer, to remain engaged and excited, and to make readers feel the same way.

# PROMPTS AND PRACTICE

1. **Define your beat.** The practice of beat reporting doesn't just apply to reporters covering various entities on a daily or weekly basis. Even a one-off story requires an element of immersive research. Even topics in which you are already immersed require an element of beat reporting. Consider, for example, a job posting from the *LA Weekly* for the position of film critic. The ad asks for a "smart and stylish" writer, but also says that "the ideal candidate will be an excellent reporter, willing to dig deeply while reporting on the film industry, its luminaries, and both the art and the industry." So whether you're interested in writing about food, love, or politics, digging deep into the topic like a beat reporter will bring knowledge, sources, and, ultimately, stories—which is what every creative nonfiction writer wants.

> **Start with questions:**
> · What are the issues within your beat or area of interest?
> · What entities does your beat include?
> · Who are the official people within your beat?
> · What kinds of public meetings/events happen in your beat?
> · What kinds of public documents are available within your beat, and how can you access them?

Most of these questions can start to be answered with a little bit of diligent online reading (in the good old days, answering these questions took a little bit longer). For instance, let's say you've just moved to Santa Fe and have decided to write about (or have been hired to write about) city government. And, for the sake of argument, let's say you've never covered city government before. After a few hours of reading previous coverage in other publications and perusing the city's website, your list would look something like this:

**Issues**: budget deficit, city politics, development, housing (it's worth noting that if you actually were covering Santa Fe city government, your list would probably look like this no matter what year it is).

**Entities**: The mayor, city councilors, city finance director, city planning director, city commissioners (planning, arts, finance), city public information officer, neighborhood groups

**Meetings/events**: city council meetings, city finance and committee meetings

**Public records**: city budget, city meeting agendas, annual reports, election statistics, development applications

Keep in mind, this is just your initial take from just a small investment of time perusing the Internet. You haven't even talked to anyone yet. But you're going to.

2. **Make a source list.** Who are the top ten people you would ideally talk to on your beat? Who are the movers and shakers in the area you want to cover? Are any of them accessible? If not, how close can you get?

3. **Attend events.** Are there any upcoming events related to your topic? If you want to write about the literary scene, make a list of all book-related events. These types of events may provide fodder, or perhaps you can pitch a preview or interview with the author. If you want to write about food, are there any food events? New restaurant openings? Happy hours?

4. **Learn your field.** What publications do you want to write for? Read them and see what they are covering and how. Know the writers who are already writing about the topics that interest you (at least know their work if you can't know them). Whether you are covering an area on an ongoing basis or jumping into a one-time

story, part of your job now is to know what is already out there. This endeavor is likely a way to generate story ideas: by seeing what isn't being written about. Read with an eye toward asking what questions have been left unanswered. For traditional reporters, organizations such as Investigative Reporters and Editors have thousands of tip sheets for various beats available to its members. Poynter's News University also has several beat-related, self-guided online trainings, some of which are currently free of charge.

5. **Start a tickler file.** As you'll learn in this book, I will always use a retro journalism term if given the opportunity. A tickler file, in a journalism context, is just a file, preferably organized in a way that makes sense to you, of potential stories or leads for potential stories. Create a system for tracking the people you want to meet with/are meeting with and what you're working on: meetings, interviews, public requests. As *SFR* Editor Julie Ann Grimm noted, the particular methodology isn't as important as simply having one. There have been numerous articles of late promoting chaos as a sign of creativity. I'm inclined to cling hopefully to that notion, as my desk/office usually look like the End Days are imminent, but my digital files are organized and useable.

6. **Now talk to people.** I majored in mental masturbation in college and enjoy a healthy helping of solipsism as much as the next person, but stories happen in the world, not in a vacuum of gray matter. If jumping right away into setting up formal interviews from your top-ten list sounds intimidating, that's fine. Just go where there are people and opportunities to hear from other people. Start by attending a lecture, a public forum, or simply sitting at a rowdy Laundromat with notebook in hand. Just get out as much as possible. Don't rely solely on the Internet for these interactions, either. While the Internet can be a great aid in finding sources, ideas, and documents, stories need characters, and people often carry more interesting information in

their minds than you'll find online (at least until the singularity; after that, all bets are off). As suggested by Frosch of the *Wall Street Journal*, don't just call people up when you need information or a quote. Develop your relationships with sources as you might develop your relationships with anyone: have a casual lunch or coffee, make time to talk just to get to know people.

7. **Use the news.** We've already discussed the importance of just reading to know the field, but the stories already being written can also help you jump in to start creating your lists and tickler files. One easy method is to read a story solely to make lists of the people who appear in them, their titles and the roles they play in the area in which you're interested. Use this extraction method for organizations, events, and documents as well.

**Read virtual and real bulletin boards to look for story ideas.**

**Sign up for email lists from organizations whose work you want to follow** (but be selective . . . I regret signing up for the Republican Party news blasts, particularly given that I can't seem to make them stop).

**Use RSS feeders to streamline your reading process.** RSS (Really Simple Syndication) allows you to feed the publications and topics you're interested in following to one spot so that you don't spend half the day trying to keep up with the Internet (a recipe for existential nausea if ever there was one). There are a gazillion readers, and chances are any I recommend will be gone or rebranded by the time you read this, but I'll throw out Feedly as one I've found to be simple to use and helpful.

**Use social media to find and track sources and stories.** My first semester teaching, I had a class on the topic of Social Movements. Right at the beginning of the semester, Occupy Wall Street began, which I knew because it dominated my

Facebook and Twitter feeds, which led me to read all the news coverage, mainstream and otherwise. I arrived at class on a Monday morning in the fall of 2011, certain the entire class would be raring to discuss the events of the weekend only to learn that no one had heard about it.

This was what some call a "teachable moment," in large part for me. I came to social media through a news job, so for me social media has largely been a tool to know what's going on in the world (and to watch cat videos, of course). I have now come to see that for many people, social media is simply that—social, cats, ranting, baby photos. That's fine (in an end-of-civilization kind of way), but don't overlook it as a tool for your reporting and research as well. Just as using news aggregators—software that streams multiple news sources in one place—can help you streamline your reading diet, using the feeder tools of sites like Twitter and even Facebook (to a lesser degree) can be a way to follow people and events of interest to you.

As the UC Berkeley Graduate School of Journalism points out in its Twitter for Journalists online tutorial, Facebook is organized across social spheres, while Twitter is organized by areas of interest. That means you can use its search functions, lists, and hashtags to follow people, topics, and events about which you want to know more. The easiest way to start (after signing up for an account) is to search the topics in which you're interested and start seeing who (or which organizations) pop up. From there, it's a matter of curating or directing your feed so that Twitter is delivering the content you want.

Once you feel you have the hang of Twitter, you may find using its interface Tweetdeck a helpful way to keep track of your Twitterverse. Tweetdeck is basically a dashboard that allows you to see all your customized columns, searches, and lists at once, which I find makes Twitter a more reading-friendly environment.

Although it's perfectly fine to use your social media in a lurking capacity, don't forget that it can also be a way to develop your sources more actively. Ask questions, reach out, and float ideas. I promise you won't be alone out there. A 2015 Poynter Institute story reported that journalists and news organizations—according to Twitter—are the most active group on Twitter. They also were reported as the top group of "verified" users, although they had far fewer followers than, say, musicians. So it goes.

# READING AND RESOURCES
## FROM THIS CHAPTER

"Beat Reporting." The Pulitzer Prizes. http://www.pulitzer.org/
prize-winners-by-category/278.

Dietz, Ben. *The Sun Never Sets*. Film. New Deal Films,
2012. http://www.newdealfilms.com/documentaries/
the-sun-never-sets.

Hacker, Scot, and Ashwin Sashigiri. "Tutorial: Twitter for
Journalists." UC Berkeley Graduate School of Journalism.
http://multimedia.journalism.berkeley.edu/tutorials/twitter.

Mullin, Benjamin. "Report: Journalists are Largest, Most
Active Verified Group on Twitter." Poynter Institute, May
26, 2015. http://www.poynter.org/2015/report-journalists-
are-largest-most-active-group-on-twitter/346957.

"Online Courses." News University, Poynter Institute. https://
www.newsu.org/courses.

Paskus, Laura, and Bryant Furlow. "Native American Youth
Face Higher Suicide Risk." *New Mexico In Depth*, May 26,
2015. http://nmindepth.com/series/choosing-life.

"Specialized Reporting." The Pulitzer Prizes.
http://www.pulitzer.org/prize-winners-by-category/273.

"Shield Laws and Protection of Sources by State." Reporters
Committee for Freedom of the Press. http://www.rcfp.org/
browse-media-law-resources/guides/reporters-privilege/
shield-laws.

Suddath, Claire. "Q&A with Author Dave Eggers." *Time*, July
22, 2009. http://content.time.com/time/arts/
article/0,8599,1912044,00.html.

Sullivan, Margaret. "The Disconnect on Anonymous Sources." *New York Times*, October 12, 2013. http://www.nytimes. com/2013/10/13/opinion/sunday/the-public-editor-the-disconnect-on-anonymous-sources.html.

"Tipsheets." *Investigative Reporters and Editors*. https://www. ire.org/resource--center/tipsheets.

Thompson, Hunter S. "Fear and Loathing in Miami: Old Bulls Meet the Butcher." *Rolling Stone*, August 17, 1971. http://www.rollingstone.com/culture/features/ fear-loathing-in-miami-old-bulls-meet-the-butcher-19720817.

# CHAPTER FOUR

# The Writer's Voice

A great photographer insists on writing poems. A brilliant essayist insists on writing novels. A singer with a voice like an angel insists on singing only her own, terrible songs. So when people tell me I should try to write this or that thing I don't want to write, I know what they mean.

—**Sarah Manguso,** *"Short Days"*

OF ALL THE elements of writing, "voice" remains the most mysterious, the literary equivalent of religion's "soul" or art's "beauty"—invariably ineffable and subjective. In a recent class, I had students read David Foster Wallace's essay "Consider the Lobster," and asked them how they would characterize Wallace's voice in the piece. Mostly they were irked by his use of footnotes, but one student—a Foster Wallace fan—said something to the effect that the voice was *very David Foster Wallace.*

I found the comment somewhat tautological, but took his point: We are drawn to writers' voices, but what do we mean by this? The writer's interests, perspective, word choices, sentence structures, tone? All of the above? Pinpointing those elements varies in degrees of difficulty depending on the writer. Here's an easy one. David Sedaris is funny. But what makes him funny? His material, his stance toward his material, the sequencing of his material, his word choice? I don't even want to answer my own questions because voice, of all the elements of craft, feels the most resistant to prescription.

A small group of friends of mine convene periodically for an event we call Book and Dish, at which we eat food and read one piece of writing written by someone else to one another. One time I brought Sedaris's "Six to Eight Black Men," about the myth of Santa Claus in Holland, and found myself unable to read it without laughing. I've just reread it now and the line "What kind of Santa spends his time pretending to kick people before stuffing them into a canvas sack?" delayed me finishing this paragraph by five full minutes. I am in the throes of a giggling fit even now while typing this sentence. Is it the material itself? No: Holland's version of the Santa Claus myth with its intrinsic racism and violence is not inherently funny. Rather, it's Sedaris's stance toward the mythology, his recognition of its racism and absurdity, his comedic timing in presenting the story, his rhetorical flourishes, which all together make it funny. But the piece doesn't just succeed because it's funny. It succeeds because of the odd humor Sedaris finds in a topic that isn't necessarily funny. It succeeds because the piece recognizes that tension and, thus, so do I. It's the same reason I like Jon Stewart, *The Onion,* and . . . Jane Austen.

But when I'm reading David Sedaris, I don't analyze why I'm laughing. I just think, *That's so David Sedaris.*

Except, of course, it isn't. It's a written version of the voice I assume Sedaris has in his head, rendered on the page. "Me Talk Pretty One Day," the titular essay of the collection, is ostensibly about Sedaris learning French but strikes me also as a decent working metaphor for the clichéd metaphor of "finding one's voice" in writing.

## ····*About That Clichéd Metaphor*

Voice in writing is a metaphor, yes? Here is the Merriam-Webster dictionary definition for voice: "sound produced by vertebrates by means of lungs, larynx, or syrinx; *especially*: sound so produced by human beings." So when we talk about the writing voice, we're talking about the idea that the voice on the page sounds a certain way. We are trying to say that the written voice is distinctive.

I thought about this a great deal when I had a radio show. I lasted one year as a daily morning talk show host, running my mouth for three hours each day, before transitioning to a weekly show. Needless to say, I became very familiar with my voice, my endless yammering voice.

At one point during this time, the station owner remarked to me, "I can tell you spend a lot of time talking in your head." I thought (but did not say), *You mean, thinking?* But, actually, that wasn't what he meant. Talking. And he was right. My inner monologue, silent narration, synaptic experience, whatever you want to call it, when I was on the radio, was suddenly significantly less mediated than normal. Thoughts that in the past might have remained inside my head had become spoken words. So. Many. Spoken. Words. I found the experience both exhilarating and debilitating. To sit down and try to mediate thoughts onto the page, basically the act of writing, became less enticing, particularly on top of teaching, which is also a type of thought-to-speech performative act. But this talking versus writing, voice-as-speech versus voice-in-writing also is instructive. The takeaway isn't that writing should necessarily sound like talking (although for some writers that is a goal), but that the goals of communication through language of our experiences, ideas, and sensibilities are the same.

In his essay "My Writing Education: A Timeline," writer George Saunders recounts a night during his time as a student in the Syracuse Creative Writing Program at his teacher Doug Unger's house during which all the students are asked to tell a story "off the cuff."

"None of us wants to be a flop and so each of us rises to the occasion by telling a story we actually find interesting, in something like our real voice, using the same assets (humor, understatement, overstatement, funny accents, whatever) that we actually use in our everyday lives to, for example, get out of trouble, or seduce someone."

For Saunders, "a light goes on" as he realizes, "What we're doing in writing is not all that different from what we've been doing all our lives, i.e., using our personalities as a way of coping with life. Writing is about charm, about finding and accessing and honing one's particular charms."

For me, this goes a long way toward understanding what we mean when we talk about "voice" in writing.

Robert Wilder talks about how telling stories aloud helped him develop the voice that characterizes his two nonfiction essay collections, *Daddy Needs a Drink* and *Tales from the Teachers' Lounge*.

"Daddy Needs a Drink" ran in column form in the *Reporter* while I was editor; as the name implies, the column discussed fatherhood from a humorous perspective (the subtitle in the book form also makes this clear: An Irreverent Look at Parenting from a Dad Who Truly Loves His Kids—Even When They're Driving Him Nuts).

What made Wilder's column funny (and popular) was his willingness to ignore the usual sacred cows of family life. For example, here's how Wilder begins a 2007 column, "The Big Splash," about taking his family to the local pool:

"Our local pool seems to be suffering from some sort of bipolar disorder.

On the first day we went this year, my family was greeted with strict instructions on how to enjoy ourselves safely. The guard at the counter told us to shower before entering the pool, which seemed fair until I saw the prison-like conditions of the locker room and the quarts of discount sunscreen the lady next to us applied before she plunged in."

Later, Wilder writes of a subsequent visit in which "the watchdogs had been replaced by a platoon of zombie lifeguards whose rulebooks must have been waterlogged in an after-hours brain drain festival."

Wilder traces the humor in his writing voice to his upbringing in a funny family.

"I grew up of as the son of a loudmouth," he says. "My dad was a big animated character, and our house was full of humor and jokes and ribbing and all that stuff. My dad, when I was younger, he listened to a lot of Henny Youngman and Victor Borge, so there was a lot of humor in the house, and that turned into Bill Cosby, and George Carlin, RIP, so there was a lot of language. It was funny because my parents didn't read very much, so it was much more oral," he said.

For Wilder, that inclination toward humor was, for a time, what he describes as his "walking around persona." As he recalls it, "I was always really verbal, and I remember sort of wanting to be quick and witty because I didn't think I had much else to offer. I was a mediocre athlete, I was a mediocre student, but I was kind of a smartass, and I was pretty quick."

In his graduate writing program, Wilder shied away from trying to write funny, instead trying to manufacture what he calls a "luminary" and "lofty" voice. That began to change, he says, as a result of teaching frequently with writer Natalie Goldberg, who would often encourage him to tell stories in class about his family.

"She'd say, 'Tell that story when London [Wilder's son] said pussy,' and I would tell them and they would always get big laughs, but I always thought that was because they were nice people and there to laugh. She kept saying to me, 'You need to write these down,' and she bugged me for like a year."

Not long after, Wilder began writing for the *Reporter*, and "What I found was when I was writing those stories primarily about my kids, I allowed myself to sound like myself because I'd been telling the stories, and I knew what got laughs. So I allowed myself permission to use that smartass, that irreverent father voice that I'd been talking in my entire adult life, and I found people really liked it, so that was sort of the beginning; people gave me permission to use my voice."

In our discussion about voice, Wilder mentioned essayist Phillip Lopate's essay "On the Necessity of Turning Oneself into a Character." Lopate's central point in this oft-cited piece is that the use of the pronoun *I* is not sufficient to establish either voice or character. Indeed, while "character" in writing is commonly associated with the invented people of fiction, the same character-building techniques are required in non-fiction, both to create dimension for the people about whom one is writing, and to provide a sense of oneself as well. This is not to say that the person on the page is a wholly fabricated self. Rather, that the persona you adopt for personal writing is a representation of the self, a written approximation of one's identity. In order to successfully translate the "I" of the real world into an "I" of some authenticity and voice on the page, one needs both acceptance of oneself and distance.

"A lot of times we think we're unworthy," Wilder says. "We think, 'my voice is not as good as this published voice,' or people want to be luminaries rather than be who they are. Someone has to tell you somewhere along the way that your voice is worth listening to."

Wilder's story about trying to write how he thought he should, rather than in his natural "voice," is a common one. (Saunders has told a similar story in interviews about trying to write like Hemingway before learning to write like himself.) These stories remind me of a scene from *Shattered Glass*, the

2003 movie based on *New Republic* writer Steven Glass's fabrication of articles.[13]

Amy Brand (Melanie Lynskey) has written an article and sits down with Caitlin Avey (Chloë Sevigny), who tells her:

"Look, I think it's good you tried this. It's good to stretch . . . I'm just, I don't think you're writing to your strengths here."

Amy looks over the edited story, covered in red ink. Caitlin asks her why she wants to "stray from" the types of articles she does so well. Amy brings up all the attention Glass has been receiving from editors, the success—financially and otherwise— he's having. She says editors don't want policy, they want "color, nuance, humor." Caitlin tells her, "Amy, you don't write funny." "It's a little funny," Amy says plaintively. "Isn't it?"

I bring this scene up not to depress anyone, but to point out that an important aspect of writing is developing an understanding of how one is being read. Do other people find you funny? Informative? Provocative? With the exception of one's private journal,[14] writing is an act that involves not just the writer, but an audience as well.

## THE IMITATION GAME

A few more words on this notion of influence and imitation. In chapter 9, I mention a student who worried that bad grammar was contagious (and that she had caught it). I don't think anyone is going to "catch" good writing, but deeply studying and experimenting with an admired writer's techniques, though it may be a step toward realizing one's own proclivities, can also function

---

13    One of my favorite movies. I've lost track of how many times I've seen it, but each time I burst into tears when the editor, Charles "Chuck" Lane, receives applause from his staff for defending the integrity of journalism.

14    And even those may end up finding an audience as well someday. Anaïs Nin's made for some good reading.

as a self-guided mentorship. Coachella Independent Publisher and Editor Jimmy Boegle says that as a young humor columnist he "aped Dave Barry a fair amount. Possibly too much, but by doing that and reading a lot of other humor columnists, I found my voice." It's the same thing with any sort of writing, Boegle continues. "Read great writers, find what works for you, and learn from them. Don't copy them, but sample their techniques here or there to help you find what works for you."

#### ••••*Many Voices*

You won't find too many writers arguing against the importance of "voice" in writing, which is perhaps why it's refreshing when one does. Noah Berlatsky's 2014 *Atlantic* magazine essay, "Voice Isn't the Point of Writing," as the title states, does just that. The gist of Berlatsky's argument is that for most writers, "writing is less about finding your own voice than about figuring out how to say something someone, somewhere will pay you for, or at least listen to. If there's a voice, it's always an adjusted and negotiated voice, rather than a pure effusion of individuality."

I don't take quite as abject a view of voice—much of what I love to read I read for voice, so it's hard to unilaterally devalue it—but certainly Berlatsky is correct in that the ability to modulate one's voice, to adhere to a specific publication or assignment's requirements, to write from different stances and points of view, demonstrates facility with voice in a way that is different from the notion of extracting one's own singular true voice.

The first month I was working on this chapter, a student came to talk with me about a memoir he'd written for a class assignment. I had noted on the piece that he had written the entirety of the experience rendered in the assignment in first-person exposition, and that to bring it more to life, he should work on identifying some places that could be written in full scene. This, I said, would allow the reader to engage more fully with the story, not to mention actually satisfy the parameters of the assignment. The student implied, however, that he believed doing so interfered with his "voice." This is not an uncommon discussion for me to have, and I'm not (wholly) without sympathy for the sense that the only authentic voice a writer has is the one that comes out of him or her unheeded or checked by considerations of craft or technique.

Put more simply, relating a story from the first-person point of view is a closer approximation of the oral tradition of telling a story and, for those of us who are comfortable yakking, translating that particular "I" to the page is perhaps the easiest act of writing. But it also assumes that each writer has only one authentic voice—the speaking voice—and only one aspect of persona or character upon which to draw. In truth, or at least ideally, a writer can experiment with various aspects of voice and persona, using attention to detail, the construction of scenes, word choice, and syntax to vary the perspective and point of view of any piece of writing as needed for editorial or other reasons. In this way, one might look at voice something like a Halloween costume. You might not dress up as a Freudian Slip every day of the week (a slip and a cigar), but you may be able to shimmy into that concept when it's appropriate.

In a post on voice to the Grammar Girl website, guest writer Julie Wildhaber compares a writer's voice to *American Idol*, noting that "Voice is what Simon Cowell is talking about when he tells *American Idol* contestants to make a song their own and not just do a note-for-note karaoke version."

I have never watched *American Idol* (reality television provokes existential nausea for me), but the notion that voice is not simply about tone/sound, but is in fact contingent upon a variety of more substantive choices, is a useful concept for writers.

To continue on with the popular culture analogies,

singer-songwriter Sia's 2016 release, *This is Acting*, is another interesting study in questions of voice and identity. The album's concept is that its songs were originally written for specific artists, who ultimately rejected them. So part of listening is trying to figure out which singer Sia might have been thinking about when writing each song, and what about the song cues that choice. And then, of course, how does having Sia sing it change that song? The notion that performers adopt shifting styles and personas isn't exactly news (see David Bowie, 1947–2016), but it is also a useful concept for writers who imagine that they have only one true voice (that must be protected against their teachers' ministrations at all costs).

Wilder tells a useful story along these lines about an assignment he once had for *Details* magazine. He had turned in a draft and was reviewing it with then *Details* Articles Editor Pete Wells. Wells told him that while the draft was good, "We look at *Details'* tone as sophisticated dickheads." Wilder thought Wells' advice "was perfect," and hearing *Details'* ideal tone described so specifically "really helped me: not only dickhead like stupid, but sophisticated dickhead." The tone and voice Wilder adopted for that article differed from that he used in an article for *Parenting* magazine, which was in turn different from his *Santa Fe Reporter* column voice. Shifting the approach for audience and for a publication's own style is part of the toolbox of being a working writer; doing it while holding onto one's distinctive outlook and voice is the challenge.

Part of this tricky equation is not just the writing aspect of writing, but also the listening and thinking part of it. As Wilder notes, one should not be a complete mystery to oneself. What do you find interesting and/or funny in the world? What situations stay with you? What do you notice and why? Understanding one's own natural aesthetic sense is a key step in developing voice, as outlook and perspective are as much a part of voice as is word choice.

Language, of course, is certainly a key element of voice, so I was curious about the challenge of developing voice in a second language. Enrique Limón, managing editor for Salt Lake City, Utah's *City Weekly*, grew up in Mexico and began working in broadcast journalism immediately after high school. Though he had always been bilingual, when he began working in print journalism in the US, he felt the need to write his pieces first in Spanish and then translate them into English.

"My thought process was always in Spanish," Limón says, "So when I started to do that crossover and do story ideas for American outlets . . . I thought it might not come out as smart or experienced or educated." That process shifted as Limón became more immersed in reporting and writing in English until, he says, "I started dreaming in English."

Learning to hone his own first-person voice in English led Limón to a love for capturing other people's voices through interviewing and feature writing.

Author Jim Ruland writes fiction and nonfiction and also has co-written memoirs for other people: 2014's *Giving the Finger: Risking It All to Fish the World's Deadliest Sea*, by Scott Campbell Jr., and in 2016, *My Damage: The Story of a Punk Rock Survivor*, by Keith Morris.

Ruland discussed cowriting in an essay for the *LA Times* published December 24, 2015, noting the difference between being a ghostwriter (in which one writes the piece behind the scenes and is uncredited, versus being a credited coauthor, saying, "The contracts remind us that the subject is the 'author,' the storyteller, the person the reader will identify as the 'I' of the story. I am the 'writer,' the individual who shapes the story." Ruland goes on to compare the experience to that of karaoke, in which one tries to embody (em-throat?) the voice of the original singer.

A key element of Ruland's process in capturing his subjects'

voices, he tells me, happens in the painstaking work of interview transcription.

"I try to view it as a labor of love and a part of the composition process," he says, "because while listening and relistening
is when I begin to organize the materials and learn the rhythms
of the subject's voice."

While voice has its ineffable qualities, it also includes numerous technical choices that can be cultivated and strengthened.

For example, syntax, "the arrangement of words and
phrases" as the dictionary says, plays a role in how our writing
(and discourse) is perceived. Sentences can be short and simple. Longer sentences—ones pulled together through clauses
and punctuation—can create a different emotive impact.
Depending on how the sentence is constructed, readers may be
rushed along or, in other cases, forced to read more slowly, more
carefully, word by word. Playing with syntax is another way of
experimenting with voice.

## POINT OF VIEW BASICS

Point of view refers on a technical level to the pronouns used
in a piece. In a broader context, the term "point of view" refers
to an individual's perspective. For writing purposes overall,
choosing a point of view should include both elements. From
whose perspective the story is being told, and, grammatically,
which pronoun that perspective uses.

### ••••First Person: I (Singular), We (Plural)

A fair amount of personal writing, such as memoir, relies on
first-person point of view. Traditional journalism, on the other
hand, tends to stay away from first person, since the reporter/

writer of the story isn't a key figure. *Vanity Fair* magazine tends to publish celebrity profiles in which the author uses first person to describe his or her experience encountering the celebrity. At any rate, first person singular makes sense when you or your perspective is central to the story. I can't think of too many instances in which first person plural makes sense in creative nonfiction. It works pretty well in the Declaration of Independence, I suppose, and it might make sense as well in a memoir about multiple personality disorder.

#### ····*Second Person: You*

One recent semester, I noticed an unprecedented number of students writing in second person for their memoirs. A fair number of these memoirs dealt with past trauma, for which second person can often be a fitting dissociative choice for perspective. Second person also works well for direct address and how-to type writing. You may notice my use of it from time to time in this book.[15]

#### ····*Third Person: He, She (Singular), They (Plural)*

As with fiction, third person in nonfiction allows for singular or multiple points of view, representing other people's views and even, at times, thoughts. As discussed in chapter 5, third person can be rendered in a variety of ways that bring the reader closer to various points of view, and which shift the perspective of the overall narrative.

---

15    In the interest of transparency, I should say I actually don't like second person point of view, but was talked into using it by my editor, who made a better argument in its favor than I was able to muster against it.

# TONE

"I like to be droll, to lull my readers and then surprise or startle them. I like using plain words in a way that gives them a renewed power in their plain-ness. I like reinventing a cliché or using it in a bold way."

— Susan Orlean, discussing her tone, *The New New Journalism*

In 1997, I wrote a story for the *Reporter* covering some Santa Fe Public Schools programs that addressed social rather than academic matters ("The ABCs of the New Social Curriculum"). These programs included one at the junior high, in which students were given an infant simulator ("Baby Think It Over") as a means of discouraging teen pregnancy. "Character Counts" seemed to involve students singing and dancing about the importance of honesty and integrity. "D.A.R.E." (Drug Abuse Resistance Education), at the time, brought police into classrooms to explain the ramifications drugs and other illegal acts would bring to students' lives. I found much of what I saw mildly ridiculous. Or, as I wrote in my opening paragraph:

"It's ten a.m. and chances are you know where your child is: school. But doing what? Math? English? Science? Maybe. It's equally likely they are practicing saying no to drugs, dancing their way to integrity, putting on a show with peaceful puppets, changing a fake baby's diaper."

The schools' public information officer and superintendent did not find much to like in this article and, if memory serves, called me in to read me a letter, the only part of which I remember was a line that said, essentially, "We don't appreciate your sarcasm."

Perhaps sarcasm is not the right tone with which to approach some of the subjects on which I've written (education, naked criminals, politicians, depression screenings), but it is pretty much my natural tone. I have occasionally written earnestly, informatively, and even with (possibly manufactured) glee and/or outrage, but my inner monologue has a heavy dose of the sardonic. Of course, certain topics simply don't inspire an ironic stance (file this under "anything with a victim"), and it's important to distinguish when one's tone is appropriate to one's subject.

For a brief time, I taught online for a school that emphasized the importance of tone in the online class forums. The general thinking was that tone is easily misinterpreted in writing so one should avoid jokes (I'm paraphrasing). This also reportedly was the thinking behind the creators of the derided "SarcMark," a revolutionary new form of punctuation that garnered universal derision and plenty of free sarcasm.[16] The SarcMark, as the name indicates, was intended as a form of punctuation delineating sarcasm so as to avoid misunderstandings.

Tone—like voice—refers to the sound of the writing and plays off the idea of verbal sounds. "I don't like your tone" is another way of saying, "I don't like your attitude." Tone it down! (Be quiet). ALL CAPS translates as screaming. White space denotes some silence, space to breathe. Many of the writers interviewed for the book *The New New Journalism* are asked and discuss, as Orlean does at the start of the chapter, the tone they take in their work. Tone, like all other aspects of writing, can be shifted and revised depending on the goal of the work, by which I mean: What does the writer want the reader to feel? Amused? Angry? Heartbroken? Sometimes tone's apparent mismatch with its subject is the key to engendering those feelings.

## SYNTAX

During one ill-fated segment in yet another class, I assigned James Baldwin's "Notes of a Native Son," assuming the students would be drawn, as I am, to Baldwin's ferocity, grief, and intellect in this personal essay that examines his relationship

---

16    Houston, Keith, "The Rise and Fall of the Infamous SarcMark," *Daily Beast*, Sept. 24, 2013.

to his father within the broader context of racism. I thought his voice—his roiling syntax, emotions, stories, memories—would carry them through the essay. I mean, how can you resist this:

"I had declined to believe in that apocalypse which had been central to my father's vision; very well, life seemed be saying, here is something that will certainly pass for an apocalypse until the real thing comes along."

The students were not drawn to Baldwin's essay and, to cover my chagrin, I launched into an impromptu, ill-advised lecture on hypotaxis and parataxis. This was ill-advised because (a) I did a poor job of explaining both, and (b) no one has ever been convinced to like a piece of writing by having the piece's use of subordinate clauses pointed out.

However, examining and playing with syntax is another way of playing with voice or, at least, of interrogating the sound of writing. Joan Didion famously did just this in her *New Yorker* piece "Last Words," in which she reprints the first paragraph of Ernest Hemingway's *A Farewell to Arms* before analyzing its "four deceptively simple sentences, one hundred and twenty-six words, the arrangement of which remains as mysterious and thrilling to me now as it did when I first read them . . . and imagined that if I studied them closely enough and practiced hard enough I might one day arrange one hundred and twenty-six words such words myself. Only one of the words has three syllables. Twenty-two have two. The other hundred and three have one. Twenty-four of the words are 'the,' fifteen are 'and.' There are four commas."

Writer Eula Biss refers to Didion's experiment in her essay "In the Syntax: Rewriting Joan Didion's 'Goodbye to All That.'" Biss writes about misreading an interview in which she thought Didion had said she learned to write by copying, word for word, Hemingway (Biss later realizes Didion said this was how she learned to type). But Biss, who had studied art, noted that in so doing "at every stage we copied the masters."

Biss sat down to rewrite Didion's "Goodbye to All That," with the notion of changing the facts of Didion's life and replacing them with her own, only to find "Those facts could not be changed without marring the syntax of the sentence, the clauses stacked with commas, with 'and' and 'and' again, the cunning repetition . . ."

This probably sounds like an argument against copying out another writer's work or borrowing another writer's syntax, but it isn't. If we are adopting the notion of "finding one's voice," we must assume some sort of search has been undertaken. Consider the exercises at the end of this chapter the equivalent of a writer's scavenger hunt.

## PROMPTS AND PRACTICE

1. **Mind meld.** Take a cue from Ruland and interview someone about his or her favorite job. Record the interview. Transcribe the interview, word for word. Can you capture enough of the subject's voice to write a paragraph in the first person, as if you were that person?

2. **Digest.** Try the same exercise with a writer you admire (or abhor, for that matter). Try to write a short (500 words or fewer) review of that author's work in the voice of the author. For inspiration, read John Crace's "Digested Read" column in the *Guardian*. As the name of this column implies, Crace condenses books into short reviews, relayed from the (exaggerated and hilarious) aped viewpoint of the author. For example, his review of Arianna Huffington's *The Sleep Revolution*, which begins, "It began in 2007 when I was on a tour to promote my worldwide bestseller, *Thrive*, in which I let the little people in on some of the secrets of the fabulously successful."

3. **Correspond.** Write a letter to your closest friend describing your ideal job. Now write a cover letter to a prospective employer for that ideal job. How did you change your language and tone based on your audience?

4. **Dearly beloved.** Write a tasteful eulogy for someone you don't like without lying.

5. **Sin against syntax.** Pick a piece of writing from a writer you admire, one whose "voice" you find distinctive. Take a paragraph or more of that writing and replace it with your own, but use the other writer's syntax: punctuation, sentence length, sentence structure. Read each out loud. How has changing the syntax changed your work?

6. **The one where you use the "Why I Write" prompt.**

"In many ways writing is the act of saying I, of imposing oneself upon other people, of saying listen to me, see it my way, change your mind. It's an aggressive, even a hostile act. You can disguise its qualifiers and tentative subjunctives, with ellipses and evasions—with the whole manner of intimating rather than claiming, of alluding rather than stating—but there's no getting around the fact that setting words on paper is the tactic of a secret bully, an invasion, an imposition of the writer's sensibility on the reader's most private space."

—Joan Didion, "Why I Write"

Many writing students will be asked, at some point, to read Joan Didion's essay, "Why I Write" (modeled on George Orwell's essay of the same title) and then asked to write their own interrogation of the writing act. Didion famously describes writing in her piece as "an aggressive, even a hostile act." Google "Why I Write," and discover others pondering this same question. I like poet Reginald Shepherd's essay, which begins, "I write because I would like to live forever. The fact of my future death offends me." Me, too. Explore the question; see where it leads you and how you experience "the act of saying I."

7. **Talk to yourself.** I knew a writer once who told me he wrote his book by speaking into a tape recorder on a cross-country drive and then transcribing it. No, you don't need to fill up the tank quite yet. But using a recorder (digital, your phone, whatever), tell a story, the kind of story you might tell if you were asked by someone you wanted to impress to tell a story (see George Saunders's previous anecdote). Listen back and transcribe. Can you shape that oral story into written form?

8. **Talk in public.** Speaking of speaking, short-form open mics, story slams, TED Talk–type events are everywhere. I was invited in 2015 to give a 140-second talk on interviewing, which was terrifying, instructive, and challenging. The instructive and challenging element of compressed live storytelling is the elimination of the written page and the way in which it requires the storyteller to learn the story inside and out, and to think about audience in a way that often eludes when sitting alone in a room with a cat (for example). For more tips on live storytelling, check out The Moth's website (listed in the resource section of this chapter).

9. **Rewrite.** Let's call this the "Weird Al" Yankovic exercise. For a couple of years, I helped rewrite songs à la Yankovic for a local melodrama musical. Just as borrowing syntax is a way of playing around with one's voice, borrowing a song's framework to rewrite lyrics provides a warm-up for voice. Pick a song you love or (more fun) a song you find mind-numbingly ridiculous. I recommend Dierks Bentley's "Drunk on a Plane."

10. **Play with words.** In his craft book *Naming the World*, Bret Anthony Johnston discusses requiring his students to write down a set number of words they both love and hate based solely on how the words sound, not their meanings. As a slight variation on this idea, review some of your writing and identify

oft-used words. Using a thesaurus, find some new words that resonate with your sensibility. Learning new words also is part of having a voice, just as is learning new information and perspectives.

## ESSAY

## Daddy Needs a Drink: Eat, Drink, Man, Woman
### Robert Wilder

One of the ways that my father shows affection during our visits with him in Florida is through sandwich making. Each morning, before we leave him for the beach, my dad happily takes orders (as long as I write them down) and expertly slathers mayo on wheat or mustard on white; lettuce, no lettuce, makes no difference. All the grandchildren love Grandpa's sandwiches and cite his handiwork as the gold standard when they refuse their own parents' attempts at feeding them upon returning home.

So after a morning of broken shell collecting and superhero sandcastle building, I opened the cooler to retrieve our lunch. My wife, Lala, was sitting on a beach towel gazing at a magazine that showcased homes with cartoonish architectural elements and throw pillows that cost as much as ten barrels of oil.

"Be careful with those," Lala said, nodding at the foodstuffs.

"Why?" I thought she might be warning me against the aggressive seagulls we had seen divebomb pale kids ferrying fries from the snack bar the day before.

"Your dad bled on some of them."

"He what?"

My wife explained that my father had cut himself during the lunch assembly process but continued on because he a) hated to waste food, b) had been tested and was clean, and c) knew I would eat the sanguine cuisine.

There was a lot to digest from that story. Wasting food is close to armed robbery in the Wilder family and, as a child, I had seen my dad freeze loaves of discounted Wonder Bread, save restaurant leftovers for weeks, and use semi-decaying vegetables and meats in soups, sauces, and stews where they'd be nicely hidden. In fact, the next day Poppy would come running to us because her beloved Grandpa served her a bagel with mold. I yawned at the news, but threw the thing out when the old man turned his back. The one thing I'd never experienced (at least to my knowledge) was blood. Spit, yes, (that's another story) but never fluid that ran in human veins. I chalked up my dad's comment about annual testing with a doctor as something old folks do in Florida to have someone to talk to, but the last reason pissed me off. My own father thought that I would eagerly eat tainted food? OK, I will add cream to my coffee after it's expired, freely employ the five-second rule with dropped tenderloin while cooking, and I just learned from the Internet that it's not a good idea to make egg salad with Easter eggs that have been sitting out a few days (a fact my dad still argues with), but blood? Who serves their child blood?

As I examined the ham and cheddar on rye with mayo, lettuce and hearty dashes of salt and pepper, I felt my salivating glands start to tingle. My dad does make damn good Dagwoods. The plasma dotted the corners as if the sandwich had been shaving and nicked itself accidentally. Just tear off those parts, I thought. It's not like it's the blood of a stranger. In fact, you could argue that it's just like eating my own life force. I ripped the tainted edges and buried the scraps in the sand. Lala was watching me closely, having already decided that neither she nor the kids would even consider eating anything that contained even the tiniest amount of my father's sap. I realized that I'd experienced as many moral dilemmas in my life as the number of shells in my son's bucket next to me, but this one seemed huge. As crazy as it sounds, I felt as though I would somehow be betraying the Wilder name by not eating my father's creation. The top of my head prickled from all this deep thought. A dark shadow passed quickly across the sun. And then, as if from God, the seagull hovering above me snatched the sandwich and flew away.

# READING AND RESOURCES
# FROM THIS CHAPTER

Berlatsky, Noah. "'Voice' Isn't the Point of Writing." *The Atlantic*, November 29, 2014. http://www.theatlantic.com/entertainment/archive/2014/11/finding-your-voice-as-a-writer-overrated/382946/.

Biss, Eula. "In the Syntax: Rewriting Joan Didion's 'Goodbye to All That.'" *Fourth Genre: Explorations In Nonfiction*, 13, no. 1 (2011): 133-37.

Boynton, Robert S. *The New New Journalism*. New York: Vintage Books, 2005.

Didion, Joan. "Last Words." *New Yorker*, November 9, 1998.

Didion, Joan. "Why I Write." *New York Times Book Review*, December 5, 1976.

Johnston, Bret Anthony. *Naming the World*. New York: Random House, 2007.

Manguso, Sarah. "Short Days." *Paris Review*, Winter 2014. http://www.theparisreview.org/letters-essays/6341/short-days-sarah-manguso.

Ray, Billy. *Shattered Glass*. Film. Bethesda, MD: Lions Gate Films, 2003.

Saunders, George. "My Writing Education: A Time Line." *New Yorker*, October 22, 2015. http://www.newyorker.com/books/page-turner/my-writing-education-a-timeline.

Sedaris, David. "Six to Eight Black Men." Chap. 14 in *Dress Your Family in Corduroy and Denim*. Boston: Little, Brown, 2004.

The Moth. "Storytelling Tips and Tricks." Moth. https://themoth.org/share-your-story/storytelling-tips-tricks.

Wilder, Robert. *Daddy Needs a Drink: An Irreverent Look at Parenting from a Dad Who Truly Loves His Kids Even When They're Driving Him Nuts.* New York: Delacorte, 2006.

———. "The Big Splash." *Santa Fe Reporter,* July 4, 2007. http://www.sfreporter.com/santafe/article-1756-daddy-needs-a-drink-the-big-splash.html.

# CHAPTER FIVE

## *People Are People*

The two blondes, who seemed to be in their middle thirties, were preened and polished, their matured bodies softly molded within tight dark suits. They sat, legs crossed, perched on the high bar stools. They listened to the music. Then one of them pulled out a Kent and Sinatra quickly placed his gold lighter under it and she held his hand, looked at his fingers: they were nubby and raw, and the pinkies protruded, being so stiff from arthritis that he could barely bend them. He was, as usual, immaculately dressed. He wore an oxford-grey suit with a vest, a suit conservatively cut on the outside but trimmed with flamboyant silk within; his shoes, British, seemed to be shined even on the bottom of the soles. He also wore, as everybody seemed to know, a remarkably convincing black hairpiece, one of sixty that he owns, most of them under the care of an inconspicuous little grey-haired lady who, holding his hair in a tiny satchel, follows him around whenever he performs. She earns $400 a week. The most distinguishing thing about Sinatra's face are his eyes, clear blue and alert,

eyes that within seconds can go cold with anger, or glow
with affection, or, as now, reflect a vague detachment that
keeps his friends silent and distant.

—**Gay Talese,** "Frank Sinatra Has a Cold"

T ALESE'S PROFILE OF Sinatra is one of the many pieces
often cited as seminal in the field of "new journalism,"
essentially literary journalism, characterized by long-
form nonfiction writing that makes use of elements normally
more associated with fiction. One of those literary journalists,
Tom Wolfe, writes extensively—if perhaps hyperbolically—
about the phenomenon in *New York* magazine in February, 1972:

> And yet in the early 1960s a curious new notion, just hot
> enough to inflame the ego, had begun to intrude into the tiny
> confines of the feature statusphere. It was in the nature of a
> discovery. This discovery, modest at first, humble, in fact, def-
> erential, you might say, was that it just might be possible to
> write journalism that would . . . read like a novel. *Like* a novel,
> if you get the picture. This was the sincerest form of homage
> to The Novel and to those greats, the novelists, of course. Not
> even the journalists who pioneered in this direction doubted
> for a moment that the novelist was the reigning literary artist,
> now and forever. All they were asking for was the privilege of
> dressing up like him . . . until the day when they themselves
> would work up their nerve and go into the shack and try it for
> real . . . They were dreamers, all right, but one thing they never
> dreamed of. They never dreamed of the approaching irony.
> They never guessed for a minute that the work they would
> do over the next ten years, as journalists, would wipe out the
> novel as literature's main event.

Contemporary long-form creative nonfiction follows the tradition Wolfe discussed in that it is nonfiction that reads like fiction

through use of the various elements of storytelling discussed in this book. Of those, characterization is often the trickiest.

In fiction, of course, characters are imaginary people. Harry Potter (despite my students' feelings to the contrary) is not a real person. Characters who seem real—whether it's J. K. Rowling's Potter or J. D. Salinger's Zooey Glass or Jane Austen's Elizabeth Bennet or Toni Morrison's Sethe—are the foundation of literature's greatest stories for most readers.[17] It's hard to tell a good story without memorable characters. That's true for fiction, and it's true for nonfiction.

Of course in nonfiction, the characters are not imagined, they are actual people, which makes rendering them on the page a different endeavor. (The middle ground, it seems, are celebrities, who are often treated—and sometimes behave—like imaginary people.)

But all stories include and need people—the people in the stories are key to engaging the people reading the stories. As Mark Zusman, owner and editor of *Willamette Week*, notes, "all stories . . . of some length and substance, no matter what the subject is, all stories are ultimately about people." When Zusman works with writers in putting together a story, "We pretty quickly get into a conversation about who are the people you are trying to bring to life."

That bringing to life makes use of what's called in fiction and creative nonfiction **direct and indirect characterization.**

## DIRECT CHARACTERIZATION

Direct characterization means using specific aspects of personality that can be directly observed to bring people to life on the page. Forms of direct characterization include people's physical attributes, their speech, their actions, and their thoughts. One useful

---

17    deconstructionists and their ilk notwithstanding

form of revision can include evaluating important people in a story to determine if there are types of direct characterization that can be added or amplified to render your subjects more vividly. Let's look at each aspect of direct characterization a bit more fully.

#### •••• *The Physical*

Physical description is one of the key elements of direct characterization. As the excerpt from Talese's profile of Sinatra demonstrates, physical description can be both visual and visceral, showing more about the character than a simple rundown of personal logistics. His "nubby and raw" fingers provide a vulnerable contrast to Sinatra's "immaculate" attire; the shoes' shined "bottom of the soles" betray both fastidiousness and control. And his eyes are not just "alert," signaling to the reader that despite Sinatra's age he is fully in command, but also have the capacity to show anger, affection, and detachment. With this physical description, Talese has done much more than bring to life the famous singer; he also has signposted the story itself, which depicts Sinatra in all of his complexity.

Emily Rapp Black, who has written often about living with a disability, says that because "a lot of what I write has to do with the body, I'm very committed to that. That's how we experience things, and I would say there aren't that many perks to having a disability, but one of them is you're never not aware of your body, and that has fed into all of my work." With students, Rapp Black emphasizes the need to remember all five senses. She asks lots of questions—regularly—requiring them to reflect: "How did you feel in that moment? What did it feel like in your body? Where were you in space? All of those five senses—people forget about that."

Describing the physical—whether it's of the body or of the environment in which events occur—isn't limited to capturing moments of pure physicality; it also means considering the physical side of emotional experience—from happiness to grief.

In his memoir, David Stuart MacLean describes with fine detail the sensory environment he experienced upon regaining consciousness in an Indian train station, unsure of where or who he was: "It was hot. My thin shirt clung to my back and shoulders, and my underwear was bunched into a sweaty wad. The heat left the ground in wavy lines, and the air was tinged blue with diesel exhaust."

In just these few sentences, MacLean conveys the intense physicality of the hot day, his own personal vulnerability and discomfort—his shirt clings and his underwear bunches—and foreshadows the hallucinatory environment he will experience: the wavy lines, as well as the way in which his life and body have been tainted by the anti-malaria drugs—the air has been tinged.

Like Rapp Black, MacLean says he always considers physicality in his writing. "I often am so amazed at writing where I feel like people just think they are disembodied brains writing for other disembodied brains," MacLean tells me. "They forget the physicality of their lives and that their bodies are weird." Focusing on the body, MacLean says, is "always sort of grounding . . . because you're just acknowledging the gravity and fragility and absurdity of our bodies and I love that stuff; I love it because it embarrasses me and it disarms me as I'm writing and once I get over the fact that I am a little chubby, I'm like, 'oh, cool, now I can access other stuff that I wasn't ready to talk about.'"

Writer Rubén Martínez's work offers painstaking detail about his subjects, such as the members of the Chávez family about whom Martínez wrote in his acclaimed 2001 book, *Crossing Over: A Mexican Family on the Migrant Trail*. In *Crossing Over*, Martínez examines Mexico-to-US immigration in large part through the tragic experiences of the Chávez family and their loss of three sons in a border accident. Throughout the book, Martínez ties the story together with sensory details and observations. In this excerpt, Martínez describes one of the Chávez daughters:

> Rosa Chávez, María Elena's daughter, is twenty-one years old. She has small black eyes set in a baby face, a round figure, and medium-brown skin. Although she isn't smiling today, over the next two years I'll get to know her smile—the slightest curling of her lips, a dimple on her right cheek—and pleasant laugh quite well. Sunday best for Rosa is what she wears most every other day of the week—a succession of T-shirts (ranging from Bruce Springsteen to CHOOSE LIFE) and jeans (today, white; she also has blue and black) and a rebozo draped across her shoulders.

For Martínez, this approach to rendering his subjects was certainly influenced, he says, by "the new journalism generation," or, he adds, "the late new journalism generation." Martínez's first features editor at *LA Weekly* was Kit Rachlis, who had been at the *Boston Phoenix* and, Martínez says, "had been mentored by early *Village Voice* editors, like really early '60s *Village Voice* editors."

Many influential nonfiction writers of the time also wrote fiction—Norman Mailer and Joan Didion, to name just two. "The influence on journalism," Martínez says, "was obvious. If you're a novelist who's writing a feature, you're going to be using all the tools in the novelist's tool bag." As Martínez asks, "How do you make a novel character come to life? For a few hundred years [to] bring a character to life . . . you need details."

As Martinez remembers it, his editor, Rachlis, handed him a copy of James Agee's *Let Us Now Praise Famous Men* and said, "Here, read this and look at how he looked at the details and look at how he goes about building up a character through detail." Agee's renowned book tells the story of his 1930s *Fortune* magazine assignment, with photographer

Walker Evans, to write about depression-era sharecroppers in the South. "He writes this insanely long piece that's never published but it becomes a book, which has an obsessive attention to detail," Martínez notes. "[Agee] sleeps in the houses of his characters, these poor sharecroppers, so he's there at midnight and can tell about the creaks in the floorboard and a plank missing on the front porch." Martínez then notes Agee's introduction to the work, in which he questions his role as a journalist, his sense of complicity at trying to render human lives in writing.

Agee's response to his own trepidations was to render the people he wrote about in, as Martínez says, "obsessive detail." Martínez himself is a particularly visual writer. While he of course works heavily with interview recordings and transcriptions, he also amasses photographs, flyers, and anything else that catches his attention while he's reporting, "so when it's really time to write a story, I can draw upon all that."

Martínez's book *Desert America* chronicles both the author's relationship to various western landscapes, and to its histories and people. One of those people, Antonio "Ike" DeVargas, is well known in northern New Mexico for his activism and political past. I have also written about DeVargas, whom I got to know when I was a reporter at the *Rio Grande Sun*. Consider the visual introduction Martínez provides for DeVargas in his book:

> He is a beautiful man. The famous shell of white hair with a slight yellow tint sits above deep furrows on his forehead. He stands about five-seven and is built lean and tough. He wears a sleeveless black T-shirt, blue-gray khakis, white socks and tennis shoes. . . . It is difficult to look into the hard beauty of Ike's eyes. Their color changes depending on the light.

By way of contrast, here is how I introduced DeVargas in a *Reporter* cover story on protracted litigation related to logging, in which he had been a central figure:

> Antonio 'Ike' DeVargas is the leader of La Compania. Outspoken, often controversial, DeVargas came to the timber industry via the unlikely route of the Vietnam War. Joining the Marines at age 17, DeVargas served in a force reconnaissance unit from 1964 to 1967, spending the bulk of his tour behind enemy lines. He returned, 20 years old and lost. For the next three years, he held more than 30 jobs, traveling between New Mexico, Colorado and California. He became political through relationships with other veterans who had started to oppose the war, but DeVargas continued to wander.

Now, granted, Martínez's characterization appears in a book; mine, in a newspaper with plenty of photos of DeVargas. But publishing context aside, Martínez has fully rendered DeVargas as a character in scene. I have summarized DeVargas's past.

Martínez also pays close attention to his subjects' environments. "Landscape is always in my notes," he says. "If I'm sitting down to interview you and we're in a room, I write down what I see in the window above your shoulder ... there's a potential for any image to play into the character's narrative."

Environmental writer Laura Paskus also privileges people and landscapes when she is reporting and writing, in part, she says, because "a lot of my stories are driven by public documents or by court cases or the sort of really boring dry things, and then what I try to do is find the best characters to tell the stories. Sometimes those characters are people or places or species."

To bring the people, places, or species to life, Paskus tries to avoid conducting interviews "over the phone, and I've stopped liking doing interviews in offices and at meetings." Instead, she says, she'll ask subjects "to go for a walk with me or go out to the places that we're talking about, which has been kind of interesting because sometimes the people who work on these issues—whether it's mining or water or land issues in particular—they don't spend a lot of time outside. So I ask them to go outside with me, and I think that helps, I hope that it helps readers; it helps me write something that a reader might be interested in, because they might remember a scene or something the person did as opposed to trying to tell a story through documents or a sit-down-in-the-office interview."

**Physical description** is one important element of direct characterization. Others include:

- **Dialogue**, discussed in chapter 2 on interviewing
- **Action**, which unfolds in large part through scene and exposition (discussed in chapter 6 on structure)

**Thought** constitutes the fourth type of direct characterization. Rendering thought can be a tricky endeavor in nonfiction writing (unless you're a psychic). It's not possible to truly know another person's thoughts but one can, of course, know what someone *says* he or she thinks or feels. As is often the case with fiction, direct quotation in nonfiction often is used to convey these thoughts and feelings. Emotion and opinion tend to make for better quotes, but in nonfiction, emotion and ideas are often more appropriately rendered in quotation or summarized quotation as only the subject can truly know his or her mind and feelings.

However, the degree to which a person/character's feelings and thoughts are presented in the narrative will depend on the point of view and distance chosen by an individual writer.

In a close third-person point of view, the author actually assumes the vantage point of someone else, writing as if from that person's internal reality. Although tricky, in my view, such writing can be very effective, particularly in terms of creating empathy for the character. Long-form literary journalism and nonfiction will often try to minimize attribution of thoughts and feelings to create a more literary effect—a story-like readability. For example, in chapter 6, I quote from the opening of Stephanie McCrummen's *Washington Post* story on Virginia State Senator Creigh Deeds as an example of scene building. I quote that opening here, as well, as an example of a close third-person point of view.

> He wakes up, and even before he opens his eyes, he can see his beautiful, delusional son.
> *Gus*, Creigh Deeds thinks.
> He lies in bed a few minutes more, trying to conjure specific images. Gus dancing. Gus playing the banjo. Gus with the puppies. Any images of Gus other than the final ones he has of his 24-year-old, mentally ill son attacking him and then walking away to kill himself, images that intrude on his days and nights along with the questions that he will begin asking himself soon, but not yet. A few minutes more. Gus fishing. Gus looking at him. Gus smiling at him. Time to start the day.

This rendering of Deeds, as if from his point of view, without attribution, makes the writing significantly more intimate and poignant.

Here's McCrummen's opening awkwardly rewritten (by me) into a more standard, objective third person point of view that relies on attribution to the subject to illustrate the difference.

> When Virginia State Senator Creigh Deeds wakes up, and even before he opens his eyes, **he says** he can see his beautiful, delusional son.
> **He says** he thinks of his son's name: Gus.
> **According to Deeds**, he often lies in bed a few minutes more, trying to conjure specific images. Gus dancing. Gus playing the banjo. Gus with the puppies. Any images

of Gus other than the final ones he has of his 24-year-old, mentally ill son attacking him and then walking away to kill himself, images that intrude on his days and nights along with the questions that he will begin asking himself soon. **Deeds says** he often lingers for a few minutes more and focuses on the more positive images: Gus fishing. Gus looking at him. Gus smiling at him.

My rewrite is obviously heavy-handed (four attributions in just a few sentences probably isn't necessary), but the point is that attribution is what creates the sense of objectivity, the filter between the subject's mind and the reader. We aren't in Deeds's mind anymore; we're being told what is in his mind.

More often, nonfiction writing, particularly journalism, uses signifiers such as "he says," or "according to," to indicate an objective third-person point of view when writing about other people. Attribution of quotes is one signifier, as are other forms of documentation. The standard use of a subject's last name in journalism also creates that distance.

As a further example, the following passage is from a long-form *New Yorker* profile of the writer Madeleine L'Engle. Throughout the piece, writer Cynthia Zarin uses a mixture of both omniscient, close, and objective third person techniques to create a sense of intimacy with the subject while still providing a sweeping, researched (if disillusioning for us L'Engle fans) portrait of the writer:

Madeleine's parents were the kind of couple whose devotion to each other can stymie children. They rose late, read aloud to each other, and went out most nights. In their apartment on the East Side, Madeleine ate her meals on a tray in her room. Her mother played the piano; her father, after a stint as a foreign correspondent, wrote potboilers. At school, she was terrible at sports and, she says, thought to be stupid (though at least one of her school reports belies this).

One morning in Switzerland, at the end of a summer spent abroad, when Madeleine was twelve years old, her parents drove through the gates of Chatelard, a boarding school for girls, introduced her to the headmistress, and left her there. She was completely unprepared. "I shook hands with the matron, and they vanished," L'Engle said.

In this excerpt, Zarin provides unattributed information in the first four sentences, giving a sense of omniscient point of view. Then: "At school, she was terrible at sports, and, **she says**, thought to be stupid (though at least one of her school reports belies this)." Here, by attributing the documentation—L'Engle's own words and her school report—the reader is back in a more standard journalistic environment. "She was completely unprepared" might, by itself, provide a sense of a close third-person point of view, except that it is followed by a supporting quotation. Throughout the piece, Zarin skillfully weaves narratives from L'Engle's history, switching back to her first name for her younger life (before she began publishing as Madeleine L'Engle) and using her last name/pen name for quotation.

In omniscient third, the author has the ability to know everything and everyone, inside and out. For obvious reasons, omniscience in nonfiction writing is an unusual stance and, when taken, is usually only done so for brief passages. It's the stance taken throughout Truman Capote's seminal true crime story, *In Cold Blood*. Capote intentionally set out to write a new kind of nonfiction work, one he referred to as a "nonfiction novel," and one of the ways he did so was by using this type of omniscience; each "character" is introduced with both exterior facts—physical appearance, history, actions—and interior "facts." The information used to create this sense of omniscience was from reporting (although facts from the book have since been disputed; more on this in chapter 8 on ethics).

Consider for example, Capote's descriptions of Herbert William Clutter:

> Always certain of what he wanted from the world, Mr. Clutter had in large measure obtained it.... In regard to his family, Mr. Clutter had just one serious cause for disquiet—his wife's health.... Mr. Clutter liked Bobby, and considered him, for a boy his age, which was seventeen, most dependable and gentlemanly.

Or consider Capote's description of killers Perry Smith and Richard Hickock's attitudes toward each other: "The two young men had little in common, but they did not realize it, for they shared a number of surface traits."

Although places in the book illuminate various sources of information, the book in its entirety reads as a novel with an omniscient and hidden narrator. This was Capote's intent; he discussed his idea of the "nonfiction novel" at length with *Paris Review* Editor George Plimpton in a 1966 *New York Times* interview, noting:

> When I first formed my theories concerning the nonfiction novel, many people with whom I discussed the matter were unsympathetic. They felt that what I proposed, a narrative form that employed all the techniques of fictional art but was nevertheless immaculately factual, was little more than a literary solution for fatigued novelists suffering from "failure of imagination." Personally, I felt that this attitude represented a "failure of imagination" on their part.

Still, Capote acknowledged in the interview, real rather than imagined people were the dividing line between fiction and nonfiction and represented challenges in the latter:

The reporter, unlike the fantasist, has to deal with actual people who have real names. If they feel maligned, or just contrary, or greedy, they enrich lawyers (though rarely themselves) by instigating libel actions. . . . The truth seems to be that no one likes to see himself described as he is, or cares to see exactly set down what he said and did. Well, even I even can understand that—because I don't like it myself when I am the sitter and not the portraitist; the frailty of egos!—and the more accurate the strokes, the greater the resentment.

Inhabiting a real person's thoughts and feelings in nonfiction writing certainly has some ethical ramifications, just as writing in a close third point of view can be technically tricky, unless the entire story is being told from that one person's point of view. There is a similar challenge writing in the first person. If I am telling you a story from my point of view, the writing may become uneven and jarring if suddenly the story shifts to the close perspective of someone else.

## IMMERSION

As previously noted, popular culture tends to depict reporters showing up in packs, screaming insensitive questions while shoving one another. While such antics can be fun and a great way to burn calories, they aren't the best approach for a story in which you want to draw closer to your subject.

Immersion reporting, on the other hand, can be a way to understand the people in your stories. For immersion reporting, the writer does not just show up, interview people about their lives, and then leave, but rather inhabits the role or job or landscape of the subject.

For example, in 2005, Nathan Dinsdale, at the time a staff writer for the *Reporter*, wrote a story about his eight hours volunteering as a bell ringer at Walmart for the Salvation Army. (I should say that in the hands of a lesser writer, this might not have been a particularly great story idea, but Dinsdale is very funny, so the piece was as much voice-driven as it was experiential). These "day in the life" stories have, in my view, as much potential to fail as succeed, but even as reporting experiments, spending more time with people in their worlds is bound to yield more characterizing information. Notable examples include journalist Ted Conover's work. Conover spent nearly a year working as a prison guard in New York after his request to shadow a guard through training was denied by the state. The result of that work became the National Book Critics Circle Award–winning book *New Jack*. In an interview on his work from the anthology *The New New Journalism*, Conover describes the distinction between interviewing prison guards and actually having the job, noting, "What I'm getting at is like the distinction between *tourist* and a *traveler*. The tourist experience is superficial and glancing. The traveler develops a deeper connection with her surroundings."

Conover, in the same interview, also points out that such immersion reporting makes it more likely for the reporter to encounter people who are not the usual suspects. A long immersion project may not always be realistic, and can have tricky ethical issues (more on this later), but also can bring the writer that much closer to authenticity as far as the type of empathy one hopes for in writing about other people.

Immersion may seem like an approach only suitable to reporting and writing on other people, but stepping into one's own life from a different vantage point also is a type of immersive experience that can yield characterizing information. For example, in his memoir *Do Over!: In Which a Forty-Eight-Year-Old Father of Three Returns to Kindergarten, Summer Camp, the Prom, and Other Embarrassments*, writer Robin Hemley, as the book's title indicates, immerses himself in the environment of his youth. In his craft book *A Field Guide for Immersion Writing*, Hemley notes that he's written both traditional journalism and traditional memoir, but the immersive memoir allowed him to satisfy "both aspects of my personality, the pensive soul with a reflective bent, and the equally strong part of me that loves to travel, to meet people, to experience the world."

# INDIRECT CHARACTERIZATION

····*Authorial Thoughts*

While it's not possible to know for sure what other people think or feel, it is conceivable—at least on a good day—to know one's own thoughts and feelings. Interpretation of people and situations in writing is a form of indirect characterization that can influence and guide the reader. For example, in his essay "Watching the Animals," Pulitzer Prize–winning nonfiction writer Richard Rhodes describes with exquisite, if excruciating, detail the slaughterhouse process for pigs in Iowa. He begins by noting, "I have great respect for the I-D Packing Company. They do a dirty job and do it as cleanly and humanely as possible, and do it well."

This short passage precedes the actual description of the slaughter, which, had I read it without Rhodes' interpretation, would not have struck me as humane or clean (although it's possible a vegetarian is not the ideal audience for this piece). Later, as Rhodes describes the pigs in their final moments, he sees the pigs' fear as they are prepared for slaughter, noting the experience "had to remind me of things no one wants to be reminded of anymore, all mobs, all death marches, all mass murders and extinctions . . ." The essay's nuance is in its mixture of straight reporting and authorial interpretation through Rhodes's personal memories of growing up on a farm; its explication of both the process and cost—to individual psyches and writ large across our society—of contemporary butchering. While Rhodes does not single out a specific person at the slaughterhouse, in his hands the reader feels as the writer does toward the men doing this work: respect and pity.

Writer Mike Sager says he tries to always create an immersive experience with his subjects to create as much empathy as possible for them. Consider the beginning of his 2001 *Esquire* magazine profile of Roseanne Barr. Sager writes:

> Over the course of our interview, in fact, she'd been astonishingly engaging—despite her occasional tendency to call me an idiot and to point out my personal flaws—revealing herself to be intelligent and well-read if somewhat grammatically challenged, holding forth articulately on a wide range of topics, citing studies, quoting references and texts. Not to mention the sense of humor: wicked and perverse and high-end, punctuated by the occasional belch.

Through Sager's interpretive stance, the reader is set up for the story to deliver on the promise of its title, "The Multitudes of Roseanne Barr," and has been directed to understand the story will demonstrate the nuance of someone in the public eye about whom one might hold previous misconceptions.

As noted in the chapter on interviewing, Sager also takes a type of immersive stance with his subjects when he's profiling them, but he does so to try to know them as deeply as possible. He will spend weeks with one person when possible. He'll ask biographical questions, but otherwise he is just there, reacting to what happens and soaking up the atmosphere.

"It's sort of like this whole getting to know someone," Sager says. "It's deeper than writing a story. . . . I become fascinated by this one person for as long as I can until I'm utterly exhausted with knowing them, and then I come home and objectify them better, but you develop a heart for someone, you really find a love for them. Maybe that's something I bring to this table; my parents loved me, they certainly damaged me quite a bit, but I know they loved me and I have no trouble loving anyone else, no matter how weird they are or even if they make me feel uncomfortable, like Roseanne, who called me an idiot every five minutes," he says. "But she also said, she told me one time, 'You have to be the one who knows.' That was so true; probably no one has said anything more true about me."

Ultimately, Sager says, "Everyone I meet equips me better to meet the next person . . . and I think journalism when done best is a higher calling. It has to be about the people you write about first."

#### ····*Other People*

The use of other people's voices in stories profiling a central figure can be used in a variety of ways. When other people describe or discuss their impressions of others, this also functions as indirect characterization. For example, in a 2013 *New York Times Magazine* profile of writer George Saunders, "George Saunders Has Written the Best Book You'll Read This Year," other writers chime in on Saunders, reinforcing the overall tenor of the piece, which, as its title indicates, is unconditionally positive:

> Tobias Wolff, who taught Saunders when he was in the graduate writing program at Syracuse in the mid-'80s, said, "He's been one of the luminous spots of our literature for the past 20 years," and then added what may be the most elegant

compliment I've ever heard paid to another person: "He's such a generous spirit, you'd be embarrassed to behave in a small way around him." And Mary Karr, who has been a colleague of Saunders's at Syracuse since he joined the faculty in the mid-'90s (and who also, incidentally, is a practicing Catholic with a wonderful singing voice and a spectacularly inventive foul mouth), told me, "I think he's the best short-story writer in English alive."

In one of my favorite books, *The Silent Woman*, by Janet Malcolm, the issue of indirect characterization arises repeatedly as Malcolm investigates the challenges of biography; in this case, specifically, the challenges faced by biographers of the late poet Sylvia Plath. Although ostensibly the story traces the specifics of various literary and legal challenges faced by Plath's biographers, the larger questions that loom relate to the issue of indirect characterization by other people. In this case, according to Malcolm, the Plath estate had assiduously guarded its holdings against those it perceived as critical to Plath's late husband, poet Ted Hughes. The divergent and often passionate impressions the legions of people involved in this story have about one another, as well as their own roles in the story, reinforce the difficulty in ever producing an objective portrait.

In one section, Malcolm looks at a passage from Anne Stevenson's biography of Plath (*Bitter Fame, A Life of Sylvia Plath*), in which Stevenson characterizes Plath's hurt at seeing Hughes with another woman as an "over-reaction," given that the woman was "in fact" one of Hughes's students.

Malcolm analyzes Stevenson's explication as an example of the impossibility of ever possessing in nonfiction the narrative authority with which Stevenson recounts the incident. Who, Malcolm asks, is Stevenson's source in explaining away Plath's hurt? Hughes? And is he reliable? Malcolm writes:

The questions raised by the passage only underscore the epistemological insecurity by which the reader of biography and autobiography (and history and journalism) is always and everywhere dogged. In a work of nonfiction we almost never know the truth of what happened. The ideal of unmediated reporting is regularly achieved only in fiction, where the writer faithfully reports on what is going on in his imagination . . . only in nonfiction does the question of what happened and how people thought and felt remain open.

The various stances the writers in this chapter, and non-fiction writers everywhere, take toward and the techniques by which they render their subjects—anthropological, empathetic, antagonistic, existential—show the challenges and possibilities of writing about real rather than invented people.

The benefits: expansion of one's world view, knowledge base, and empathetic capacity are but a few. Plus, thinking about other people allows respite from thinking about oneself, if but for a short time.

## ····People Are People

I titled this chapter People Are People, in part, because who can resist a Depeche Mode reference, right? In writing, however, people play different roles in stories. As in literature, where E. M. Forster conceived the idea of "flat" and "round" characters to differentiate their levels of complexity and importance, you as the writer need people to play different roles in your nonfiction.

Narratives that focus on a central person often use as many types of direct and indirect characterization as possible in order to create a sense of three-dimensionality. Such stories also will rely on other character-dependent literary devices, such as plot. Jimmy Boegle, editor and publisher of the *Coachella Valley*

*Independent*, says finding people whose lives—rather than whose opinions—are the focus of a story is what he sees as the key difference between articles and stories.

"No matter what you're writing, be it a wine column or a hard news story or a feature, the best stories are actually just that: stories," Boegle says. "Doing a traditional style article where you talk to one person on the left side and one person on the right side and an academic in the middle, that's OK, but it's not going to be as readable and compelling as an actual story." In an actual story, characters need an arc and "there has to be some sort of conflict or adversity, either overcoming the adversity or being overcome by that adversity."

As an example, during his time as editor of the *Tucson Weekly*, Boegle oversaw a great deal of reporting on immigration issues in Arizona. While pundits and politicians had (and continue to have) much to say on the topic of immigration, Boegle and his staff focused on finding the people behind the stories, whether it was immigrants suffering as a result of US border policy, or border residents themselves. "Those were where the stories were that illustrated the issue," Boegle says. "More than anything John McCain or Jon Kyl (current and former US senators for Arizona) had to say."

A challenge for nonfiction writers, particularly those working in journalism, is to branch outside the "usual suspects" for subjects. Celebrity and politician profiles, though entertaining at times, have their own particular sets of benefits and drawbacks. Profiling someone with a hefty public record means a plethora of available background material, which can ease the crafting of a narrative. On the other hand, people in the public eye can be difficult to interview simply because as subjects, they have been interviewed so many times; they have already crafted their narratives and learned how to perform them.

But perhaps this is the case for everyone, regardless of their level of exposure to having their lives re-created on the page.

Recently I was reading (despite my better instincts) an *Atlantic* magazine article, "The Mind of Donald Trump." In it, writer Dan P. McAdams aims to use what he describes as "well-validated concepts in the fields of personality, developmental, and social psychology" to "develop a dispassionate and analytical perspective on Trump." Trump wasn't willing to be interviewed, so McAdams uses documented interviews and other material for his piece. I won't spoil the conclusions but, needless to say, I wasn't shocked—although the article was quite interesting.

One section, though, stood out to me, less for what it says about Trump and more for how it speaks to the challenge for the nonfiction writer encountering real-life subjects:

> As brainy social animals, human beings evolved to be consummate actors whose survival and ability to reproduce depend on the quality of our performances. We enter the world prepared to perform roles and manage the impressions of others, with the ultimate evolutionary aim of getting along and getting ahead in the social groups that define who we are.

Everyone has a story to tell and, likely, has already fixed upon his or her own personal narrative. The challenge for the nonfiction writer is to find a truth that is not just a reiteration. Telling the story your subject wants told isn't really an act of creative nonfiction or journalism; rather, it's called public relations. Truman Capote sympathized with the real-life subjects who disliked their renderings. But I suspect somewhere between what journalists refer to as blow jobs and what critics call hatchet jobs, greater truths that make use of facts, empathy, and craft are possible for (almost) every subject.

# PROMPTS AND PRACTICE

1. **Photo op.** If available, use an old photo of a member of your family for this exercise. Relying solely on the photograph, describe your (mother, father, aunt, sister, etc.) using physical details. If an old photograph isn't available, use a current one.

2. **Self-inventory.** In his essay "On the Necessity of Turning Oneself into a Character," from his book *To Show and to Tell*, Phillip Lopate discusses the need for a writer to take his or her own inventory—not necessarily in an AA way, but as a means of presenting "that self to the reader as a specific legible character." Write out a list of your traits; be as specific as possible, avoiding generalities like "nice" or "smart" or "tall." From this list, pick one characteristic and write a short scene from your life that exemplifies the trait you've identified.

3. **Q&A.** Conduct an interview—either formally or informally—at someone's home. Take notes on the person's environment, and identify at least three physical details that either reinforce or contradict (or both) your impressions of this person. In writing, render these descriptions in relation to your subject to show either a reinforcing or conflicting element of the person's character.

For example, in Janet Malcolm's *A Silent Woman*, she describes Stevenson, during their meeting at the University Women's Club in London, as appearing "defeated and ground down," and her environs reinforcing this impression: "The room had a dour and pinched character; its faded beige wallpaper and sagging brown armchairs seemed gratuitously dismal."

4. **Objectify.** Speaking of objects, this prompt is inspired by Dinah Lenney's wonderful essay collection, *The Object Parade*, in which each essay begins with some sort of, yes, "object," through which Lenney explores a memory, idea, or question. In

a self-interview on the *Nervous Breakdown*, Lenney notes that objects can also be referred to as talismans or belongings, writing, "They're loaded with history and memory and meaning." So pick one of your talismans; all that matters is that it has value for you. Begin by describing it with as much tactile detail as possible, and consider how its value also helps define its owner (you). Read Lenney's "Object Parade: Little Black Dress" for inspiration.

5. **Scare tactics.** Interview someone about the most frightening experience he or she has ever had, and ask for both a description of the event and the thoughts and feelings that occurred during it. Now write two versions of the story as told to you, one in a limited third-person point of view, and another in a closer third-person point of view, as if in the mind of the person you've interviewed. Read through these to gauge a sense of the difference in mood and style. Be brave, and ask your subject to read what you've written and assess how well he or she feels you captured the experience.

6. **Watch music.** Watch a video (or many videos) featuring your favorite musician. Write at least one paragraph that describes the musician physically, how he or she looks—from clothes to gestures to expressions—while performing.

7. **Gossip.** Practice indirect characterization. Interview a person who knows someone you know. Ask for a secondhand story about the first person or a memory. Take notes. How do their impressions add to or change your understanding of the initial person? Write a short profile of your main subject, using the indirect characterization you've gathered to enhance the story.

8. **Role play.** One year, I was asked to participate in "principal-for-a-day" at a local elementary school. I agreed, thinking it might yield a story, but it only reinforced my belief that I should never

be a principal at an elementary school. Still, stepping into someone else's shoes is a useful exercise in experiencing other people's
viewpoints and lives. Search for an opportunity to spend a day in
another person's occupation or life. This could mean volunteering
somewhere or just asking someone you know if you can shadow
him or her. Many law enforcement agencies have ride-along
opportunities with local police departments (a rare opportunity to
voluntarily enter a police car). If all else fails, consider bell-ringing
at the holidays. Use this immersion experience not just as fodder
to write about your own experience, but an opportunity to talk to
others whose lives and work differ from your own.

9. **Watch out.** Just as eavesdropping is a useful way to train your
ear for speech patterns (and possibly to find story ideas), people
watching (eye-dropping?) creates opportunities without pressure
to practice looking. Head to a park bench, coffeehouse, beach—any
place where you can observe and make notes on people's physical
attributes and movements. What can you recognize not only about
other people but about your own tendencies in observation?

10. **Final words.** In her 2015 nonfiction book *Find the Good:
Unexpected Life Lessons from a Small-Town Obituary Writer*,
Heather Lende writes that she begins each obituary with a
phone call, followed by a visit, in which she takes notes and tries
to look for the good in the life of the deceased. This means looking at photos and listening for stories so that even the saddest
end—a mother who dies of cancer and leaves twin girls, a young
man who commits suicide—is not the only story. "People lead
all kinds of interesting and fulfilling lives," Lende writes, "but
they all end. My task is investigating the deeds, characteristics,
occupations, and commitments." So, write either your own obituary, or employ research and interviewing skills to write one for
another person (possibly warn that person of what you're doing
and why so it doesn't set off any alarms).

# READING AND RESOURCES
# FROM THIS CHAPTER

Boynton, Robert S. *The New New Journalism: Conversations with America's Best Nonfiction Writers on Their Craft*. New York: Vintage, 2005.

Capote, Truman. *In Cold Blood: A True Account of a Multiple Murder and Its Consequences*. New York: Vintage, 1965.

Conover, Ted. *Newjack: Guarding Sing Sing*. New York: Vintage, 2001.

Goldberg, Julia. "La Manga: Finding the People Among the Trees," *Santa Fe Reporter*, October 15, 1997.

Hemley, Robin. *Do-over!: In Which a Forty-Eight-Year-Old Father of Three Returns to Kindergarten, Summer Camp, the Prom, and Other Embarrassments*. New York: Little, Brown, 2009.

———. *A Field Guide for Immersion Writing: Memoir, Journalism, And Travel*. Athens: University of Georgia Press, 2012.

Lenney, Dinah. "Little Black Dress." In *The Object Parade*. Berkeley: Counterpoint, 2014.

———. "The TNB Self-Interview." *Nervous Breakdown*, April 21, 2014. http://www.thenervousbreakdown.com/tnbnonfiction/2014/04/dinah-lenney-the-tnb-self-interview.

Lopate, Phillip. *To Show and to Tell: The Craft of Literary Nonfiction*. New York: Free Press, 2013.

Lovell, Joel. "George Saunders Has Written the Best Book You'll Read This Year." *New York Times*, January 3, 2013. http://www.nytimes.com/2013/01/06/magazine/george-saunders-just-wrote-the-best-book-youll-read -this-year.html.

Malcolm, Janet. *The Silent Woman: Sylvia Plath & Ted Hughes*. New York: A.A. Knopf, 1994.

Martínez, Rubén. *Crossing Over: A Mexican Family on the Migrant Trail*. New York: Metropolitan Books, 2001.

———. *Desert America: Boom and Bust in the New Old West*. New York: Metropolitan Books, 2012.

McAdams, Dan P. "The Mind of Donald Trump." *The Atlantic*, June 2016. http://www.theatlantic.com/magazine/archive/2016/06/the-mind-of-donald-trump/480771/.

Sager, Mike. "The Multitudes of Roseanne Barr." *Esquire*, August 2001. http://longform.org/stories/the-multitudes-of-roseanne.

Talese, Gay. "Frank Sinatra Has a Cold." *Esquire*, May 14, 2016. http://www.esquire.com/news-politics/a638/frank-sinatra-has-a-cold-gay-talese/.

Wolfe, Tom. "The Birth of 'The New Journalism'; Eyewitness Report." *New York Magazine*, February 14, 1972. nymag.com/news/media/47353/index3.html.

Zarin, Cynthia. "The Storyteller." *New Yorker*, April 12, 2004. http:// www.newyorker.com/magazine/2004/04/12/the-storyteller-cynthia-zarin.

# CHAPTER SIX

# Constructive Construction

The presence of structure reassures readers that they are in the hands of a skilled storyteller, someone they can trust with their time and interest. They know they are going somewhere, which means they can relax and enjoy the journey.

**—James B. Stewart,** *Follow the Story*

For me, form is always an accident. It's always this suppressed byproduct of the actual writing, so it's not something that I go into when I sit down to write—it's something that is the aftermath of what's been written. So I often happen upon the correct form somewhere in the process.

**—Jenny Boully,** *The Form Our Curiosity Takes*

IN A 2013 *New York Times* essay, architect and writer Matteo Pericoli proposed, "Great architects build structures that can make us feel enclosed, liberated or suspended. They lead us through space, make us slow down, speed up or stop to contemplate. Great writers, in devising their literary structures, do exactly the same." Pericoli went on to describe a class he had taught, in which students analyzed the structural elements of various pieces of writing (fiction, poetry, and nonfiction) and then teamed up with architectural students to render these works in three-dimensional forms. My favorite of those pictured was the rendering of David Foster Wallace's essay "A Supposedly Fun Thing I'll Never Do Again," structured as a series of parenthetical cuts and glass floors (side note: Ayn Rand's novel *Atlas Shrugged* seems better as a building).

Architecture metaphors, spatial ideas, and physicality appear often in discussions of writing structure. It's probable Ernest Hemingway said something about this. Writing is a form of communication and it manifests formally, on the page or the screen, in large chunks or small bits, in long narratives or fractured segments, in stories or essays or hybrids made from white space, footnotes, and JavaScript. The discrepancy between Stewart's and Boully's quotes earlier in this chapter may be simply accounted for by the types of writing each does: journalism in the case of Stewart, and lyric essay in Boully's case. Or perhaps the type of nonfiction in which a specific writer engages is directly correlated to the way individual brains and sensibilities engage with the world. Or all of the above.

The initial exercise Pericoli assigned his students, to take a piece of writing and analyze its structure, is an excellent task for any writer who encounters work he or she admires. All writing takes some form, and identifying and playing around with form can be both challenging and liberating. Arguably, it should be both.

#### ••••*Pre-Structure Structure*

I am always intimidated by writers whose writing processes include meticulous preparation toward cohesiveness. I operate under a strange hybrid system of extreme control and crazy-making chaos. Right now, for example, this book is heavily

outlined with all my interviews and notes annotated and organized in folders on my computer. But I am sitting in my office
barely able to move due to the piles of books and paper that I
have incrementally retrieved over the last six months from bookshelves, files, and closets; all have come to rest within inches
of my computer. Five minutes ago, I accidentally knocked over
John D'Agata's *The Lost Origins of the Essay*, and the book's
heft caused an avalanche of other books onto the floor, terrifying the cat and causing me to lose my train of thought and, for
a moment, all hope of accomplishing anything this morning.

To cheer myself up, I reread John McPhee's *New Yorker*
essay on structure, which tells of the writer "surrounded by
drifts of undifferentiated paper, and near tears in a catatonic
swivet" before he utilizes the outlining techniques drilled into
him in high school to get on track. Except rather than follow his
lead and attack chaos with order, I decided to instead reread
Ander Monson's essay-in-outline-form, "Outline toward a
Theory of the Mine Versus the Mind and the Harvard Outline,"
and then to reread his essay "Essay as Hack," which formally
interrogates form, considers the essay in relation to hacking,
games, and dreams, and, finally, to "Vanilla Mint–flavored
Benadryl Quick Dissolve Strips."

I knew as soon as I read the last line of the piece—"I don't
know what this means"—that I was ready to return to hours of
uninterrupted focused work, although I had no idea why. Some
form of the events I just described happens in small and large
ways when I write, particularly on deadline. I can't exactly recommend this meandering lunacy as a formal process, although
it is ingrained in how I work.

Each of the writers I talked to for this book have a writing
process. This isn't to say one shouldn't try to, perhaps, improve or
shake it up (Monson, in "Essay as Hack," talks about assigning
"mind-hacks" to students to force their brains to work differently
in the generative writing stage. For example: writing hungry,

writing tired, dictating into microphones, using a typewriter instead of a computer), but once it's time to work (particularly on deadline), a process toward organizing one's material is essential.

Some writers prefer to write a draft cold and then, in the editing and revision process, make structural decisions. Some writers prefer to make organizational decisions ahead of time so that they know where they are going.

*Willamette Week's* Mark Zusman emphasizes the importance he places on discussing stories with reporters prior to writing as part of the structure decision-making process.

"I think sometimes people don't appreciate enough how much editing can be done before a reporter actually writes a first draft," Zusman says. "In other words, my experience has been a lot of times editors will start working on structure after they see a first draft. I find it helpful to have those conversations prior to getting a first draft, in talking to the reporter about both what the story is, secondly what's their focus and then how are they going to tell it; how are they going to unpeel that onion. And in the consequence of them talking, oftentimes a structure becomes clear." Of course, he adds, "Sometimes it becomes clear and they write a first draft and you realize they have to start all over."

Mike Sager compares the stages of gathering material and writing to collecting and spilling water. While he's reporting, he's filling up, and only when he's preparing the material does he start thinking about how to tell the story.

"Think of a bucket underneath a well, and if you're pouring it out you can't spill it. I fill it and then I spill it," Sager says. "It's kind of like why I chose to be a history major instead of political science. History is over and I could take a look at what it meant in the context of the times. I want to wait until after my reporting is done, then I often find within a story a little story arc of what was happening during the time I was there. Do the perspiration and then the inspiration comes. You can't scrimp on your secondary work. There's the primary work, which is the gathering; the secondary work is the preparing."

My colleague Matt Donovan, author of the essay collection *A Cloud of Unusual Size and Shape*, describes a similar approach, although his work was more rooted in immersion and research than journalistic reporting:

"I take copious notes without any privileging about what's important, or any conscious worries about what might ultimately belong. I don't discriminate, and have taken on a more-is-more approach. I've learned to trust any tug on the sleeve I feel during my initial readings, or, to mix metaphors, find myself intuitively taking on the magpie role of chasing after any possible gleam, no matter what I may have thought I had set out to pursue. At the same time, no matter how gleaming any discovered fact or anecdote might be, in the end I'm still willing to cut it loose from the final version if I don't feel that it's working to serve the piece as a whole."

Whether working from notes, outlines, Post-its, or index cards, eventually formal decisions will need to be made, pehaps before writing, perhaps in revision. What follows are discussions of various (though hardly exhaustive) types of structure, from journalistic to literary to disjunctive to interactive.

#### ····*Preamble*

*Creative Nonfiction* magazine describes "scenes and stories" as the "building blocks" of creative nonfiction. Scenes and stories are what people—and by people I mean writing teachers—are sometimes talking about when they say to "show" rather than "tell" what happened.

When an event is rendered in scene, the goal is to recreate the experience so that the reader is in the moment.

Exposition is the "tell," the sharing of reflections, theories, ideas, and questions. When exposition is used to render time rather than scenes, it compresses time. My colleague James Reich says he sometimes uses the opening prologues at the beginning of the *Star Wars* movies to delineate exposition from scene ("A long time ago, in a galaxy far, far away . . ."). That opening crawl is both a summary of events and what's known as "backstory."

Let's look at a few examples:

> Chunks of the doorframe fly through the air and fall on either side of me. I stand there, immobile. A hundred cops outside, some in uniform, some not, guns drawn, faces and bodies tense. A tall, heavyset blonde police officer steps forward through the doorway and smacks me in the face with the butt of her shotgun as more cops push past her and into the apartment. I lie on the floor, a foot across my throat, a knee in my groin, a shotgun and a 9mm leveled at my head.
>
> —Patrick O'Neil, *Gun, Needle, Spoon*

This excerpt from O'Neil's memoir is rendered in **scene**. Events are happening in real time, and the concrete details reinforce the visceral experience O'Neil describes.

> Though both the musician and the graduate student could tell you stories, I can tell only mine: I was twenty-four, and my father had recently died. Daddy worked hard at being a writer and a drinker, but was successful only in the drinking. He shouted at me when he drank, but he was Daddy, so I loved him. I was just starting to be adult enough to reconcile the complicated feelings I had for my father, but he died before I realized his drinking did not mean he didn't love me. He died feeling like he had failed me. And that has always made me feel that, really, it was I who failed him.
>
> —Suzanne Roberts, "Mistakes"

This excerpt from Roberts's award-winning essay is **expository**. Although there are scenes in the essay, in this particular portion, Roberts has summarized events, told them, compressed time. The reader is not in a scene in which the narrator's father is yelling at her; we are being told that it happened.

As is hopefully obvious, both of these examples are compelling writing, because both types of writing can be used effectively depending on the writer's material, approach, and sensibility.

# STRUCTURES, SHAPES, AND APPROACHES

···· *The Inverted Pyramid*

Perhaps because I never went to journalism school, I learned the concept of the "inverted pyramid" structure late in life (like after I'd written for newspapers for fifteen years). When I look back at stories I wrote for the *Rio Grande Sun,* a community weekly, many utilize traditional inverted pyramid structure, although I am sure this was simply a result of having to write as many stories as fast as I could rather than any formal decision-making process.

As concepts go, the inverted pyramid is easy: it just means structuring a story so that the most important information is at the top of the article. This is a reasonable choice for stories in which the information—the news—is the reason for the story, and has the added benefit of allowing the reader to learn the key aspect of the story first. This practice apparently originated with reporters' dictation of news through faulty telegraphs[18] (so maybe not totally relevant to today's world). Even post-telegraph, organizing stories this way meant that stories that were too long for allotted space in print could be easily cut from the bottom.

Pick up any daily newspaper on any day of the week and you will find stories in which the main point of the story—the news—is where the story begins (and is the key point of the

18    Bruce DeSilva, "Endings," in *Telling True Stories: A Nonfiction Writers' Guide* (New York: Penguin Group, 2007), 116-124.

headline). As the story progresses, the least important facts of the story appear lower in the piece. Although there are exceptions, this type of structure tends to emphasize information over storytelling and is thus primarily expository. A major downfall to using this type of structure is its format doesn't incentivize the reader to finish. On the other hand, this also creates a challenge for the writer.

## ···· *Narrative Storytelling*

Narrative structure, on the other hand, is driven by story and typically is built upon both scenes and exposition. In stories, events happen; this is why narrative stories frequently use chronology as their structural spine. But chronology does not have to mean linear time. Narratives can move forward and backward in time as befits the story being told. Ordering those events to create a sense of significance creates what is traditionally referred to as plot. Plot basically refers to causality, meaning. Janet Burroway describes it clearly in *Writing Fiction*: "A plot is a series of events deliberately arranged so as to reveal their dramatic, thematic, and emotional significance."

When I was editor of the *Reporter*, a staff writer embarked on a moving piece about the aftermath of a family whose daughter had been brutally murdered. In that case, we chose to structure the story chronologically, but backward: The story began in present day and worked itself regressively to the day the young woman was killed. Using chronology as a structural element has the added benefit of making the story easier to outline, and the use of time can create a built-in element of momentum and suspense.

As noted earlier, David Stuart MacLean's book *The Answer to the Riddle Is Me* begins with his traumatic experience of awakening on a train platform in India with no idea who or where he is.

The decision to begin in that moment was not born simply out of a chronological sense that this was the "beginning" of the story, MacLean says.

"One of the things when I was writing the book was sort of getting over the first scene," he says, "because the first scene is sort of the big splashy event." MacLean likens the role of the "big splashy event" to a scene in Plato's *Republic*, in which Leontius "is passing by the executioner's slab and he keeps trying not to look and his head keeps wanting to look at the executioner's slab and finally he opens his eyes and runs at the slab and says, 'take your fill!'" In "the trauma memoir," he says, "Sometimes I think you have that issue, which is the executioner's slab, the big event, and I decided I just wanted to get the big event out of the way quickly rather than be coy about it."

The "event" in this case was a "crazy story," but ultimately MacLean "was more interested in living with trauma and this sort of nonendingness of trauma; the event is good for a dinner topic . . . but I wanted to do more than just tell that crazy story."

Emily Rapp Black's first memoir, on the other hand, began as a series of essays, which she later added to and edited into a more chronological, narrative memoir. Her second memoir began as a blog and also was ultimately edited into book-length form. In addition to each book beginning in a different form, the structural choices she made were entirely different. The first book, Rapp Black says, was largely linear; the second had a more thematic structure.

## Thematic/Associative

Many different types of essays follow nonchronological schematics. Academic papers, editorials and argumentative essays, lyric and other types of personal essays may follow trajectories in which logic, ideas, or just the individual mind's associative thinking create the structure of the piece. These can range from hyperlogical to highly formal to stream-of-consciousness. Perhaps it is the wide-ranging disparities between these types of writing that creates all the hoopla regarding terminology in creative nonfiction. It is strange to think that a newspaper editorial on Donald Trump, Jonathan Swift's "A Modest Proposal," Dinty W. Moore's abecedarian essay "Son of Mr. Green Jeans," and Anne Carson's extended prose poetry "The Glass Essay" all somehow share the same genre. Strange, but liberating.

#### ••••Braided Stories

Jo Ann Beard's "Fourth State of Matter" is an excellent example of a braided narrative. The piece (spoiler alert) tells the personal story of Beard's separation from her husband, ailing dog, and attic of squirrels intertwined with the story of the workplace shooting of her colleagues at the University of Iowa in 1991. The story weaves back and forth between these different narratives, unifying them all through Beard's primary metaphor—plasma, the fourth state of matter—which provides both a structural and emotive conclusion about the connectivity of the human experience.

#### ••••Character Driven

As can be the case in fiction, character-driven nonfiction frequently focuses on an individual person. In some cases, this may mean profiling a life story (this often is the case for people who have accomplished something noteworthy, either for good or ill). For example, Gay Talese's "Frank Sinatra Has a Cold" (discussed in chapter 5) hones in on specific details of Sinatra's life and image to write a portrait of a man who occupies a very specific space in culture.

On the other end of the spectrum, consider Andrew Solomon's 2014 *New Yorker* profile of Peter Lanza, whose son Adam Lanza killed himself, his mother, and 26 people at Sandy Hook Elementary School. The story is ostensibly a profile of Peter Lanza but, of course, also a story about his son and the horrific tragedy he inflicted (and about mass violence and all the questions it engenders).

Another type of character-driven story—often seen in newspaper features—is one in which one or more people help illustrate the topic of the story. To use an example from a story I worked on, in 2004 Dan Frosch wrote a piece that was published in numerous alternative newsweeklies around the country, "Soldier's Heart," about Operation Iraqi Freedom soldiers returning home with PTSD. To humanize this situation, which was also sourced with relevant data, reports, and expert commentary, Frosch found several soldiers whose stories and experiences provided lived experience to the narrative.

## ····Circles (and Other Shapes)

In his essay "Picturing the Personal Essay: A Visual Guide," Tim Bascom describes (and draws) the circular structure as one that allows the writer to connect the beginning of a piece and its end in a way that creates a sense of closure. Bascom uses as an example from Annie Dillard's essay "Living Like Weasels," in which Dillard both begins and ends the piece with reference to a weasel skull, creating a sense of circular closure. Bascom's essay illustrates (literally) various other ways of "seeing" structure with examples that include useful ways of thinking about focus, reflection, and layering. Brian Kiteley's craft book *The 3 a.m. Epiphany* is aimed at writing fiction, but I think his exercises for internal structure, which include "shapes" such as parallel lines, also provide interesting fodder for using shapes to, yes, shape your writing.

#### ····*Segmentation*

Segmentation is a structural device used in a variety of creative nonfiction, but perhaps most notably in various types of lyric essays. The lyric essay is most easily described as a popular type of genre hybrid for nonfiction, in which the lyricism of poetry is given equal weight to the analytic elements of the essay. As a genre, it is mostly credited—at least in its modern form—to the *Seneca Review*, where it was championed by John D'Agata and Deborah Tall in a 1997 issue devoted to such pieces.

These days, lyric essay also is a terminology sometimes used when an essay breaks entirely from the normal organizational constraints of traditional nonfiction writing. In the case of segmentation, this can mean stitching together fragments rather than writing in a more traditional narrative manner. One of the more notable examples is David Shields's essay "Life Story," which is comprised entirely of bumper sticker slogans. Writer Carl Klaus (founder of the University of Iowa's Nonfiction Writing Program) has described this type of writing as "disjunctive," and notes the way such pieces can require the reader to read the segments as autonomous, as well as consider their relationship to one another.

Segmentation also takes cues from poetry by employing white space and line breaks less often associated with prose. In *The Answer to the Riddle Is Me*, MacLean used white space and short chapters in portions of the book to structurally emphasize the way in which he was experiencing reality in the wake of his response to Lariam. MacLean describes the process of using white space as a difficult one "because I get grumpy about white space sometimes because I feel that it's pretentious." And, once he'd decided to use it, he then "had to fight for my white space" later. Ultimately, though, "I liked the idea of the clipped-ness of the short little blips," which grow longer as the book progresses "because I feel like that's mostly how I experience life," and because they create "almost like a strobe light effect, which I wanted."

····*Hermit Crabs/Received Forms*

The "hermit crab" moniker was created, as best I can tell, by writers Brenda Miller and Suzanne Paola in their book *Tell It Slant: Creating, Refining, and Publishing Creative Nonfiction*. Miller and Paola classify the hermit crab as a type of lyric essay, in large part because of the way it breaks from the traditional strictures of nonfiction writing and to some degree elevates reading the form of the essay in conjunction with the content. In the hermit crab essay, the writer repurposes an existing type of "shell" for his or her content (in, apparently, the way a hermit crab uses another creature's shell for its home; I'm not that up on the behavior of crustaceous creatures).

I prefer the term "received forms," which acknowledges the way in which this type of writing takes an established container and uses it as a formal constraint. Margot Singer's essay "On Scaffolding, the Hermit Crabs, and the Real False Document" offers an insightful examination of this type of writing and its roots in the tradition of using received forms such as imagined documents, letters, and such:

> The use of "found form" in creative nonfiction reminds us that the literary text is always a construction, not a transparent window onto "reality" or "truth."
>
> Said another way: the truth lies in the form. In the structure and the scaffolding. In the exposed ducts and pipes

and beams. In space as well as time. In the reminder that all writing forms an artificial shell.

In a 2015 article for *TriQuarterly* magazine, "Finding a Form Before a Form Finds You," Patrick Madden interviewed several writers who had appropriated a specific form for an essay to discuss the pitfalls and payoffs of such formal experiments. The pitfall is that such experiments (like all writing) may not work. The payoff is perhaps best expressed in the article by Ander Monson, whose essay in the form of an outline, "Outline toward a Theory of the Mine Versus the Mind and the Harvard Outline" is a notable example of writing using a received form, in this case, the Harvard Outline. Monson told Madden that while one is constrained in such experiments:

"Being constrained is the whole point! That's why you choose a received form, to see what pressures present themselves and what architectures you have to work within or erect to keep the thing from collapsing."

There are several notable contemporary examples that I like to use in class when teaching this specific type of essay:

"Writer Michael Martone's Leftover Water," by Patrick Madden, in which Madden used an eBay listing as his structure (and it was an actual eBay listing that was then published as an essay).

"Mr. Plimpton's Revenge," by Dinty W. Moore, uses Google Maps to write a Google Maps essay about his experience and encounters with George Plimpton when the latter visited the University of Pittsburgh in the 1970s. Moore's essay is available online, as is the Google Maps essay one of my classes created. Imagine a Google map that locates specific places as maps do. In this case, instead of just providing typical map information, each location has a short written segment that correlates to the place. Taken together, the piece is an interactive essay that makes great use of Google Maps to enhance a story that is rooted in both time and space.

"An Index for *Bi the Book: How to Become Bisexual In Less than a Month*," by Chelsey Clammer, is an essay written in the form of a book index. This piece is available at the end of this chapter.

Several of my students have conceived and executed a variety of interesting received forms essays, including ones in the form of online real estate listings, screenplays, and one on the process of making a dress that investigated body image and was written on both paper and a dress.

*Amaya Hoke models essay as dress*

····*Flash Nonfiction*

Writing long-form has its own set of challenges (I'm experiencing some of them as I write this chapter: exhaustion, carpel-tunnel syndrome, crippling self-doubt, dirty hair), but writing short is, in my view, more difficult. Flash creative nonfiction in many ways takes its cue from the popular flash fiction genre. It is compressed writing—pieces that are constrained by word count—but ones that must still deliver the goods: a story, an emotional response, striking language, for example. Flash, along with its tiny sibling micro-narrative, don't have hard and fast rules in terms of the major constraint of word count. But as a general rule, look to *Brevity* magazine, which solicits essays of 750 words or less. *Brevity*'s editor, Dinty W. Moore, described the "imperatives" of flash nonfiction in an interview with *River Teeth Journal*, saying, "The imperatives are the same, but everything is dialed up in a shorter piece." In other words, flash is not simply an excerpt from something longer or a story told faster; it's a complete piece of writing that requires the writer to be concise, to say the least.

While flash may evoke ideas about specific types of literary writing, writing short is a skill that is useful in a variety of nonfiction settings. Vanessa Martinez, editor of the *Colorado Springs Independent*, says she encourages her writers, especially younger ones, to follow the *New Yorker*'s short-form (approximately 800 words or so) Talk of the Town column. "That style gives them an opportunity to tell a short-form narrative, and I think a lot of young writers aren't familiar with that; they think if they're going to do narrative, they have to go very long."

# STORYTELLING ACROSS PLATFORMS

····*Multimedia*

Storytelling Across Platforms is the name of a class I teach, in which students use a variety of online open-source tools to tell stories in different ways. This includes using Instagram to tell micro stories, Storify to curate stories, and Soundslides to make audio-visual projects such as video essays. They also build WordPress blogs to showcase their work. I was editor of a newspaper during the time we transitioned from print-only to print/web and had to do things like learn HTML in order to use Blogger, so I am still awed at the availability of free tools and how invigorating it can be to find new ways to tell stories.

The audio-visual projects can be challenging, although the form itself has received some attention in the last few years from literary publications such as *Blackbird*, *TriQuarterly*, and *The Normal School*. Writing about the form in *TriQuarterly*, Marilyn Freeman notes that "As a form the video essay tests the mettle of the literary essay—personal, lyrical, contemplative, improvisational, performative, critical—not on the page but on the *screen*."

One of the most popular class projects has been working with *Atavist*. The magazine itself is a National Magazine Award–winning publication privileging long-form storytelling across a spectrum of topics. *Atavist* also is an online software that allows anyone to create an interactive story of any length and incorporate images, video, maps, slideshows, and audio.

····*Visualizations*

As the cliché goes, a data visualization is worth a thousand words. As with multimedia, facility in telling stories with non-narrative methods has multiple benefits, from learning new skills to finding hidden stories. Rani Molla, a data columnist at *Bloomberg Gadfly*, collects numbers, makes data visualizations, and then analyzes them in her columns. I first met Molla when I hired her as a copy editor and then arts writer and then arts editor at the *Reporter*. During that time period, the *Reporter* had begun to play around with finding non-narrative ways to tell stories by experimenting with format, charts, and other types of visual storytelling. After leaving the *Reporter*, Molla went to Columbia University Graduate School of Journalism to study data visualization. Prior to *Bloomberg*, she worked at the *Wall Street Journal*. Molla has found that working with data and charts alongside her writing allows her to explore topics in fresh ways, whether she's writing about culture or business. She describes her epiphany about the value of working in multiple mediums during her graduate work when she was reporting on the Bronx. "It's low on everything, it's very poor, it has all these problems, and I expected it to not have that much data, too. But it's New York, so there was data and I was able to see that most of the [Bronx's] Wi-Fi came from McDonald's. I thought that in and of itself, that was a powerful thing."

Data journalism and data visualizations are booming in the investigative reporting sector as well, as chapter 7 discusses.

But even writers who don't want to immerse themselves in the world of spreadsheets and data sets will find many free and easy tools to make charts and other data visualizations, such as those available through Infogr.am, Google Charts, and Timeline JS.

I think of fooling around with other types of storytelling akin to Ander Monson's idea of the brain hack. Even if the end result isn't becoming a professional data journalist, the process may open up new ideas or ways of thinking. Monson's magazine, *Diagram*, also features a variety of "schematics," along with text, images, and other types of creative works.

## ····*Beginnings and Endings or, as I Like to Call Them, Ledes and Kickers*

Like many journalists who have never seen a linotype machine, I have always used the variant spelling "lede" because I thought it was a tradition of journalism, dating back to a time in which an alternative spelling was required to distinguish "lede" from "lead" for reasons related to the aforementioned linotype machine. This belief seems to have been somewhat debunked (or at least it has been the subject of some rousing Internet debate among journalists with greater historical knowledge than I possess) and filed under the headings of romanticism and nostalgia. I can live with that. A kicker, then, is an ending. Regardless of the type of nonfiction, beginnings and endings, ledes and kickers, play important roles in narrative writing (perhaps in non-narrative writing as well, but maybe not as much) because they often determine if a reader will be drawn into a piece and, having finished, if the piece will resonate and satisfy. And yes, you may also spell it "lead," but I figure if I am going to be nostalgic, I might as well go all in.

*Wall Street Journal* reporter Dan Frosch calls ledes his "biggest challenge," and says, "Oftentimes I find myself saying ledes out loud, toying with them in my head, toying with them out loud."

The lede—the beginning of the story—is a crucial element of any piece, not only because it can determine whether a reader keeps going, but because it also in a large way dictates the entire structure and tone of the story itself.

Here are some lede options. It's worth pointing out that if you knocked on a hundred journalists' doors (a terrifying proposition, although perhaps it would make for a good story), you'd find many diverging opinions on the nomenclature and descriptions for ledes, and you'd find more types than I'm listing here.

## 1. **News-Breaking Summary**

"A group of anti-government militia members have occupied the headquarters and visitor center of Malheur National Wildlife Refuge in Harney County, Ore., apparently seeking to provoke a standoff with the federal government."

> —Aaron Mesh, "Militia Group Takes Over Federal Building
>      in Eastern Oregon Because 'The Lord Was Not Pleased'"

As you can see, this is a traditional lede, used for a news-breaking and/or time-sensitive story, in which one sentence tells the reader the basics of the story, including the **who** (anti-government militia), **what** (occupation/standoff) **where** (Malheur National Wildlife Refuge in Oregon) and **why** (trying to provoke a standoff) of the situation. In theory, the reader could read one line and have the basic gist of the story—certainly enough to make conversation while in line at Whole Foods:

"Hey, did you hear about that standoff in Oregon?"

"I know! It's crazy!"

Putting aside the news-breaking lede's value as a conversation starter, it's also an organizational cue to the rest of the story, which then gives the chronology of the situation and the background of the people involved.

Here's another straightforward example:

"A U.S. Special Forces member was killed and two others wounded in fighting in Afghanistan's Helmand province on Tuesday, a U.S. military spokesman said."

> —Jessica Donati and Felicia Schwartz, "U.S. Soldier
>                                            Killed in Afghanistan"

Again, this is a lede concerned with the who/what/when/where of the situation. If the reader wants more—the how and the why—the lede is a fast entryway into the larger story.

## 2. **Compression of Entire Story**

"Despite a federal judge's rulings legalizing same-sex marriage, most probate judges in Alabama on Monday refused to issue marriage licenses to gay and lesbian couples, escalating a legal showdown that echoed the battles over desegregation here in the 1960s."

—Alan Blinder, "Gay Marriage in Alabama Begins,
but Only in Parts"

The difference between this compressed lede and, say, a news-breaking lede is that it hints at a story larger simply than the facts of what's happening currently, but additionally points toward a larger context (the echoes of the desegregation battles in Alabama) that will be explained later in the story.

## 3. **The Tease**

"No human being has caught it in New York City for at least a century, but still, there it was, researchers said, in places touched by hundreds, maybe thousands, of people every day."
—Anemona Hartocollis, "Bubonic Plague in Subway System?"

This teasing lede, or "blind" lede, is predicated on telling readers the situation but withholding a key piece of information, in this case the "what" (which turns out to be the bubonic plague), and the "where" (which turns out to be the subway system).

## 4. **Descriptive**

"Passersby of the Standard hotel on Manhattan's Washington Street will encounter an inflatable rainbow structure of indeterminate shape, beginning this week. At night it lights up like an alien pod that's just set down from a planet located in the artist James Turrell's high-school locker."

—Rachel Tashjian, "What Is That Glowing Orb
in Manhattan's Meatpacking District?"

"It is one of those perfect Colorado mornings — the sky a brilliant cerulean stretching for miles over a rough-and-tumble landscape of high desert and red rocks, the blue snow-capped peaks of the Rockies barely visible to the east. I am descending the high bluffs above the Colorado River just west of Hot Sulphur Springs, decked out in hip waders, determined to improve my fly-fishing game."
 —Deborah Huso, "For the Quieter Side of the Rockies, Go West"

Both of these examples rely more heavily on imagery than on information. In the first example, from *Vanity Fair*, the reader is drawn into a central visual image, and the lede also has a bit of a "blind tease," in that it does not explain what the "inflatable rainbow structure" is, thus prompting the reader to continue reading in order to learn more.

In the second example, from the *Washington Post*, the lede relies on a sense of environment and place, both pulling the reader into a landscape but also setting the pace for a more narrative and personal story, as signaled by the use of the first person "I."

### 5. **Scene**

"He wakes up, and even before he opens his eyes, he can see his beautiful, delusional son.

*Gus*, Creigh Deeds thinks.

He lies in bed a few minutes more, trying to conjure specific images. Gus dancing. Gus playing the banjo. Gus with the puppies. Any images of Gus other than the final ones he has of his 24-year-old, mentally ill son attacking him and then walking away to kill himself, images that intrude on his days and nights along with the questions that he will begin asking himself soon, but not yet. A few minutes more. Gus fishing. Gus looking at him. Gus smiling at him. Time to start the day."
                    —Stephanie McCrummen, "A Father's Scars"

In this extended lede, writer Stephanie McCrummen employs what might be described as close limited third person (discussed at greater length in chapter 5), in which the story begins within the mind of the story's protagonist, Virginia State Senator Creigh Deeds.

Presumably from her interviews, McCrummen heard this story from Deeds and chose to render it in a real-time scene, rather than a summarized anecdote told from the point of view of the writer. This type of lede certainly draws in the reader in some of the traditional ways a lede should—the reader learns that Senator Deeds had a mentally ill son who killed himself— but it also signals that this piece will be a deeper story and provide a longer narrative that focuses on the senator.

## 6. Anecdotal

"Ilene Waterstone, actor-comedian Steve Martin's personal assistant, moved into a tower at the Park La Brea Apartments on April Fools' Day in 1992. She wasn't sure what to expect. 'I used to think of Park La Brea as being the old people's complex,' she recalls.

It wasn't long before she fell in love with it. The grounds were lush and well-maintained, her neighbors respectful and neat. Then about two years ago, things went to hell."
—Jonathan Tolliver, "L.A.'s Biggest Apartment Complex Has Broken Elevators, Insect Infestations and a Waiting List"

The anecdotal lede is just that, a short complete story, or anecdote, that illustrates the entire story's focus. The lede may focus on one person who may or may not be central to the piece or just illustrative of a larger issue.

## 7. The Question

"All good things come in threes, right?"
— Lamarco McClendon, "'Tetris' Movie Will be a Sci-Fi Trilogy"

Should you start a story with a question?

Only if you have the answer! (In the example above, the answer also is provided in the lede: "That's certainly what producer Larry Kasanoff is banking on with his latest video game adaptation, *Tetris*.")

Even when the question is easily answered, many writers and editors shy away from the question lede. Although questions are used fairly often in headlines and subheds, they are considered—and rightfully, I think—both clichéd and gimmicky. With that said, beginning with a question is an option.

## 8. **The Quote**

"When I first came out to L.A. [in 1968], my friend [photographer] Joel Bernstein found an old book in a flea market that said: Ask anyone in America where the craziest people live and they'll tell you California. Ask anyone in California where the craziest people live and they'll say Los Angeles. Ask anyone in Los Angeles where the craziest people live and they'll tell you Hollywood. Ask anyone in Hollywood where the craziest people live and they'll say Laurel Canyon. And ask anyone in Laurel Canyon where the craziest people live and they'll say Lookout Mountain. So I bought a house on Lookout Mountain."
—Lisa Robinson quoting Joni Mitchell, "An Oral History of
Laurel Canyon, the 60s and 70s Music Mecca"

As with the question lede, many argue that beginning stories with quotes is overdone and clichéd. I think it can work sometimes. In this case, there are a lot of reasons it makes sense that this particular story begins with a quote from Joni Mitchell. For one, it's a great quote that immediately pulls the reader into wanting to know more about Laurel Canyon. For another, it's a story that is structured around quotes from others—thus, the oral history of the story's title.

## 9. **The Personal**

"I arrived in Tirana, Albania, on a Sunday evening in late August, on a flight from Istanbul. The sun had set while the plane was midflight, and as we landed in the dark, images of fading light still filled my mind. The man next to me, a young, red-haired American wearing a straw hat, asked me if I knew how to get into town from the airport. I shook my head, put the book I had been reading into my backpack, got up, lifted my suitcase out of the overhead compartment and stood waiting in the aisle for the door up ahead to open."

—Karl Ove Knausgaard, "The Terrible Beauty of Brain Surgery"

"As we walked among the empty houses of Zalesye, the last thing I expected to see was an inhabitant. But suddenly there she was. Striding from her cottage in heavy boots, a scarf tied on her head, Rosalia greeted us in Ukrainian and proudly showed us her potato patch."

—George Johnson, "'Babushkas of Chernobyl' Finds Life Thriving in Scarred Land"

Knausgaard is the notable author of a six-volume autobiographical novel, so I would imagine that writing from the personal point of view comes rather naturally to him at this point (also, for the record, this story was translated from Norwegian). Johnson is a brilliant science writer, who is able to write both for scientists and the layperson about complex and difficult subjects. His use of the first person in the story cited above draws the reader into a challenging subject with voice, character, and visceral detail.

Perhaps the intimacy of voice afforded by first person is its main draw. But first person also contains the promise that the story is not only about the topic at hand (in this case, brain surgery and nuclear devastation), but also about the perceptions and observations of the narrator. Obviously, writing in the first person won't fly for certain kinds of stories (or for certain kinds of writers for that matter), but for stories that are driven more by voice and perspective than by breaking news, it is certainly a viable option with which to experiment. And certainly for personal essays and memoir, first person is probably the obvious choice for the overall point of view, even if the lede or beginning starts elsewhere.

All of the options mentioned for entry into a story apply as well to endings. The "quote" ending has been oft-criticized as being overused in journalism to the point of cliché, so if having your writing criticized as clichéd bothers you, then perhaps avoid that. Having a deadline can help with finding an ending, as can having a word limit.

An excellent way to improve both ledes and kickers is to read nonfiction with a special eye toward beginnings and ends that work for you as a reader, and try different approaches. Don't feel locked into a specific beginning or ending; feel free to move elements around.

## PROMPTS AND PRACTICE

1. **Collage.** Take a pile of magazines. (If you don't have any, go to the library and take some of the free ones or ask friends to give you their old ones. Trust me: someone has old ones lying around . . . unless you are by chance reading this on a digital display embedded in your arm in the future, in which case, disregard this exercise.) Leaf through them and cut out any portions of articles or ads that catch your attention. Once you have a nice pile, try arranging them and re-arranging them. No, you are not writing a ransom note (although you could if so inspired). Rather, use these fragments as the start for an essay. If so driven, find even more fragments to create a collage essay.

2. **Place make**. Choose five places in your city (or somewhere you've visited), and write short (100-300 words) about each of them. Find photos you've taken or (and this is easier) that are available online. Write a Google Maps essay using these five segments. This can also be done as a group activity if you have some friend-writers who would like to collaborate.

3. **Cut up.** You may possibly have encountered cut-ups in a classroom at some point as a frenzied instructor (ahem) attempted to teach you sentence and paragraph transitions. Although as a general rule I advise writers to stay away from scissors, this is an exception. Take a longer piece you've written and cut all the paragraphs into separate pieces. Put them back together. Does it make sense, or are you missing transitions from idea to idea? If you have an extra-tolerant friend, ask him or her to reassemble your piece. You may find that someone else making those connections (or failing to make them) helps you see the piece in a new way. For an added challenge, cut every sentence into its own strip and put the piece back together. This is a way of not only testing the connectivity of what you've already written, but possibly finding a new way of revising the piece.

4. **Shape up.** Pick one of the shapes from Tim Bascom's essay or a different type of shape (I vaguely recall from geometry class that there are several more). Write or repurpose part of a story in such a way that you try to shape the piece to follow the shape you've chosen. Keep in mind, you may decide the shape doesn't make sense for the piece. The goal here is to force your brain to see your piece in a new way, an essential if sometimes difficult aspect in revision.

5. **Make note.** I call this the *Memento* exercise, based on the film in which a man with no memory has to write everything important down as he searches for his wife's killer, even tattooing some

of the critical data on his body (don't worry: this prompt does not
involve any permanent ink). To start, pick one day in which you
have a little time/space. Set an alarm on your phone (or your . . .
other device with an alarm) for every hour (or less frequently if
this seems like too much, or more often; the time doesn't matter). At each interval, write your observations for a few moments.
These observations can be your thoughts, an encounter you've
had, what you're seeing. What you write should be what seems
pressing/important to you at that moment. Don't look at these
fragments until the end of the day/week/month. Is there a driving narrative idea here? Do the fragments hold together in an
interesting way? Is there the start of something here?

6. **Kill time.** *Memento*, of course, also is a study of fragmenting
time in a story (it's basically a braided narrative, with one of the
narratives told in reverse time), but it's not the only film from
which one might take a cue in experimenting with structure.
One of my favorite novels, Jennifer Egan's *A Visit from the Goon
Squad*, was, she has said, influenced by her viewing of Quentin
Tarantino's chronologically fragmented *Pulp Fiction*. Try apply-
ing a similar technique to a linear narrative you've written or
would like to write. Tell a story with a beginning, middle, and
end. If you need a prompt, pick three important dates from your
life and write a few paragraphs about each. Now scramble the
narrative, eliminating the linear from the story.

7. **Constrain yourself.** This exercise may play the same role
as practicing scales serves musicians. Perhaps it will produce
something brilliant. I'm talking about Oulipo. Oulipo stands for
Ouvroir de Littérature Potentielle, and was created in the early
1960s by—wait for it—French people: mathematician François
Le Lionnais and writer Raymond Queneau. Oulipo basically
puts formal constraints on a piece of writing, often leading to
unexpected results but always forcing the writer to slow down

and think through word choice and diction more carefully. For example, the Oulipo exercise "N+7" requires taking an existing poem and substituting each of its nouns with the noun that is seven words later in the dictionary. These exercises can also be used in a creative nonfiction capacity. Writer Daniel Nester's teaching blog has a wide collection of Oulipo exercises. I'm stealing one for this exercise, which is called "The beautiful in-law." Write a real letter to someone you know, but do not use any of the letters in the recipient's name within the letter. You may find that this exercise results in a piece of creative nonfiction that can be shaped into an actual piece. Or you'll have a finely crafted letter to send someone. Just one more structured way of approaching writing.

8. **List it**. Despite my occasional sense that lists have ruined society, I also believe as a structural device lists can be used for good—and sometimes funny—writing. For inspiration, read some *McSweeney's* lists. Maybe start with Laura Merli's "Five Excuses to Get Out of Reading a Friend's Poetry," and go from there. You'll find the link in the Resources and Readings section of this chapter. Now write a few lists of your own.

9. **Connect interstices**. Emily Rapp Black shared this exercise, which she says was shared with her by writer Stephen Elliott. Thank you Emily and Stephen! "Choose five moments from your life that are indicative of your life," Rapp Black says, "the five most crucial moments; not milestone, like marriage, divorce, graduations, but five small moments that really sum up your life. Those are harder to identify but are usually much more interesting and deeply singular to the person that's writing them. Take those five things and put them in a linear order; they'll make a kind of narrative order that makes sense that you can then build a story around, but gets you away from the clichés because it's so deeply singular."

I'll add on to this exercise and say, once completed, take the story you've written from the previous exercise built around the five linear moments. Break its linear order and try at least three different beginnings and three different endings.

10. **Create white space**. Erase and annotate or footnote portions of the text you've created.[19]

---

19      I was meandering around the Association of Writers and Writing Programs Book Fair in March 2016 when a woman asked me if I had seen any booths or books specifical-ly on erasure. I had seen, by this point, approximately three million booths and books on just about everything and felt as though my head was going to explode at any moment. I imagined spontaneously combusting while yelling as final words: "Poof! Erasure!"

Erasure is actually a mode of writing in which the writer takes an existing text and erases portions of it to create a new text. It normally does not include human sponta-neous combustion.

Later, I did in fact spot a booth privileging erasure writing and then, somehow, also spotted the woman and sent her toward it. Soon thereafter, I learned that Ander Mon-son's magazine, *Diagram*, was soliciting erasures for a special issue, and right after that I ran across poet Jenni B. Baker's website, erasinginfinite.com, in which she is erasing David Foster Wallace's *Infinite Jest* one page at a time to create new poems.

All this sent me thinking, naturally (or at least associatively) about Jenny Boully's book *The Body*. Boully's text consists solely of footnotes; the "body" of the text is miss-ing, erased. When I teach from it, I ask students if they are able to extrapolate what the missing content might be and then share Boully's words from an interview in which she says, "*The Body* is based on what was my life at the time. So it is autobiographical. I left out the actual story, of course, but I feel as if I give so much of it away in the footnotes themselves. I feel as if I've given the right clues and that the astute reader will recon-struct the narrative."

*The Body*, of course, is a specific writer's work and formal experiment, but perhaps may also function as an exercise on both erasure and white space. Hence, I have footnot-ed the entire explanation for this exercise and hopefully left some white space up above. I would recommend reading *The Body* in its entirety, but you can also find an excerpt of it online by searching Boully's name and the title.

# ESSAY

## An Index for *Bi the Book: How to Become Bisexual In Less than a Month*
### Chelsey Clammer

## READING AND RESOURCES
## FROM THIS CHAPTER

Atavist. https://atavist.com

Bascom, Tim. "Picturing the Personal Essay: A Visual
    Guide." *Creative Nonfiction,* Summer 2013. https://
    www.creativenonfiction.org/online-reading/
    picturing-personal-essay-visual-guide.

Beard, Jo Ann. "The Fourth State of Matter." *New
    Yorker*, June 24, 1996. http://www.newyorker.com/
    magazine/1996/06/24/the-fourth-state-of-matter.

Boully, Jenny. *The Body: An Essay*. Athens, Ohio: Essay Press,
    2007.

Chapman, J'yln, comp. *The Form Our Curiosity Takes: A
    Pedagogy of Conversation*. Essay Press, 2014. https://issuu.
    com/essaypress/docs/chapmansingle.

Clammer, Chelsey. "An Index for *Bi the Book: How to Become
    Bisexual In Less than a Month*." *The Drunken Odyssey*,
    November 20, 2014. https://thedrunkenodyssey.
    com/2014/11/20/the-lists-8-an-index-for-bi-the-book-how-
    to-become-a-bisexual-in-less-than-a-month/.

*Diagram Magazine*. http://thediagram.com.

Freeman, Marilyn. "On the Form of the Video Essay."
    *TriQuarterly*, January 16, 2012. http://www.triquarterly.org/
    essay/on-the-form-of-video-essay.

Google. My Maps. https://www.google.com/mymaps.

Hare, Kristen. "Gallery of Good Ledes,
    Recommendation Edition." *Poynter*, April 18, 2014.
    http://www.poynter.org/2014/
    gallery-of-good-ledes-recommendation-edition/248323/.

Hartocollis, Anemona. "Bubonic Plague in the Subway System? Don't Worry About It." *New York Times*, February 6, 2015. http://www.nytimes.com/2015/02/07/nyregion/bubonic-plague-in-the-subway-system-dont-worry-about-it.html.

Macy, Beth. "New York Times Editor Bill Keller on Narrative's Future: Three 'Threats' to It He's Not Buying." *Nieman Storyboard*, April 27, 2010. http://niemanstoryboard.org/stories/new-york-times-editor-bill-keller-on-the-future-of-narrative-journalism-and-three-threats-to-it-he-doesnt-buy/.

Madden, Patrick. "Writer Michael Martone's Leftover Water." *The Normal School*, Fall 2010. http://www.thenormal-school.com/PDFs/madden_normal_school_fall10.pdf.

———. "Finding a Form Before a Form Finds You." *TriQuarterly*, September 29, 2015. http://www.triquarterly.org/craft-essays/finding-form-form-finds-you.

McCrummen, Stephanie. "A Father's Scars: For Va.'s Creigh Deeds, Tragedy Brings Unending Questions." *Washington Post*, November 1, 2014. https://www.washingtonpost.com/national/a-fathers-scars-for-deeds-every-day-brings-questions/2014/11/01/2217a604-593c-11e4-8264-deed-989ae9a2_story.html.

McPhee, John. "Structure." *New Yorker*, January 14, 2013. http://www.newyorker.com/magazine/2013/01/14/structure.

Merli, Laura. "Five Excuses to Get Out of Reading a Friend's Poetry." *McSweeney's*. http://www.mcsweeneys.net/articles/five-excuses-to-get-out-of-reading-a-friends-poetry.

Moore, Dinty W. "Mr. Plimpton's Revenge: A Google Maps Essay, in Which George Plimpton Delivers My Belated and Well-Deserved Comeuppance." *The Normal School*, January 2010. tinyurl.com/plimptonmap.

Monson, Ander. "Outline Toward a Theory of the Mine Versus the Mind and the Harvard Outline." *Neck Deep and Other Predicaments*. Minnesota: Graywolf, 2007.

———. "Essay as Hack." Otherelectricities.com, May 21, 2008. http://otherelectricities.com/swarm/essayashack.html.

Myers, Steve. "Calling the Beginning of a Story a 'Lede' Is Just Another Form of Nostalgia." *Poynter*, September 19, 2011. http://www.poynter.org/2011/calling-the-beginning-of-a-story-a-lede-is-just-another-form-of-nostalgia/146464.

Nolan, Christopher. *Memento*. Film. Santa Monica, CA: Newmarket Films, 2000.

O'Neil, Patrick. *Gun, Needle, Spoon*. Ann Arbor, MI: Dzank Books, 2015.

Patton, Jenny. "Focusing on Flash Nonfiction: An Interview with Dinty Moore." *River Teeth Journal*, January 9, 2012. http://www.riverteethjournal.com/blog/2012/01/09/focusing-on-flash-nonfiction-an-interview-with-dinty-moore.

Roberts, Suzanne. "The Same Story." *Creative Nonfiction*, Fall 2014. https://www.creativenonfiction.org/online-reading/same-story.

Robinson, Lisa. "An Oral History of Laurel Canyon, the 60s and 70s Music Mecca." *Vanity Fair*, March 2015. http://www.vanityfair.com/culture/2015/02/laurel-canyon-music-scene.

Singer, Margot, and Nicole Walker, eds. *Bending Genre: Essays on Creative Nonfiction*. New York: Bloomsbury, 2013.

Solomon, Andrew. "The Reckoning." *New Yorker*, March 17 2014. http://www.newyorker.com/magazine/2014/03/17/the-reckoning.

Tolliver, Jonathan. "L.A.'s Biggest Apartment Complex Has Broken Elevators, Insect Infestations and a Waiting List." *LA Weekly*, April 7, 2015. http://www.laweekly.com/news/las-biggest-apartment-complex-has-broken-elevators-insect-infestations-and-a-waiting-list-5475916.

# CHAPTER SEVEN

# The Paper Chase and Muckraking in the Information Age

In a mass democratic society such as ours, in which there are strong tendencies toward the concentration of power in political and economic institutions, the abuse of power has deep public consequences. It is especially important, therefore, for a vital and vigilant press to hold the leaders of such institutions accountable to preserve a dynamic and participatory democratic society.

—**Lila Weinberg,** *The Muckrakers*

IN 2014, I went to an exhibit in Zurich, Switzerland, titled "Delivery for Mr. Assange." Put together by the art collective Mediengruppe Bitnik, the show featured a reconstruction of WikiLeaks founder Julian Assange's office at the Ecuadorian Embassy in London. The exhibit was pre-*Mr. Robot* but explored the same themes as the unlikely hit TV show: surveillance versus privacy. It asked the same endemic questions about the dichotomy of transparency and secrecy in the intelligence age.

I had been pondering then—and continue to ponder—the same issues. The amount of online information available to today's reporters, not to mention everyone else, is staggering. At the same time, secrecy among government officials flourishes.[20] Some days this seems like a paradox, others like a logical progression. I normally don't have the mental energy for elaborate conspiracy theories, but I will say if I were inclined to want to rule the world and needed to distract the populace, creating a sleight-of-hand glut-of-information age wouldn't be a bad way to go.

Conspiracy theories aside, for any writer engaged in research, the volume of available information and the modes of retrieving it can be both exciting and overwhelming. As a reporter in the late 1990s, I would file a request for a school budget and pore over the subsequent paper document with rabid (also geeky) excitement. Within a decade, I was scraping lobbyist information off the New Mexico's Secretary of State website and exporting it into a custom-made searchable online spreadsheet. Government budgets, legislation, public health data, crime reports, business licenses—the types of public information are not endless, but in this day and age of online information, they can often seem as though they are.

Seemingly limitless access to information sounds good on the front end but also raises a plethora of challenges for the writer or reporter in search of information. I think these challenges can be particularly intimidating to those for whom the Internet primarily represents a standard unholy trinity of Google searches/email/social media, but even professional muckrakers have been known to waste hours looking for something that is either not there or not easy to find.

The term muckraker sometimes sounds like a pejorative and, indeed, was not intended as a compliment when Theodore

---

20    In addition to local and state challenges for public records, the National Freedom for Information Coalition reports that 2015 had more federal legal challenges for public information than any year since at least 2001: http://www.nfoic.org/sunshine-week-2016.

Roosevelt evoked it in the early 1900s. In his speech, Roosevelt distinguished between those who exposed wrongdoing to better society versus those who practiced "indiscriminate assault." Needless to say, politicians' (one in particular . . . who seems to be the president of the United States) antagonism toward the media is certainly alive and well today. Fortunately, so is the accompanying crusade of journalists to use the power of the press to expose waste, graft, and lies in the public sector.

In between writing funny lists about cats, of course.

One of the main tools investigative journalists, political reporters, public service journalists, and indeed writers of all bents use to go after stories are state and federal laws that govern what information is public. The general belief is that the best way to have clean government is to ensure that the practices of government—its spending, its lawmaking, its procedures—are transparent. Or, to put it more concisely, "Sunlight is said to be the best of disinfectants," as Supreme Court Justice Louis Brandeis said in 1913.

Of course, the Internet has wreaked havoc not just on journalism, our attention span, and the overall civility of society, but also on the sunshine metaphor to a degree. While it is the nature of politics that someone will always be trying to hide something, we aren't exactly suffering right now from a dearth of information. As Eric Newton puts it in his digital book *Searchlights and Sunglasses: Field Notes from the Digital Age of Journalism,* "Shining a light works when information is scarce, and it still is, at times. But today news also can be abundant. When everything is already all lit up, a searchlight is just another thing you can't see."

Even if you're not interested in investigative journalism as either a citizen journalist or professional writer, the tools used to ferret out information are useful for research on myriad topics. Facts—whether in the form of numbers, historical documents, or research—play a vital role in nonfiction writing. Understanding where to find information can enhance your own writing projects—or come in handy should you find yourself yearning to rake a little muck yourself.

#### ···· *The Basics*

Local and state governments all have some form of public records and open meeting laws. These laws make it theoretically possible for anyone—journalists and citizens—to request information and govern the amount of time public officials have to provide that information. Open meeting laws ensure that when public officials make decisions that impact the public, they do so publicly. There are comparable federal laws in the United States, the keystone of which is the 1967 Freedom of Information Act, or FOIA.

I say theoretically because, unfortunately, there are numerous and ongoing instances of public officials thwarting these laws, and no shortage of stories in which newspapers and private citizens have had to battle head-to-head with government officials to extract information that was never meant to be secret in the first place. In "Fifty Years of FOIA," writer John Dyer looks at the investigative journalism that has been made possible by FOIA as well as the inconsistencies and shifting legal and cultural landscape in which the law operates. An April 2016 report, "In Defense of the First Amendment," found that 65 percent "of the editors who responded reported that the news industry is weaker in its ability to pursue legal activity around First Amendment–related issues than it was 10 years ago." On the bright side, in May 2016, The John S. and James L. Knight Foundation and Columbia University announced a $60 million initiative to build the Knight First Amendment Institute at Columbia University "to preserve and expand First Amendment rights in the digital age through research and education, and by supporting litigation in favor of protecting freedom of expression and the press."[21]

These battles to preserve access to information wage on at the national and local levels. In New Mexico, my former employer, the *Santa Fe Reporter*, initiated litigation against New Mexico Governor Susana Martinez in 2013—litigation that continues today. The basis for the original lawsuit is the *Reporter*'s contention that Martinez's office is violating both the Inspection of Public Records Act by denying access to public records and the "freedom of the press" provision of the state constitution "by unlawfully discriminating and retaliating" against the paper, according to a September 2013 *Reporter* article initially announcing the lawsuit.[22] These lawsuits are, obviously, time intensive and expensive—not just for the journalists and advocacy groups who sue for records, but for taxpayers, who foot the bill for the government to defend itself. In other words, when public officials violate laws that require them to make public records public, the public then pays for the government to defend themselves.

Those costs have themselves made news. In April 2016, the *NM Political Report* carried an update on open records litigation against the office of New Mexico's Secretary of State by the ACLU that reported lawyers' fees in the case expected to top $90,000.

Nonetheless, fighting for these records in the courts is all too commonplace—and necessary. "Journalists all over in the state are facing the same challenges," *Santa Fe Reporter* Editor Julie Ann Grimm said when I spoke with her about the *Reporter*'s ongoing suit against the governor's office. "Even though we're

---

21    Knight Foundation, "Knight Foundation, Columbia University launch First Amendment Institute, $60 million project to promote free expression in the digital age, press release," May 17, 2016, http://www.knightfoundation.org/press-room/press-release/knight-foundation-columbia-university-launch-first/.

22    Horwath, Justin and Joey Peters, "You've Been Served: *SFR* court case alleges governor violated IPRA, state constitution," *Santa Fe Reporter*, Sept. 3, 2013, http://www.sfreporter.com/santafe/article-7677-you%E2%80%99ve-been-served.html.

in a competitive environment and I want my newspaper to get
the story, I want all the other journalists and all of the public
to have access to the information that the law says we should
have access to." Because ultimately, she says, "It's important for
our society and important for free speech and public discourse.
And regular average citizens don't always have the time and
the resources to deal with it."

#### •••• *The Public Good*

Freelance journalist Peter St. Cyr, who was honored in 2015
by the New Mexico Foundation for Open Government with
its prestigious Dixon First Amendment Award for his work
using public records (and became director of the New Mexico
Foundation for Open Government at the beginning of 2017).
He also has mounted several lawsuits against the government,
seeking out information such as the names of people granted
pardons by former Governor Bill Richardson, the Albuquerque
Police Department's weapons' inventory, and the state's medical
marijuana licenses. St. Cyr took a roundabout path to becoming an investigative reporter. He worked as a sports stringer for
the *Albuquerque Journal* in high school, ended up in PR after
college, and then began working for Albuquerque radio (I first
met St. Cyr during those early radio years, as he reached out
to me for a weekly radio call-in on Santa Fe news). From there,
St. Cyr had several stints in television, working as an assign-
ments editor and even winning an Emmy for his work, but, as he
says, "I hated every second of television. There were times I sat
down on the bench and was told I couldn't work on a story and
decided I didn't become a journalist to sit on a bench and watch
others do stories that I had first or watch history go by."

St. Cyr's transition to investigative journalism began in
large part with a story he wrote for the *Santa Fe Reporter* on

abusive tactics inflicted on state prisoners. The story, "Nuts to Butts," relied on St. Cyr's review of hundreds of legal and other public documents to tell the story of inmates at the state's Los Lunas correctional facility who had been forced "to sit single file on the floor, legs splayed, each inmate straddling the man in front of him."

The story of how St. Cyr reported this piece illustrates the tenacity often needed when following a paper trail (digital or otherwise). The story began when St. Cyr heard about the situation from a source he had made when working for the television station. St. Cyr learned that the inhumane tactics at the prison had led to a lawsuit, and "I just thought it was huge because I was told there were videos and pictures. My first reaction was if that really happened and there's video and pictures, this is bigger than Abu Ghraib because it shouldn't be happening in the US for sure [given] our constitutional rights." As "any reporter or journalist who has tried to cover prison stories" knows, corrections are a difficult area to cover "because it's really hard to scrutinize what's going on behind locked gates."

St. Cyr "knew I was going to have to rely on documents and interviews," but initially the interviews fell apart. The Department of Corrections said, "We're not going to try this case in the press." St. Cyr didn't have access to the inmates, and the inmates' lawyer also, at that point, was unwilling to talk. Some reporters would have given up, but St. Cyr says, "I was very curious because I'm concerned; we send inmates away but they don't give up their core American constitutional rights." He knew the first thing he wanted to find were pictures and videos from the incident, so he filed an Inspection of Public Records Act request with the Corrections Department and was told "they had no pictures and they had no video." This response "didn't jibe" with what St. Cyr had been told, so he took another route. He had learned during his time at the television station that court reporters also are present during depositions in litigation. He used the legal search website *Pacer* to search through federal documents and lucked out when he discovered that the court reporter who had taken depositions on the corrections lawsuit was someone he knew. That court reporter told St. Cyr that not only were the depositions public record, but he sent St. Cyr the documents and the program to read them, export them, and search them by keywords.

St. Cyr had the documents, all four hundred or so pages of them. "I made the decision that I really wanted to be able to absorb them all," so after helping a friend relocate to Boston, St. Cyr, rather than fly home, "took the slow train from Boston to Albuquerque and I read the depositions on the train trip." As a result, he learned "all sorts of things," such as the existence of a special incident report from the night of the "nuts to butts" incident. From there, he spoke with the public information officer for the Corrections Department and requested the special incident report, which St. Cyr says mentioned photos and videos. St. Cyr's requests did not yield results, so he then turned to the Internet.

Using techniques he had learned at an Investigative Reporters and Editors boot camp on computer-assisted reporting, St. Cyr employed Google's Advanced Search functions to find "blind links" that led him to the department's confidential plans for emergency response situations. As a result of being able to review those plans, St. Cyr was able to file new public records requests that targeted specific forms used in such situations. The videos and photos never materialized—they hadn't been preserved—but eventually the mother lode of information St. Cyr gathered through both paper and online records yielded critical details he was able to use in the story. Within six months of his story publishing, the Corrections Department settled the lawsuit with the inmates.

## ····*Beyond the Paper Trail*

When I was first starting out as a reporter, pre-Internet, the current abundance of online information would have seemed like heaven (assuming your idea of heaven involves massive amounts of documents). As I've said, I didn't go to journalism school, but I worked at the *Rio Grande Sun* early in my career, which arguably is the equivalent of journalism school, as the late Bob Trapp trained all his reporters to follow the money, use public documents, and watchdog public institutions. For me, this included stories on topics ranging from Rio Arriba County's expenditures for filling inmate prescriptions to indictments over election-fraud litigation.

I reported in the late 1990s a story for the *Reporter* about land-use in Santa Fe County and a particular public official's questionable relationship with family members' land divisions. The story eventually received a first-place investigative reporting award from the state press association (although it had no perceptible impact on the public official's career). The story involved, for me, many hours at the county clerk's office looking at land records—plats, deeds, etc.—on microfiche. Not long ago, a student came to me because the word "microfiche" had come up in conversation and, though he had looked it up on the Internet, he still didn't have any idea what it was. As I tried to explain the idea of microfiche (I'm not sure anything can make a person feel more old than trying to explain microfiche to someone who has had email since he was a child), I thought about how exciting it seemed at the time to search, in a tactile way, for documented proof of the story in which I was engaged. At the *Sun*, people used to leak me public officials' phone records. I could not have imagined at the time that in less than a decade, sorting through massive amounts of online information would be de rigueur.

These giant stores of data have bolstered a great deal of data-driven storytelling, both online and in print. In the mid

2000s while I was editor of the *Reporter*, we began experimenting with using not just the available data but also the new and often free open-source tools available to find new ways of presenting information that broke with traditional narrative storytelling, and perhaps better positioned the information for accessibility and interactive use by our readers. Our efforts were rewarded with several national awards (no small feat given the tiny size of *SFR*'s staff and budget). The rewards were also the less tangible sense of a growing understanding of the ways in which information, when made accessible and useable, could serve the public good.

An early effort to bolster and educate the public about public information and transparency was spearheaded by Dave Maass, then a reporter at the *Santa Fe Reporter*. Maass wrote a January 2008 cover story for the *Reporter* titled "The Citizen Muckraker's Guide to New Mexico," which was then followed with an online repository of information organized by category, allowing users to research anything from legislative action to campaign finance to criminal records.

Maass currently is an investigative researcher for the Electronic Frontier Foundation, a nonprofit organization that describes itself as "defending civil liberties in the digital world"; he describes the job as one of both muckraking and noise-making. The organization's projects are myriad and diverse, running the gamut from examining how police use mobile devices to scan biometric details to a variety of surveillance and privacy projects. Maass uses public records extensively in his position at EFF, as well as in his capacity as a freelance reporter. Public records, for example, played heavily into the joint-award-winning reporting projects Maass worked on at *San Diego CityBeat* related to jail deaths and juvenile justice.

Maass views public records as a resource that may not necessarily answer questions but "raises questions." "It's like having a huge interview you've just transcribed or a book you've checked out from the library; it's somewhere between an academic book and a person; it's like a primary source and it has voice to it and characters to it and it has information."

Maass was inspired in 2008 to create the Muckrakers Guide by an impulse to foster the online tools available to everyone.

"There's a ton of information out there now, and this information isn't just sitting in folders in bureaucrats' offices; a lot of it is online . . . and there's so much out there but not necessarily a lot of reporters to dig through it. It requires a community to find this information and look through it. That's where you find accountability."

While professional journalists have long known to follow paper trails as part of the reporting process, public engagement has become enormous. At his role at EFF, Maass sees such "citizen journalism" as a robust part of the work he does. "I look through the window of surveillance issues and police accountability, and if you look at what we know, a lot of that information didn't come from reporters."

Beyond using public information to find stories or to answer questions, there is a way in which examining the records of the digital age provides the same important context as historical research.

"We don't exist anymore as people who just talk on the phone and send each other letters," Maass said. "The way that people communicate isn't just a meeting; it's over text messages, it's over email, it's over Skype, over all kinds of technology. Sometimes you get a better view of how things are transpiring in history by following the paper trail."

After I spoke with Maass, my thoughts turned to the 2015 film *Spotlight*, which won an Oscar for best picture and tells the story of the *Boston Globe* reporters who uncovered the decades-long cover-up of pedophiliac priests in the Catholic Church. The movie was praised by journalists for showing the shoe-leather behind investigative reporting: the interviews, the spreadsheets, the fight for public documents. But as Sacha Pfeiffer—one of the reporters depicted in the film (played by Rachel McAdams)—points out, the Internet also played a role because the story was published in the early days of the Internet, 2002, which gave it a national reach and brought other survivors and their stories to the Globe.[23] Hundreds of stories, the original documents, the database, and more are all available online through the *Boston Globe*'s website.

Every day, journalists from publications like the *Sun* to large metros like the *Boston Globe* to online reporters for *ProPublica* to citizen journalists working from home use various combinations and levels of doggedness and skill to dig for information to tell stories that can help people understand their communities better and, sometimes, help improve them. The two-year investigation on Native American youth suicide that Laura Paskus and Bryant Furlow conducted for the online investigative reporting magazine *New Mexico In Depth* began simply by an awareness of the data, and led to stories about the people behind those numbers.

I have always felt admiration and allegiance for investigative journalists, but am perhaps feeling it more so this year, as I'm writing during the 2016 election season and undergoing alternatively apoplectic and paralytic responses to the volume of unmitigated, unsubstantiated . . . stuff that is posing as journalism.

---

23    Mike Pesca, "Seeing Yourself in *Spotlight*," *The Gist* podcast, *Slate*, January 29, 2016.    http://www.slate.com/articles/podcasts/gist/2016/01/the_gist_spotlight_film_and_boston_globe_reporters_and_jeb_bush.html.

#### ····*Expanding Your Skill Set*

I'm not an Excel whiz. I'm not a hacker. I am certainly no math prodigy. But given enough motivation, I've hunkered down with spreadsheets, tinkered with code, and crunched numbers. I'm not here to proselytize to writers about the value of using the other side of one's brain (particularly because then I'd have to research which functions the left governs versus the right and fall down some rabbit hole in which I'd no doubt learn that the entire construct is an urban legend). I will say that I have experienced, and have watched many creative writers experience, the energizing thrill of what we might call "trying something new." Online resources for dipping a toe, a foot, one's entire corporeal being into document/data research are plentiful. See the resource list at the end of this chapter.

#### ····*Social Media*

Just as social media has become a medium for short-form storytelling, so is it a player in the muckraking/transparency arena. Consider, for example, the news at the end of 2015 that Sunlight Foundation, Open State Foundation, and Access Now had come to an agreement with Twitter to re-launch Politwoops, a project the Sunlight Foundation had run for several years using Twitter's API to publish deleted tweets by politicians. Regarding the agreement, Twitter's CEO Jack Dorsey publicly said that Twitter holds "a responsibility to continue to empower organizations that bring more transparency to public dialogue, such as Politwoops."

Politwoops, of course, is just one very small example of the ways in which social media is a key player in the citizen journalism world. Consider the *New York Times*' report on the National Security Agency's use of Facebook to track Americans' social connections[24] for a larger and more alarming example. From Occupy Wall Street to the Arab Spring to the sadly ongoing instances of police brutality and public shootings in the US, social media has become not just a place to vent or share, but also a key tool for writers and journalists to find sources, follow stories, and share information.

Rani Molla, the *Bloomberg Gadfly* columnist, both writes about and creates data visualizations to report and opine on a variety of hard-news topics—her areas of coverage for Bloomberg are corporations and markets. But she's also used data in past pieces to look at issues of culture. For example, in July 2015, Molla penned a story for *WSJ* about the most popular songs of the summer, as assessed through Twitter's own internal data. That's a data-driven story that was driven by a simple question Molla had about what had been the most popular song of the summer. Sometimes starting with a question leads to "the best data because it's not already out there," Molla said. "But they collect it and they're willing to give it to you as a journalist, because it shows they are a good data source, and then you have a data source that no one else has." Using data for cultural stories, Molla noted, "is a great way to report on culture because it's a way of quantifying the unquantifiable."

#### ····*Getting Personal*

Journalists think of public records as one of many checks in the watchdogging of public officials, but public records also play a role in most people's lives. Years ago, I was asked to speak on a panel addressing a roomful of lawyers (there's a joke somewhere in this setup) to pontificate on how lawyers could work better

---

24    James Risen, and Laura Poitras, "NSA Gathers Data on Social Connections of US Citizens," *New York Times*, September 28, 2013, http://www.nytimes.com/2013/09/29/us/nsa-examines-social-networks-of-us-citizens.html.

with the media. I said they might want to warn their clients about the public nature of litigation. Over the years, I've dealt with numerous people whose names appeared in lawsuits and arrest records, who were caught seemingly unaware that their allegations and foibles had become part of the public record.

For writers, this is something worth knowing as well, particularly in the nonfiction arena. A notable example of a lapse of judgment in this realm is the case of James Frey, author of the 2003 memoir *A Million Little Pieces,* who was publicly and loudly exposed as having fabricated and/or exaggerated numerous elements of his life story. As the *Smoking Gun* wrote in its report, "A Million Little Lies," "Police reports, court records, interviews with law enforcement personnel, and other sources have put the lie to many key sections of Frey's book." (You can read more on the ethical implications of all this in chapter 8.)

An obvious takeaway from the Frey fiasco might be "don't lie in a memoir." The late David Carr, a reporter and media columnist for the *New York Times,* took accountability a step further in his 2008 memoir, *The Night of the Gun.* Employing the tools of his trade as a reporter, Carr utilized public records, interviews, and other documents to tell his life story of addict to journalist. Carr, who died in 2015, made these materials available online in an interactive, multimedia timeline. These include, for example, a police report on domestic abuse, the court custody agreement for his children, and medical records.

Like Carr, David Stuart MacLean employs a fair amount of self-reportage in his memoir *The Answer to the Riddle Is Me,* as he searches to rediscover his own identity after his Lariam-induced memory loss. But the book also delves into reportage on the drug itself.

MacLean utilizes research not as the main spoke of his story but, as he describes it, as a "handrail" throughout the narrative that allows the reader to experience an organic understanding of Lariam's impact on MacLean.

"I feel like when people write research they let the research overtake the book or the essay," MacLean says, noting that at one point he had an editor who wanted MacLean's research on Lariam concentrated in one place in the book rather than dispersed throughout. MacLean notes that he understands the reasoning behind this type of organizational choice in which writers "hand over the reins to the research," but "that's not interesting to me. The interesting thing to me is my relationship of myself to the search, and the writerly narrator self to the research, and how the narrator self accumulates and is expected to understand what's now going on." As for the research itself, MacLean described his process as one that was ongoing while he was writing, noting that he would send the more scientific papers to friends who helped him understand the science in lay terms.

## ····*Beyond Data*

For much of my reporting life, I thought of information as a specific commodity needed for a specific purpose; if I could find records, documents, and budgets that showed X, that information would allow me or another reporter to prove Y (that's supposed to be an algebra reference, by the way).

But some creative nonfiction relies on facts less as proof and more for ballast, depth, and metaphor. In MacLean's case, for example, certainly the research on Lariam helps ground the reader in the reality of this drug's harmful history. But more importantly, it connects the reader to MacLean's own personal reckonings, not all of which are solved by understanding the medical reason for his trauma. In other words, Lariam is the "why," the handrail that helps explain what has happened to MacLean. But for the nonfiction writer, "why" is not the only question.

Leslie Jamison, author of *The Empathy Exams*, discussed her view of the relationship between the personal and the reported in a talk she gave at the annual The Power of Storytelling conference in Europe, noting:

"This is one of the central imperatives of combining personal material with history or criticism or reportage: each thread must do some work that isn't being done by another, that can't be done by another."

In other words, information, research, and facts frequently fuel more lyric investigations, such as Eula Biss's *On Immunity*, which explores the issue of vaccination, or Maggie Nelson's *Jane: A Murder*, a poetic, collaged, and reported inquiry into the murder of her aunt.

Matt Donovan's collection *A Cloud of Unusual Size and Shape*, includes many essays lyrical in both form and use of language, but they also are heavily researched. The essay subjects are far ranging, from explorations of the devastation of the United States.' nuclear age to the destruction wrought by Vesuvius. Donovan describes his own research strategy as one of "amassment" and says, "Part of that tendency comes from simply feeling passionate about the topics I'm researching, and wanting to personally find out as much as possible about the material. But I also never know where I'm going to find details or small anecdotes or quotations or any corner of some esoteric element that's going to somehow afford thematic resonance within the essay." Donovan says new material he finds while researching always ends up shaping his work. "I've also learned that what triggers the imagination, or ultimately serves as a central metaphor, can't ever be predicted. I read several books about the Trinity Site and Oppenheimer, for instance, before happening to stumble upon a single obscure footnote about a radio broadcast during the bomb's detonation that became one of the lynchpins for my meditations."

# ONLINE RESOURCES

In 2010, I delivered a presentation on Computer Assisted Reporting at an Association of Alternative Newsweeklies writers' conference in Las Vegas, Nevada. Within a frighteningly short period of time, most of the resources I shared, which I was actively using at the time, were either defunct or no longer free. Thanks, Silicon Valley. Let this serve as a caveat that I can't guarantee this small collection of resources for finding information will be available in perpetuity, and they are indeed only a small sampling of what is available. They are, however, keystones in my use of the Internet for information gathering, and I hope they will be useful to those who don't already use them.

**Data.gov**
Data.gov houses the US government's data sets—close to two hundred thousand of them. Users can search information by topics, ranging from agriculture to business to oceans to public safety. For example, let's say you're interested in climate change (and, certainly, we should all have at least a passing interest in this topic). Under the topic climate change, a user can dig down into underlying topics such as coastal flooding, food resilience, and energy infrastructure. Under food resilience, one might then explore a food access research atlas, and look at a variety of maps and data sets related to places where people are vulnerable to food shortages. And then, before you know it, eight hours have passed and you are still looking at data! The site allows users to search the databases, while providing a seemingly endless list of apps that have been developed using this public information. Needless to say, if you're a developer, or looking to create an app, this site is a rich depository of information available to all.

**Electronic Frontier Foundation, www.eff.org**
Remember that whole Apple versus the Justice Department battle in which it was entirely unclear who even won, but abundantly clear that legal/ethical battles over privacy vs. security in the digital age are bound to continue, and the legal framework around these issues is very much a work in progress? Enter EFF, whose work "defending civil liberties in the digital world" includes litigation, policy papers, and a variety of projects all aimed at promoting both transparency by government and privacy rights for individuals. For example, it hosts extensive resources for understanding and following the NSA spying program. At the same time, it has a copyright education program geared at students (or anyone) seeking clear understanding of how copyright works, and its own Transparency Project—complete with FOIA-driven info—aimed at using FOIA to increase government oversight.

*Extra, Extra,* **http://ire.org/blog/extra-extra**
This blog from Investigative Reporters and Editors shares stories and other investigative projects that make use of public information, data, and computer-assisted reporting. It's a good place to see inspiring examples of investigative journalism and/or get ideas for your own investigative projects.

**Foia.gov**
Foia.gov is a Department of Justice website that provides background, user information, and data about the Freedom of Information Act. It's certainly a good first stop for learning about the law. You can use the site's simple interactive database to look up various government agencies and assess their status with receipt and processing of FOIA reports (yes, I realize this function probably has limited appeal, but I thought it was interesting). Perhaps more helpfully, the site offers—albeit

limitedly—assistance in determining where to file FOIA requests for various agencies.

**GitHub, https://github.com**

GitHub is an online repository and active collaborative space for coding projects of various types and degrees of difficulty. It's basically a social website for coding. As Emily Ferber points out in her article "Getting GitHub: Why Journalists Should Know and Use the Social Coding Site," GitHub also can be a place for a reporter (or writer or anyone) to learn more about coding and find options for making his or her own online projects.

**MuckRock, https://www.muckrock.com**

Self-described as "a collaborative news site that brings together journalists, researchers, activists, and regular citizens to request, analyze, and share government documents, making politics more transparent and democracies more informed," MuckRock has vast amounts of public information available, as well as instructional material for anyone wanting to initiate public records requests. The site has a reasonable tiered paid system that will file public requests for users. Muckrock works directly with citizens, news organizations, and others seeking public information, as the process of doing so has grown increasingly challenging both logistically (so much information!) and legally (so much stonewalling!)

**National Freedom of Information Coalition, www.nfoic.org**

NFOIC is a national nonprofit that includes state and regional partners ranging from journalists to lawyers to citizen groups. It provides a variety of resources, including news, education, funding, and an annual Freedom of Information summit.

**The National Institute for Computer-Assisted Reporting, https://www.ire.org/nicar**

Although not free, NICAR's datasets and other information are a program through the national Investigative Reporters and Editors association. Membership to IRE, particularly if you're interested specifically in developing as an investigative journalist, is money well spent. In addition to the NICAR data sets, IRE provides a variety of reporting tools and general tip sheets. As far as public information goes, its FOIA page is accessible to non-members, and is a great starting place for learning more about public information.

### New Mexico Foundation for Open Government, http://nmfog.org

If you happen to be in New Mexico, this organization is invaluable in both understanding and using New Mexico's public records and open meetings law, and has a helpful online training for understanding both. The organization supports New Mexico journalists in holding government accountable to these laws. The site also has a compendium of national resources for accessing and using public information. If you're not in New Mexico, never fear: your state has comparable resources. The National Freedom of Information Coalition, in addition to providing a variety of tools and information about protecting transparency on the national level, has a round-up of resources for each state: (nfoic.org/state-foi-resources).

### Open Data Handbook, http://opendatahandbook.org

The Open Data Handbook is a resource from Open Knowledge (https://okfn.org), a nonprofit network that focuses on transparency and the use of data across networks to promote open society. Data can sometimes seem like kryptonite to creative writers, but as a former data-coward, I can attest that even someone with a lifelong fear of math can become comfortable and even excited about learning to use data. Open Knowledge's Open Data Handbook is a helpful primer to get started.

**ProPublica, www.propublica.org**
Despite skepticism about the merging of nonprofits and journalism, the nonprofit ProPublica is alive and well nearly a
decade after its inception, and has won a variety of awards for
its investigative and muckraking journalism, including multiple Pulitzers. ProPublica openly describes itself as doing work
that focuses "exclusively on truly important stories, stories with
'moral force.' We do this by producing journalism that shines a
light on exploitation of the weak by the strong and on the fail-
ures of those with power to vindicate the trust placed in them."
In addition to reading ProPublica's own investigations, the
site makes available data, tip sheets, and guides to a variety of
topics, as well as its stories for reprint at no charge. Users can
access datasets requested by ProPublica for free, or purchase
"premium" data sets (data sets that have already been cleaned
up by ProPublica).

**Reporters Committee for Freedom of the Press,**
**http://www.rcfp.org**
This nonprofit provides excellent background on public information laws, as well as specific guides on areas of media law. It
regularly posts news stories on issues related to press freedoms
and staffs a hotline for reporters.

**The Sunlight Foundation, sunlightfoundation.com**
In its own words, The Sunlight Foundation is a nonprofit "that
uses the tools of civic tech, open data, policy analysis and journalism to make our government and politics more accountable
and transparent to all." The site includes a variety of useful
tools, such as "Hall of Justice," which has nearly ten thousand
datasets related to criminal justice for individual states and
nationally. I'm also fond of its PoliticalSleuth.com project,
which invites the public to help determine who is paying for
various political ads around the country. These are just two of

the organization's projects. The Sunlight Foundation provides a wealth of background information on public information-related policy, as well as APIs for the more advanced data wranglers out there.

**SearchReSearch**, http://searchresearch1.blogspot.com
This site from Google research scientist Dan Russell is a great spot to find tips for using the Internet in a focused and investigative way. Russell, who has presented on smart searching at past Investigative Reporters and Editors conferences, goes beyond standard Google search tips with advanced lessons for using Google, along with quizzes to test your ability to dig deep.

**Searchlights and Sunglasses**,
**http://searchlightsandsunglasses.org**
*Searchlights and Sunglasses* is a digital book by Eric Newton, produced by the John S. and James L. Knight Foundation and the Reynolds Journalism Institute. Interactive and beautifully designed, the book is a wonderful and provocative primer that examines the ways in which the digital landscape has shifted the priorities and challenges for reporters, while reaffirming the basic tenets of gathering information and storytelling. Check it out!

**"The Art and Science of Data-Driven**
**Journalism,"** http://towcenter.org/research/
**the-art-and-science-of-data-driven-journalism**
This report from The Tow Center for Digital Journalism takes an extensive look at the historical and current practice of data in journalism, with discussions of its ethical ramifications and practical applications.

# PROMPTS AND PRACTICE

1. **Poke around.** Pick a nonprofit you support (or are curious about). Take a look at the organization's tax returns and see how it's doing by searching ProPublica's Nonprofit Explorer. https:// projects.propublica.org/nonprofits.

2. **Watchdog.** Suss how your state senators and congressional representatives are voting (or if they are). Use https://www .govtrack.us to check up on your elected officials (or find them if you're not sure who they are).

3. **Date yourself.** Were any great songs released on your birth-day? Find out, and dig up other interesting historical music facts at http://calendar.songfacts.com.

4. **Pro search.** Using Google Advanced Search, look up all the articles on "Prince" which include the words "Tidal" and "Spotify" that appear on the site: nytimes.com. (Now use Google Advanced Search to find something you're actually interested in researching.)

5. **Request records.** File a public records request with a city or state agency (or a federal one). If you don't have a particular burning request need, file a request for your mayor's calendar and see what he or she is up to day to day.

6. **Code 101.** Sign up for GitHub (it has free options) and complete the "create a repository" tutorial. https://github.com.

7. **Up your skills.** UC Berkeley's Advanced Media Institute offers a variety of online tutorials that range from multimedia to data to social media tools. Try one. https://multimedia .journalism.berkeley.edu/tutorials.

8. **MuckRock it.** Browse through Muckrock.com's projects. Pick one. Participate.

9. **Time in.** Make a timeline, either telling a personal story or a story based on reporting or research using Knight Lab's Timeline JS. No coding required, and the site has plenty of detailed tutorials. http://timeline.knightlab.com.

## Julia's Fundamental Needs While Writing

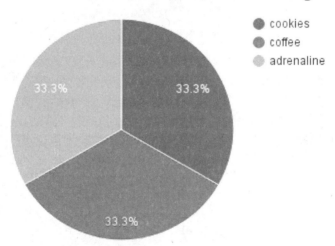

● cookies
● coffee
● adrenaline

33.3%  33.3%  33.3%

10. **Charticle.** Use Google to practice making charts. You can use real data or what professionals call "silly data." You can access Google charts simply through Google Drive. Create a new spreadsheet, keep it simple, and then use the "insert" function to translate your spreadsheet into visual form. For more info on using Google Sheets or any of Google's doc forms, just use Google Help (or google your question). If you're anti-Google, you can make a variety of charts (and other visual forms) using https://infogr.am.

# READING AND RESOURCES
# FROM THIS CHAPTER

Biss, Eula. *On Immunity: an Inoculation*. Minnesota: Graywolf, 2015.

Boston Globe. Spotlight coverage. http://www.bostonglobe. com/arts/movies/spotlight-movie#spotlight.

Crowell, Colin. "Holding Public Officials Accountable with Twitter and Politwoops." Twitter, December 31, 2015. https://blog.twitter.com/2015/holding-public-officials-accountable-with-twitter-and-politwoops.

Davis, Kelly, and Dave Maass. "60 Dead Inmates." *San Diego CityBeat*, October 29, 2014 http://sdcitybeat.com/flex-261-60-dead-inmates.html.

Dyer, John. "Fifty Years of FOIA." *Nieman Reports*, January 12, 2016. http://niemanreports.org/articles/fifty-years-of-foia.

Ferber, Emily. "Getting GitHub: Why Journalists Should Know and Use the Social Coding Site." *Knight Lab*, June 13, 2013. http://knightlab.northwestern.edu/2013/06/13/getting-github-why-journalists-should-know-and-use-the-social-coding-site/.

Goldberg, Julia. "$55,000 Spent for Inmates' Drugs." *Rio Grande Sun*, July 4, 1996.

Goldberg, Julia. "Subdivided Loyalties." *Santa Fe Reporter*, April 1, 1998.

Jamison, Leslie. "The Possibilities of the Personal." *Nieman Storyboard*, October 21, 2015. http://niemanstoryboard. org/stories/leslie-jamison-the-possibilities-of-the-personal.

Knight Foundation. "In Defense of the First Amendment," *Knight Foundation*, April 2, 2016. http://www.knightfoundation.org/media/uploads/ publication_pdfs/KF-editors-survey-final_1.pdf.

MacLean, David Stuart. "Crazy Pills." *New York Times*, August 7, 2013. http://www.nytimes.com/2013/08/08/opinion/cra- zy-pills.htm.

Molla, Rani. "Songs of the Summer, According to Twitter." *Wall Street Journal*, July 9, 2015. http://blogs.wsj.com/speakeasy/2015/07/09/ songs-of-the-summer-according-to-twitter.

Nelson, Maggie. *Jane: A Murder*. Berkeley: Soft Skull ShortLit, 2006.

Reichbach, Matthew. "After Appeal, SoS' Office Has to Pay Big in Open Records Case." *NM Political Report*, April 21, 2016. http://nmpoliticalreport.com/40922/ after-appeal-sos-office-has-to-pay-big-in-open-records-case.

Roosevelt, Theodore. "The Man with the Muck Rake." PBS, April 15, 1906. http://www.pbs.org/wgbh/ americanexperience/features/primary-resources/ tr-muckrake.

St. Cyr, Peter. "Nuts to Butts: Controversial Prisoner Shakedowns Could Leave Taxpayers on the Hook for Damages." *Santa Fe Reporter*, April 2, 2013. http://www. sfreporter.com/santafe/article-7339-nuts-to-butts.html.

Weinberg, Arthur and Lila Weinberg. *The Muckrakers*. Chicago: University of Illinois Press, 2001.

# CHAPTER EIGHT

# *Ethical Frameworks*

The only judgment any of us really ought to make about one another's work is whether or not it's good, whether or not it affects us, whether or not we are transported by it emotionally, intellectually, or perhaps even just technically.

—**John D'Agata**[25]

In a novel, a house or person has his meaning, his existence, entirely through the writer. Here, a house or a person has only the most limited of his meaning through me: his true meaning is much huger. It is that he exists, in actual being, as you do and as I do, and as no character of the imagination can possibly exist. His great weight, mystery, and dignity are in this fact. As for me, I can tell you of him only what I saw, only so accurately as in my terms I know how: and this in turn has its chief stature not in any ability of mine but in the fact that I too exist, not as a work of fiction but as a human being.

—**James Agee,** *Let Us Now Praise Famous Men: A Death in the Family, Shorter Fiction*

---

25   Weston Cutter, "Doubling Down: An Interview with John D'Agata," *Kenyon Review*, February 23, 2012, www.kenyonreview.org/2012/02/doubling-down-an-interview-with-john-dagata-and-jim-fingal.

EVERY NONFICTION WRITER who is not James Frey or Stephen Glass or Jayson Blair knows that what he or she is doing by writing nonfiction is declaring, at varying levels: This is a story about people and events that actually happened.

Right? Maybe not.

In theory, with this multi-clause axiom that starts this chapter, the ethics of writing nonfiction should be as simple as: Don't make shit up. I personally think this is a decent rule of thumb.

Nonfiction writing, however, can be trickier than kindergarten rules (isn't that where we first learned it's wrong to make shit up?)—its customs variable from subgenre to subgenre, writer to writer. Many esteemed memoirists allow for a little leeway in their stories in the name of art and distinguish "truth" from "true"; some distinguish too much (see Frey). Even trustworthy journalists, who presumably understand the need to firmly avoid any sort of fabrication, engage in small acts of treachery such as cleaning up quotes—and sometimes larger acts such as feigning sympathy. In other words, if you're looking for a literary categorical imperative in this genre, you're out of luck. If you're looking for fodder for interesting discussions and thought, read on.

## WITHIN GENRES

•••• *Memoir*

In his memoir *Night of the Gun*, David Carr writes, "Memoir is a very personal form of creation myth." As discussed in chapter 7, Carr, a former drug addict turned media writer for the *New York Times*, took the tack with his memoir of rereporting his own life through a combination of interviews and public records.

Five years earlier, in 2003, James Frey had published *A Million Little Pieces*, also the story of his years as an addict, which later became an international best seller when Oprah Winfrey championed it. That was Frey's high point. The low point began in 2006 when the website *The Smoking Gun* revealed a six-week investigation of Frey's story that showed much of what Frey had written was either fabricated or exaggerated. This report led eventually to an awkward televised confrontation (more awkward than most daytime television, that is) in which Oprah schooled Frey on the meaning of truth. Oprah felt betrayed by Frey's lack of adherence to truth in his true story. Fair enough. [26]

The first time I showed my students the video of Oprah's face-off with Frey ("I have to say it is difficult for me to talk to you because I really feel duped," she told him), some laughed and others were baffled by Oprah's outrage. Why did it matter so much, some wondered, if Frey exaggerated or lied? Wasn't it his story to tell as he saw fit? Would people be so angry if a fiction ultimately turned out to be true? And so on. Those are some of the questions many writers have pondered and responded to in the realm of memoir and truth.

Memoir, after all, is distinct from other types of nonfiction writing, such as autobiography and biography. The latter two are generally characterized by an adherence to an external chronology based on reportable facts. Memoir, on the other hand, is generally focused less on an entire life story and more on a facet of a life story. In working terms, this ends up looking like:

**Autobiography:** This is the story of my life as it happened.

**Memoir:** This is a story from my life as I remember it.

This is not to say that works in the biography tract won't make use of literary devices. But memoir, whose name is obviously

---

26 (Oprah reportedly apologized to Frey a few years later for her on-air smackdown, for what that's worth).

rooted in the same Latin word that brought us "memory," implies an intrinsic reliance on internal recollections and impressions, rather than documented and reported information. In other words, memoir may be rooted in emotional truths rather than, say, actual ones.

These distinctions are, obviously, a little fuzzy and hardly universally accepted. Frey's publisher, after all, offered refunds to those who'd read *A Million Little Pieces* and felt "frauded" by the revelation that the book wasn't, in fact, all true. And even writers who defend their rights to rely on memory and impressions tend not to defend Frey's transgressions.

I imagine it's because of my journalism background, but I can't imagine actively fabricating material and calling it non-fiction. I can imagine inadvertently screwing up any number of things, but asserting, as Frey did, that I'd spent weeks in jail when I'd only spent a few hours or that my girlfriend had died in one way when she actually died in another feels not just aggressively dishonest but also actively self-destructive. These are the types of things that can be fact-checked, after all.[27]

**Ethical takeaway**: Don't lie about things that can be fact-checked.

I'm kidding. Kind of. Certainly fabricating facts that are part of a public record or easily disputed seems to be both provocative and self-destructive, although perhaps a self-destructive act emerging from a book about a self-destructive person isn't all that shocking after all.

Frey aside, smaller acts of finesse, art, and reworking of "fact," happen frequently in nonfiction with far less fanfare.

Dialogue in fiction is, presumably, invented. Dialogue in nonfiction is generally recorded—electronically or through notes—transcribed and edited. So what to make of all the dialogue in memoirs that sometimes recount events from decades

---

27   For the record, I've never spent any time in jail.

past, from childhood? Do Natural Born Writers all come with the capacity for perfect recall of all conversations?

Not so much. Writer Daniel Nester takes up this question in his essay "Notes on Frey," writing that when younger he had also imagined that writers had some level of photographic memory. "Since then, I have become well aware that the arbiters of creative nonfiction, essay, autobiography, memoir, and lyrical whatchamacallits have all convened somewhere and given 'quoted dialogue' a free pass on the authenticity highway."

Certainly not all memoirists create dialogue based on likely conversations. Others do and include disclaimers to that end. To the non-memoirist (and the journalist), these distinctions may seem conflated. Aren't facts facts? Perhaps, but as André Aciman writes in his 2013 *New York Times* essay "How Memoirists Mold the Truth," "Writing the past is never a neutral act." The decision to write a memoir is a decision to focus on a particular story for a particular reason. And in so doing, Aciman says, "What we want is a narrative, not a log; a tale not a trial."

Many memoir writers speak of emotional truth as the guiding force in writing one's personal stories, and some, such as Dani Shapiro, have (rightly, I think) drawn the line between telling a story and telling all. In her 2014 *Salon* piece "Dear Disillusioned Reader Who Contacted Me on Facebook," Shapiro sharply distinguishes writing a memoir that does not include every aspect of her life from fabricating events, noting, "When a writer sits down to write memoir, she is not sharing her diary. She is not confessing. She is not doing some sort of public striptease."

And then there's John D'Agata.

D'Agata, who has edited several of everyone's favorite creative nonfiction anthologies,[28] also is the coauthor of a notable book that takes up the issue of veracity in creative nonfiction, *Lifespan of a Fact*. The book is the purported saga of a multi-year

---

28    Rightfully so. Among them, *The Next American Essay*, Graywolf Press, 2003, is a particular favorite of mine.

fact-checking war for a piece he wrote for the *Believer* ("What Happens There") after it was rejected by *Harper's* magazine due to its factual shortcomings. I say purported, as the actual manuscript is itself a constructed piece, not a verbatim transcript of the fact-checking experience between D'Agata and fact-checker Jim Fingal. The antagonism was crafted; D'Agata and Fingal finessed from people into characters.

"My hope, which has not been fulfilled, is that readers would satirically recognize that hysteria which we always fall into when this issue comes up," D'Agata said in a 2012 interview with *Interview* magazine.

In the same interview, D'Agata elaborates on his belief that it makes little sense to pigeonhole "nonfiction" as the genre whose primary "goal" is to deliver facts "as opposed to the other sorts of experiences that we get from the other genres in literature, or really from any other medium in art."

D'Agata also found the "Frey incident illustrated yet again the hysteria that people bring to this issue," and his own experiences with *Lifespan of a Fact* reiterated to him "that we are really nowhere when it comes to reading this genre."

D'Agata also is not a fan of the term "nonfiction," preferring the word "essay," and continues to push back at the strictures he believes most readers bring to it. He writes in the preface to *The Next American Essay*, "Please do not consider these 'nonfictions.' I want you preoccupied with art in this book, not with facts for the sake of facts." To drive that message home, perhaps, the prologue for this essay collection is "And," by Guy Davenport, which originally appeared in Davenport's book *A Table of Green Fields*, a collection of short fiction.

D'Agata obviously does not consider himself a journalist or a reporter. Nonetheless, the original *Believer* article ("What Happens There") does have what might be considered a journalistic premise: sixteen-year-old Levi Presley's 2002 suicide; he jumped to his death from a Las Vegas hotel. Is it hysterical to presume that a story with a teenager's death at its heart would adhere to basic journalistic premises in reporting the facts of the situation? Is it impossible to also privilege language and ideas while getting names and dates correct? Many reviewers thought not.

In her review for the *New York Times Sunday Book Review*, Jennifer B. McDonald writes, "D'Agata's rejection of 'nonfiction' still fails to support his conviction that fact and art are mutually exclusive. Furthermore, his implication that something calling itself 'nonfiction' and trying to hew to fact cannot also rise to the level of literature is at the least confounding and at worst insulting to some of our finest writers."

I'm less worried about the world's finest writers' feelings, but do agree with McDonald that pitting facts against art creates a false dichotomy. In terms of an ethical framework, however, D'Agata (and others) are simply responding to the classic question: Do the ends justify the means? In this case, the end is Art. The means include playing loose with facts that, in the writer's eyes, are detrimental to the final work.

These are concerns not limited solely to the world of memoir, nor even to the world of literary nonfiction.

···· *Journalism*

". . . on the whole, journalism is the most underestimated, the least explored of literary mediums."
—George Plimpton quoting Truman Capote, "The Story Behind a Nonfiction Novel"

I end each semester in my introductory nonfiction class with Janet Malcolm's *The Journalist and the Murderer*. It's long been one of my favorite books about journalism, and tends to spark good discussions and interesting papers.

Initially published in 1989 as a two-part series in the *New Yorker*, *The Journalist and the Murderer* dissects the fall-out from Joe McGinniss's true-crime book, *Fatal Vision*, the story of Jeffrey MacDonald, convicted in 1979 of murdering his wife and two young daughters. McGinniss had essentially embedded with MacDonald and his legal team during the trial; his relationship with MacDonald—the journalist/subject relationship—is the focal point of Malcolm's story. She famously begins: "Every journalist who is not too stupid or too full of himself to notice what is going on knows that what he does is morally indefensible."[29]

She continues to characterize the journalist as "a kind of confidence man," who will do whatever necessary to gain the trust of a subject, only to turn around and write a story that may not (although Malcolm seems to imply will not) be particularly sympathetic.

At first glance, the book seems to be directed specifically at the question of how much candor journalists owe their sub-jects and the degree to which the general public understands the writing process. MacDonald felt duped by McGinniss—he thought the latter man believed in his innocence; he thought they were friends. MacDonald sued McGinniss for fraud and breach of contract. Even though MacDonald was a man con-victed of murdering his wife and children, the jurors were sym-pathetic enough (or confused enough) in the fraud case that they were unable to render a verdict.

Malcolm re-reports aspects of the trial, but a key one comes when writer Joseph Wambaugh, who also had been approached, initially, to write MacDonald's story, takes the stand. MacDonald's lawyer asks Wambaugh to disclose whether it is customary for a writer to lie to his or her subject in order to get the story. Wambaugh essentially says that he doesn't disclose his actual thoughts and feelings to subjects

---

29   Yes, I riffed off Malcolm's opening for the opening of this chapter.

as it can have a detrimental impact on the story itself. He tells a specific story that illustrates that point, noting that "my ultimate responsibility was not to that person, my responsibility was to the book."

There was no retrial, but McGinniss did eventually settle the case with MacDonald. McGinniss did not think much of Malcolm's book; actually, that's an understatement. McGinniss, who died in 2014, in fact wrote an epilogue to a reissued edition of *Fatal Vision* that addresses *The Journalist and the Murderer*. That epilogue remains on McGinniss's website and is preceded by a note from McGinniss that reads:

"So numerous and egregious were Malcolm's omissions, distortions and outright misstatements of fact that I felt compelled to set the record straight. . . . There is no statute of limitations on truth. Even now, twenty-three years later, Malcolm's fictions ought not to be accepted uncritically. I reprint my 1989 response to her here."

Malcolm's book does convey her sense that McGinniss deceived MacDonald, convicted murderer though he was. McGinniss takes issue not only with Malcolm's conclusion, but with her use of his situation as a premise for investigating the journalist/subject relationship.

*The Journalist and the Murderer* remains a seminal book on journalism despite McGinniss's refutations of its specifics. Journalistically, of course, these facts should be all that matter, but the issues Malcolm raises—such as what level of candor is required by reporters in pursuit of the truth—are of greater interest.

Well, I suppose I should say they are of greater interest to me than trying to wrestle with the voluminous details of the MacDonald murder case, which are now close to 50 years old. As it happens, MacDonald's case is the subject of Errol Morris's 2012 book *A Wilderness of Error*. In it, Morris provides a detailed—forensic, really—look at the murder case. He also takes aim at both McGinniss's reportage of that case and Malcolm's meditations on MacDonald and McGinniss's relationship, and her conclusion of McGinniss's bad faith.

In addition to his detailed examination of the MacDonald case, Morris also takes aim at media "narratives," at the notion that truth is in the eye of the beholder. Toward the end of the book, he includes a transcript of a discussion he had with MacDonald about the role the media had played in MacDonald's case. Morris says he called Malcolm because he was disturbed by a passage in *The Journalist and the Murderer* in which Malcolm admits to not reading much of the material MacDonald had sent her about the case—transcripts, reports, etc.—describing herself as "oppressed by the mountain of documents that formed in my office." She writes:

"I know I cannot learn anything about MacDonald's guilt or innocence from this material. . . . it all depends on how you read the evidence. . . . The material does not 'speak for itself.'"

Morris finds Malcolm's attitude—that truth is mutable and depends on the lens of the viewer—objectionable, to say the least. "It comes down to an issue of truth. Is there such a thing? And yes, there is such a thing," he relates saying to MacDonald in the book. Morris goes on to discuss the way in which, for example, police collect evidence at a crime scene and interpret it in order to create a "narrative" of what happened. In MacDonald's case, Morris says, "Part of telling your story is a story about how that narrative came into being" and the role the media played.

Morris has little patience for either McGinniss or Malcolm and includes an exchange between Malcolm and MacDonald about the subject of facts and narrative. MacDonald writes back to Malcolm, presumably quoting words from her own letter, and says:

"Not every work 'that imposes some form on the flux of disorder of actuality' is a fiction masquerading as nonfiction." Narratives, MacDonald writes, do have "as you put it, an element of choice, but that is not the same as 'fiction.' . . . every narrative requires judgment and probably some choices by the author—but the narrative doesn't require artful lying, crucial deletions to force the reader only one way, and fictional creations by the author damaging to the truth-seeking process of nonfiction writing."

Morris agrees with his subject, asking, "Is this what it all comes down to? Two journalists—one who betrays MacDonald by twisting the facts and another who tells him facts don't make a difference?"

I have read *The Journalist and the Murderer* many, many times; I could and likely will read it again for my classes. I have read *A Wilderness of Error* only once and, though I found its doggedness admirable and compelling, I admit it would take perseverance to read it again. I just didn't find it as interesting, as readable, as Malcolm's book. For what it's worth, I also read *Fatal Vision*, once, and though propulsive, the book wasn't one I wanted to reread either. It turns out, though I bristle against D'Agata's stance against facts, as a reader I, too, am less compelled by information than story.

When I first read Janet Malcolm's book, I had trouble believing a jury would have greater sympathy for a convicted murderer than for the writer who wrote about him. When I read MacDonald's letter to Malcolm, I found myself agreeing with him to a degree. Constructing an interesting narrative isn't the same as writing fiction; choosing how to tell a story and which elements to include isn't the same as lying. But once those choices and omissions are made, have we breached readers' trust? And what is the cost of doing so?

For the most part, my students read *The Journalist and the Murderer* and are appalled by the behavior of everyone involved. Needless to say, faith in the honesty of our culture's gatekeepers—be they journalists, law enforcement, or politicians—isn't at an all-time high. Perhaps one's ethical stance can only truly be found by interrogating one's own allegiances: Art?

Truth with a capital *T* and the belief that it exists? Journalism and its basic tenets?

As a journalist, I am stuck with believing, as I said at the beginning of this chapter: "don't make shit up." I also believe that people and their stories, with all their inconvenient unartful facts, can still be rendered artfully without gross misrepresentation. As the MacDonald/McGinniss/Malcolm/Morris situation makes clear, sometimes this is easier said/understood than done/understood.

From a philosophical or ethical viewpoint, I suppose this means I support an Aristotelian view that ethical situations should at least require some reasoning and consideration (I'm paraphrasing), and that absolutes are unattainable. That being said, the degree to which narrative may be artful is not the only ethical issue that can arise from writing nonfiction.

···· *True Crime*

True crime is not the only journalistic milieu in which ethical issues arise, but it sure is a notable one. *In Cold Blood*, though still considered groundbreaking for its formal experimentation with narrative, also has been the subject of numerous criticisms alleging mistakes and fabrications, pretty much from the time it was released in 1966. Media writer Jack Shafer documents this history in a 2012 blog for Reuters, "Dismantling the Capote Myth," actually comparing Capote to D'Agata, and concluding: "What joins D'Agata and Capote is this: Both love 'real' facts, but when blocked by journalistic convention from the literary effects they desire, they willingly leapt that fence to create whatever rules they needed to enhance their work. Because he admits to his shape shifting, D'Agata's work is harmless. Capote's book, on the other hand, continues to be taught in journalism classes, is celebrated as a masterpiece, and I would guess that it has been read by 50 percent of Americans who consider themselves educated."

(Interrogation of Capote's work hasn't desisted since: A 2013 *Wall Street Journal* article, "Capote Classic 'In Cold Blood' Tainted by Long-Lost Files," reports on then-new files from the Kansas Bureau of Investigation that undermine key chapters in the book and indicate Capote showed blatant favoritism toward certain people characterized in his "nonfiction novel."[30])

I sometimes teach *In Cold Blood* in my journalism classes, though not as an example of veracity. Capote claimed to have trained himself to transcribe conversations verbatim without a tape recorder—I don't really understand why anyone ever believed his claim that the book was "immaculately factual."[31]

Rather, I teach it to show its role in shifting how writers and readers perceived the strictures of nonfiction narrative. My syllabus for a recent course called Storytelling Across Platforms included both *In Cold Blood* and the first season of the podcast *Serial* from *This American Life*. Both stories, though separated by decades and utilizing different mediums, make use of similar standard techniques of storytelling: plot, characterization, voice, point of view.

Although we did discuss these issues (and the students wrote about each work's craft elements), season one of *Serial* in particular raised interesting lines of ethical inquiry, not just in my classroom, of course, but nationally. If you missed it somehow,

---

30    Capote's errors—however one wishes to characterize them—become even more interesting given that the book was initially published in installments in the *New Yorker*, which has a notable fact-checking department. *Slate* magazine followed down this rabbit hole in a March 2013 article, "Fact Checking 'In Cold Blood.'" Writer Ben Yagoda concludes that at the time the *New Yorker*'s fact-checking policies would have covered mostly verifiable facts such as dates, locations, and spellings. He looks at the fact-checking file and concludes, "There is nothing in the file to suggest that [fact-checker Sandy] Campbell tried to verify the dialogue or action with which the article was packed."

31    From George Plimpton's oft-cited New York Times' 1966 interview with Capote. See end notes.

season one of *Serial* reinvestigates the 1999 Baltimore murder of Hae Min Lee and the subsequent conviction of her ex-boyfriend Adnan Syed, who remains incarcerated for the crime. *This American Life* journalist Sarah Koenig set out to re-report the story after a friend of Syed who maintains his innocence contacted her. *Serial* was released in 12 weekly podcast installments in 2014 and became a national phenomenon. In a media column, the late David Carr wrote that the podcast's "numbers are impressive for any media platform."

*Serial* also spawned podcasts about the podcast,[32] not to mention a *Saturday Night Live* spoof and numerous national interviews for Koenig. It also may have contributed to motions for a new trial for Syed; at least, Syed's attorney credited the podcast, and the interest it garnered for doing so. In a February 10, 2016, *People* magazine article, lawyer C. Justin Brown said, "As a result of *Serial*, more information became available to us . . . more information than we otherwise may have gotten." Brown also noted that the information came from people "all over the country . . . investigating this case." That investigation in part took the form of an intensive Reddit thread, as well as other podcasts and web forums. And, on June 30, 2016, Syed's conviction was vacated and a judge ordered him a new trial, writing in his decision that "This case represents a unique juncture between the criminal justice system and a phenomenally strong public interest caused by modern media."[33]

I was both addicted to and troubled by *Serial*. It was very well produced and made for fascinating (if occasionally confusing) listening. As Josh Levin writes in *Slate*, "In most cases, the narrative is more cohesive when you don't show your work—when

---

32    Most notably, *Undisclosed*, which is credited with finding information that the judge cited as a reason for granting a new trial.

33    Fenton, Justin and Justin George, "Conviction Vacated, New Trial Ordered for Adnan Syed of 'Serial,'" *Baltimore Sun*, July 1, 2016, http://www.baltimoresun.com/news/maryland/crime/bs-md-ci-adnan-syed-new-trial-20160630-story.html.

readers or listeners don't know about the missed connections, the people who agree to talk to you but then back out, the protracted searches for facts that might not even matter."

I was bothered, though, by *Serial*'s popularity. On the one hand: great! Millions of supporters turning up for excellent journalism delivered via a podcast. On the other hand, was there not something off in the moral universe about people following reportage of an actual murder as if it were the latest thriller from Netflix? Yes, it was propulsive and addictive. But it also was reportedly upsetting to the victim's family, and the victim herself was barely a character in the podcast. Wasn't it just out-and-out bad taste—moral relativism be damned—to broadcast a spoof, no matter how funny (and it was funny) based on a podcast that had at its heart the murder of a teenage girl? Was there not something skewed about holding narrative expectations that the "story" would resolve in a satisfying way when the story was a real crime? (As a side note, *Slate's Serial Spoiler Special* podcast is excellent, overall, and also delves into some of these issues at great length; but listen to *Serial* first).

I have no answers to these questions, other than I think they are the right questions to ask. As Adrienne LaFrance writes in the *Atlantic*, "What is it, exactly, that people are participating in here? Are *Serial* listeners in it for the important examination of the criminal justice system? Or are we trawling through a grieving family's pain as a form of entertainment?"

*Serial*, of course, is not the only example of this type of true-crimertainment in recent years—and reportedly the rabid response to *Serial* took its producers and reporters by surprise. No more. From Netflix's *Making a Murderer*, to FX's *The People v. O.J. Simpson: American Crime Story*, cultural fascination with true crime seems rooted and established.

Billy Jensen is the supervising producer/digital for the WB show *True Crime Daily*. He is a former altweekly newspaper editor, which is basically how I know him, and has written several true crime stories. He spearheaded a 2014 South by Southwest panel on "Citizen Dicks: Solving Murders with Social Media." He also has written true crime stories for *Rolling Stone* magazine, *LA* magazine, and numerous other publications, some focusing on the role "citizen detectives" have played in unsolved crimes.

Jensen is a strong proponent of crowdsourcing for crime solving and has written stories about citizen detective work that paid off. He believes it's a trend that's going to continue to increase.

"We've seen what the crowd can do for journalism and how when there is a natural disaster, when there's a terrorist attack, the images that you see are not usually from professional news organizations, they're from citizens who are carrying their phones and take pictures of them. I think the next step in the evolution is something along these lines," he says.

But as for the ethics of using true crime to entertain people, Jensen says, *Serial*'s use of narrative plot techniques, from red herrings to misdirection, is "no different" from any other news program reporting on similar issues, whether it's *20/20* or *Sixty Minutes*. "Everybody does it," he says. The only difference, he says, is that *Serial* unfolded over weeks, rather than two hours, giving the public time to engage on the Internet in a way they wouldn't for a two-hour program. What he sees as a greater failure by *Serial*, as well as other similar efforts, are that "the victim is not at the center of any of this; it's always the villain at the center of all of these crimes that they're talking about." Even though in *Serial*, for example, Hae Min Lee's family didn't participate in the podcast, Jensen says, "You could have painted a better picture of this woman without the family and made viewers care about the victim more."

Jensen said in his case he has dropped stories at families' requests, but doing so would depend on the case. "At the end of the day I want to solve the crime more than I want to tell a good story," he says. "If the crime gets solved before I get to tell the story, I'm more happy than if I write a good story." Moreover, he adds, "There are so many cases, so many stories I want to tell that if I tell one in a way that's over-the-top insensitive and doesn't do anything to push forward the story, I'm not going to get the next person to want to talk if they think I'm just being salacious for salaciousness' sake."

The *New Yorker* took up the issue of the victims in both *Serial* and *Making a Murderer*. I should say that although I'm talking about both pieces, I don't think they are equal. *Serial* seemed to clearly take pains with its investigative journalism, while *Making a Murderer*, despite its creators' protests to the contrary, seemed . . . less a work of journalism. But arguably neither, as Kathryn Schulz writes in "Dead Certainty," "ever addresses the question of what rights and considerations should be extended to victims of violent crime, and under what circumstances those might justifiably be suspended. Instead, both creators and viewers tacitly dismiss the pain caused by such shows as collateral damage, unfortunate but unavoidable. Here, too, the end is taken to justify the means; someone else's anguish comes to seem like a trifling price to pay for the greater cause a documentary claims to serve."

These issues lead me to think about the Dart Center, a Columbia Journalism program that offers a plethora of resources for reporting on victims and tragedies. It advises: "Focus on the person's life. Find out what made the person special: personality, beliefs, environment (surroundings, hobbies, family and friends), and likes and dislikes. Treat the person's life as carefully as a photographer does in framing a portrait."

But these shows really weren't about their victims; not even, really, about the accused. Instead, they seemed to be about the justice system and to be tapping into the deep (often rightful) mistrust of law enforcement, the judicial system and, yes, the media.

I asked Jensen if he thought systemic mistrust of authority was why true crime was so popular right now, and he said that perhaps it was part of it, but that true crime's allure also spoke to something deeper and more universal. "People want to see resolution because they want to see order out of chaos," Jensen says. "That's what true crime stories bring; potentially, this is what could happen to you and you realize there's a reason why it happened, however twisted it was, and then order is brought back."

If there is any takeaway from all this murkiness, it's that testing one's own biases, responses, and tendencies certainly can't hurt. In their two-year investigation for *New Mexico In Depth* of the high youth suicide rate among Native Americans, reporters Laura Paskus and Bryant Furlow made a conscious choice at the outset regarding the ethical framework for their stories. Paskus says a close friend of hers, who is Native American and involved in the issue, had shared with Paskus "his thoughts about media coverage on Native American youth suicide and how destructive that coverage could be sometimes because it made people in communities feel even worse about their situations and their lives and had this negative effect on communities." As a result, Paskus says, "We wanted to look at the problem and to do it in a way that we hoped wouldn't make those vulnerable people feel even worse, so we were going at it with this 'do no harm' way, and we really consciously avoided having scenes in the stories that were grief porn; we stayed away from that."

The series, "Choosing Life," was transparent about its reporting and ethical framework with an editorial note that reads, in part, "We spent so much time on this project because we wanted to delve deep and treat the people we were reporting on with sensitivity and compassion. We tried to listen to feedback from Native Americans and others about how to responsibly report on suicide."

While most major publications have extensive ethical guidebooks for reporters (many of which are online), specific stories or areas of reporting can, as the Paskus and Furlow story demonstrates, require individual calibration.

# TYPES OF ISSUES

#### ····*Conflicts of Interest*

The notion that journalists are "objective" has been widely discussed and is still, often, misunderstood. Journalists are people, not robots (not robots *yet*, I should say) and, as such, fundamentally incapable of being objective. To be objective is to lack bias. Bias means one has certain inclinations, views, and beliefs. These don't necessarily have to be pejorative—I have a bias toward liking the beach, for example. In a journalistic context, objectivity refers to the practice of journalism, not the person practicing it. As Bill Kovach and Tom Rosenstiel write in their book *The Elements of Journalism,* "In the recognition that everyone is biased . . . the news, like science, should flow from a process for reporting that is defensible, rigorous, and transparent."

Conflicts of interest are cases in which a writer has an obvious bias or the potential for one: writing about a company at which one worked, reporting on a friend, reviewing a relative's book/album, etc. In most cases, conflicts of interest are easily avoidable (the examples I've given are easily avoidable). Others may seem surprising, such as a writer having relatives who actively support political candidates, a writer being a part of civic organizations, a writer being married to an elected official.

OK, the last one seems like an obvious potential area of conflict. I am thinking of *Willamette Week*; one of the paper's owners, Richard Meeker, is married to Oregon's attorney general and, because of this potential conflict, the paper didn't cover the primary election for the race. When she was elected in 2012, *WW*'s editor, Mark Zusman, printed an editor's note acknowledging his long-term relationship with Meeker and his wife, Ellen Rosenblum:

"Because Meeker and I have jointly owned *WW* for nearly 30 years, there's a perception—and perhaps a reality—that it would be difficult for me to objectively assign or edit stories involving his wife."

As such, Zusman wrote, he would be delegating all coverage decisions about Rosenblum to the paper's managing editor. In 2015, Zusman took over as publisher for *Willamette Week*; Meeker for the *Santa Fe Reporter* and the company's other paper, *Indy Weekly*, in Durham, North Carolina. Zusman verified to me via email that while there were a variety of reasons for the shift, avoiding ongoing conflicts of interest was among them.

This is but one example of the many types of conflicts that can occur in news media, and one way in which such a situation can be handled. In general, avoid conflicts. When unavoidable, disclose them. If unsure if a conflict exists, discuss it and decide. If you work for a specific publication or news agency, it will make its parameters clear. For example, the Associated Press does not allow its employees to "serve as official scorers at sports events." I'm not sure if this includes children's Little League games; you'd have to ask.

Zusman was my boss when I was at the *Reporter* and used to emphasize to me that the perception of a conflict of interest is as important as whether or not the conflict exists or will present a problem in the reporting.

Preserving these rules of striving toward objectivity and transparency has always been a key element for professional journalists, but perhaps is more important now than ever given the proliferation of information sources in the digital age. As Kovach and Rosenstiel write, in the current climate in which traditional media organizations compete with all sorts of sources—from excellent citizen journalists to financially motivated propaganda—"one of the most profound questions for a democratic society is whether news can survive as a source of independent and trustworthy information."

That's not a simple question to answer (nor do the authors portend to have easy solutions), but avoiding conflicts of interest and fostering transparency when they might exist is one step.

Many news organizations post their ethical standards online should you wish for a more extended look at how media institutions handle such issues. A link for the *New York Times'* Standards and Ethics guidelines is included at the end of this chapter, as is the entirety of The Code of Ethics of the Society of Professional Journalists.

Other conflicts to avoid:

- Taking money, favors, or anything of value from a source
- Paying sources for their stories
- Writing about a publication's advertisers in exchange for their ads

## ····*Plagiarism*

Don't do it, intentionally or otherwise. Keep notes on where your information is coming from, and use citation to avoid misrepresenting someone else's work as your own, including press releases. While many variables exist across the spectrum of nonfiction, plagiarism has no defenders (as far as I know).

## ····*Fabrication*

It's worth stating again that regardless of one's feelings about *In Cold Blood*, fabrication in journalism is taboo. Stephen Glass and Jayson Blair, both mentioned in the opening of this chapter, are two famous fabricators whose lies were so outrageous they continue to reverberate. Glass was a staff writer at the *New Republic* in the 1990s whose work I deeply admired at the time (less so when it turned out that twenty-seven of his forty-one pieces had been wholly or partially made up.[34] As mentioned previously in this book, Glass's deceptions are the subject of the film *Shattered Glass*. Jayson Blair was a *New York Times* reporter who in 2003 turned out also to be fabricating material for his coverage of the war in Iraq. Blair's malfeasance led the *New York Times* to investigate and in some cases overhaul its editorial processes; in the end, some senior managers resigned over the situation. Society of Professional Journalists offers on its website a deeper look at the Blair case in its ethics case studies. Unfortunately, journalistic scandals relating to plagiarism and fabrication have not disappeared in the intervening years. For editors, ensuring the work they publish is original and accurate is of paramount concern, and most reputable organizations have numerous failsafe policies to try to avoid problems. Still, they happen. The Poynter Institute has a helpful online guide for addressing allegations of plagiarism and fabrication, the link to which is included at the end of this chapter.

···· *Privacy*

When you write about yourself, you are the arbiter of how much you want to reveal or shield about your life. When you are writing about other people in the form of memoir or personal essay, you have the option to ask them if they are comfortable with what you are writing; you also have the option to not do so and accept the consequences that they may not be happy with how you have chosen to portray them. You may run the risk at times of violating people's privacy in a legal sense.

People do have certain legal rights to privacy (believe it or

---

34    Michael Hiltzik, "Stephen Glass Is Still Retracting His Stories—18 Years Later," *Los Angeles Times*, December 15, 2015, http://www.latimes.com/business/hiltzik/la-fi-mh-stephen-glass-is-still-retracting-20151215-column.html.

not), although some of these rights vary from state to state. For example, in some states it is legal to tape a telephone discussion with someone without that person's consent; in others, it isn't. Most news organizations protect the names of certain types of people: victims of sexual abuse or other severe crimes, and juveniles involved in crimes. Exceptions are sometimes made in the first instance when victims voluntarily identify themselves and in the latter, when the crimes are deemed by individual editors to justify doing so. As a general rule, if you're unsure if what you are writing invades someone's privacy to a degree that may lead to legal action—and certainly if you have been threatened with legal action—call a lawyer. If you would like to read more on the legal issues of privacy, the Reporters Committee for Freedom of the Press has excellent resources on this and other legal topics.

## ····*Fairness and Libel*

A basic tenet of news writing is fairness, as in doing one's best to report all sides of a story. This means if a city councilor insults the mayor's proposal, a reporter is expected to call the mayor and give him or her a chance to respond. Sometimes, depending on deadlines, a reporter may be unable to reach someone for response; this is when you see the statement: "_____ was unavailable for comment." Reporters are required to call people for comments, even if the person is a public official who has refused to respond for four years running (for example).

Libel is the legal term for defaming someone in print. I should make it clear that I am not a lawyer and nothing I am saying here constitutes legal advice (and, yes, I am legally required to say that ... I think). Defamation comes in two forms: libel and slander (slander refers to defamation in oral form). In a very small nutshell, libel is the act of printing as fact non-factual statements about someone that hurt that person's reputation.

Writers are not protected from libel through quotation—meaning if someone else makes a damaging and incorrect statement about another person, a writer who quotes that statement is not exempt from the consequences of the libelous statement. Though it would be nice to believe one can avoid allegations or litigation of libel simply by never printing inaccurate injurious statements, this isn't true. The *Reporter* was never sued while I was editor, but I was threatened with lawsuits several times. Fortunately, the *Reporter* had an excellent lawyer who wrote excellent scary letters to people and made them go away. At any rate, the point is, anyone can sue anyone they want whenever they want. However, certainly one can strive to avoid libel lawsuits by avoiding printing libelous statements. The Associated Press Stylebook is a good place for a primer on libel, privacy, and other legal issues that can arise when writing in the real world. However, if you have an actual situation, and you are not working for an organization with legal counsel, be sure to call an actual lawyer. The Reporters Committee for Freedom of the Press also is an excellent resource for understanding legal issues related to reporting—including journalists' rights for information—and provides a legal hotline.

## ····*Bottom Lines*

If you are writing on your own, you will have to make your own decisions about how to navigate some of this terrain. If you are working for a publication, you will need to follow its rules. Standard news publications follow fairly basic tenets that ban any use of fabricated information or composited characters. Attribution is always required for information. Anonymous sources are only used when the information is vital, can't be secured in any other way, and the source has a legitimate reason for asking for his or her identity to be protected. Obviously, there have been notable and controversial exceptions to these rules. Some publications employ "public editors" who respond to readers' concerns and allegations about perceived problems—from bias to inaccuracies—in reporting. I find the *New York Times'* Public Editor column to be an informative read as it helps improve my understanding of the public perception of how media works, as well as my own shortcomings: past, present, probably future.

#### ····*Source Protection*

As mentioned in chapter 3, anonymous sources are people who provide information or quotes for a story but are granted the right to do so without attribution. By granting anonymity, journalists are shielded, to various degrees, from revealing the names of their sources should they be subpoenaed or otherwise compelled to do so.[35] Many journalists have gone to jail rather than reveal their sources, in both high profile and lesser-known instances of journalists adhering to the ethical belief that, once granted, confidentiality must be absolute. While reporters have some type of protection at the state level, these rights vary from

---

35   I was called to testify before a grand jury in an election fraud case circa the late 1990s in Rio Arriba County while working as a reporter. I did end up going, and it was like being an extra in a super boring episode of *Law and Order*. I did not reveal anything, confidential or otherwise, because I didn't actually know the answers to any of their questions. There had been some talk that the district attorney was going to ask for/subpoena my reporting notes, but they never did. I am pretty sure I know why this all went down. I had heard that people were being called to testify before a grand jury in this case, but grand jury proceedings are secret. Since I had a pretty good idea of who *would* be called in such a case, I started calling people and faking them out with statements like, "So I see you're on the list to testify before the grand jury." They would confirm it since they thought I already knew it was true. Then I reported on it. Then the DA thought I knew more than I did. There are two takeaways from this story. The first is that you can sometimes obtain information by pretending to have it already. The second is that if you seem to know something in a legal case that the authorities want to know, you may end up in their sightlines. This is not an anecdote of legal or journalistic significance; it's just my example. The Reporters Committee for Freedom of the Press has a compendium of journalists jailed and otherwise punished for protecting their sources here: http://www.rcfp.org/jailed-journalists.

state to state, and there is no federal law protecting a reporter's privilege to protect sources. While reporters working for news organizations can (usually) rely on their publication's legal support, reporting privilege can be murkier for freelancers or for writers who are not working in a traditional media setting or milieu. Again, see the Reporters Committee for Freedom of the Press for an extensive guide to understanding these laws.

## ADDITIONAL READING

Although The Code of Ethics of the Society of Professional Journalists isn't a universal code for reporters, it's pretty close to it and certainly an excellent touchstone for anyone faced with confusion in a specific situation. SPJ has excellent online ethics resources, including case studies, which I have used many times in my classes.

## The Code of Ethics of the Society of Professional Journalists

### Preamble

Members of the Society of Professional Journalists believe that public enlightenment is the forerunner of justice and the foundation of democracy. Ethical journalism strives to ensure the free exchange of information that is accurate, fair and thorough. An ethical journalist acts with integrity.

The Society declares these four principles as the foundation of ethical journalism and encourages their use in its practice by all people in all media.

The SPJ Code of Ethics is a statement of abiding principles supported by explanations and position papers that address changing journalistic practices. It is not a set of rules, rather a guide that encourages all who engage in journalism to take responsibility for the information they provide, regardless of medium. The code should be read as a whole; individual principles should not be taken out of context. It is not, nor can it be under the First Amendment, legally enforceable.

### Seek Truth and Report It

Ethical journalism should be accurate and fair. Journalists should be honest and courageous in gathering, reporting and interpreting information.

Journalists should:

- Take responsibility for the accuracy of their work. Verify information before releasing it. Use original sources whenever possible.
- Remember that neither speed nor format excuses inaccuracy.
- Provide context. Take special care not to misrepresent or oversimplify in promoting, previewing or summarizing a story.
- Gather, update and correct information throughout the life of a news story.

- Be cautious when making promises, but keep the promises they make.
- Identify sources clearly. The public is entitled to as much information as possible to judge the reliability and motivations of sources.
- Consider sources' motives before promising anonymity. Reserve anonymity for sources who may face danger, retribution or other harm, and have information that cannot be obtained elsewhere. Explain why anonymity was granted.
- Diligently seek subjects of news coverage to allow them to respond to criticism or allegations of wrongdoing.
- Avoid undercover or other surreptitious methods of gathering information unless traditional, open methods will not yield information vital to the public.
- Be vigilant and courageous about holding those with power accountable. Give voice to the voiceless.
- Support the open and civil exchange of views, even views they find repugnant.
- Recognize a special obligation to serve as watchdogs over public affairs and government. Seek to ensure that the public's business is conducted in the open, and that public records are open to all.
- Provide access to source material when it is relevant and appropriate.
- Boldly tell the story of the diversity and magnitude of the human experience. Seek sources whose voices we seldom hear.
- Avoid stereotyping. Journalists should examine the ways their values and experiences may shape their reporting.
- Label advocacy and commentary.
- Never deliberately distort facts or context, including visual information. Clearly label illustrations and re-enactments.
- Never plagiarize. Always attribute.

## Minimize Harm
Ethical journalism treats sources, subjects, colleagues and members of the public as human beings deserving of respect.

Journalists should:
- Balance the public's need for information against potential harm or discomfort. Pursuit of the news is not a license for arrogance or undue intrusiveness.
- Show compassion for those who may be affected by news coverage. Use heightened sensitivity when dealing with juveniles, victims of sex crimes, and sources or subjects who are inexperienced or unable to give consent. Consider cultural differences in approach and treatment.
- Recognize that legal access to information differs from an ethical justification to publish or broadcast.

- Realize that private people have a greater right to control information about themselves than public figures and others who seek power, influence or attention. Weigh the consequences of publishing or broadcasting personal information.
- Avoid pandering to lurid curiosity, even if others do.
- Balance a suspect's right to a fair trial with the public's right to know. Consider the implications of identifying criminal suspects before they face legal charges.
- Consider the long-term implications of the extended reach and permanence of publication. Provide updated and more complete information as appropriate.

## Act Independently
The highest and primary obligation of ethical journalism is to serve the public.

Journalists should:
- Avoid conflicts of interest, real or perceived. Disclose unavoidable conflicts.
- Refuse gifts, favors, fees, free travel and special treatment, and avoid political and other outside activities that may compromise integrity or impartiality, or may damage credibility.
- Be wary of sources offering information for favors or money; do not pay for access to news. Identify content provided by outside sources, whether paid or not.
- Deny favored treatment to advertisers, donors or any other special interests, and resist internal and external pressure to influence coverage.
- Distinguish news from advertising and shun hybrids that blur the lines between the two. Prominently label sponsored content.

## Be Accountable and Transparent
Ethical journalism means taking responsibility for one's work and explaining one's decisions to the public.

Journalists should:
- Explain ethical choices and processes to audiences. Encourage a civil dialogue with the public about journalistic practices, coverage and news content.
- Respond quickly to questions about accuracy, clarity and fairness.
- Acknowledge mistakes and correct them promptly and prominently. Explain corrections and clarifications carefully and clearly.
- Expose unethical conduct in journalism, including within their organizations.
- Abide by the same high standards they expect of others.

# READING AND RESOURCES
# FROM THIS CHAPTER

Aciman, André. "How Memoirists Mold the Truth." *New York Times Opionator Blog*, April 6, 2013. http://opinionator.blogs.nytimes.com/2013/04/06/how-memoirists-mold-the-truth.

Carr, David. *The Night of the Gun: A Reporter Investigates the Darkest Story of His Life, His Own.* New York: Simon & Schuster, 2008.

———. "'Serial,' Podcasting's First Breakout Hit, Sets Stage for More." *New York Times*, November 23, 2014. http://www.nytimes.com/2014/11/24/business/media/serial-podcastings-first-breakout-hit-sets-stage-for-more.html.

D'Agata, John. "What Happens There." *The Believer*, January 2010.  http://www.believermag.com/issues/201001/?read=article_dagata.

Dart Center. "Working With Victims and Survivors." *Dart Center*, February 22, 2011. http://dartcenter.org/content/working-with-victims-and-survivors.

Glaister, Dan. "Million Little Pieces May Cost Publishers Millions in Refunds." *The Guardian*, September 8, 2006. http://www.theguardian.com/world/2006/sep/08/books.usa.

Griffin, Lisa Kern. "'Making a Murderer' Is About Justice, Not Truth." *New York Times*, January 12, 2016. http://www.nytimes.com/2016/01/12/opinion/making-a-murderer-is-about-justice-not-truth.html.

Helliker, Kevin. "Capote Classic 'In Cold Blood' Tainted by Long-Lost Files." *Wall Street Journal*, February 8, 2013. http://www.wsj.com/articles/SB10001424127887323951904578290341604113984.

Herbst, Diane. "As Serial Case Concludes, Adnan Syed Says He Will 'Keep Fighting to Prove My Innocence.'" *People* magazine, February 10, 2016. http://www.people.com/article/adnan-syed-serial-hearing-ended-tuesday-baltimore.

Hiltzik, Michael. "Stephen Glass Is Still Retracting His Stories—18 Years Later." *Los Angeles Times*, December 15, 2015. http://www.latimes.com/business/hiltzik/la-fi-mh-stephen-glass-is-still-retracting-20151215-column.html.

Jensen, Billy. "Solving Murders with Citizen Dicks." *Slideshare*, July 26, 2013. http://www.slideshare.net/billyjensen1/solving-murders-with-social-media.

Kovach, Bill, and Tom Rosenstiel. *The Elements of Journalism: What Newspeople Should Know and the Public Should Expect.* New York: Three Rivers, 2014.

LaFrance, Adrienne. "Is It Wrong to be Hooked on Serial?" *The Atlantic*, November 8, 2014. http://www.theatlantic.com/technology/archive/2014/11/is-it-wrong-to-be-hooked-on-serial/382500.

Malcolm, Janet. *The Journalist and the Murderer.* New York: Knopf, 1990.

McDonald, Jennifer B. "In the Details: 'The Lifespan of a Fact,' by John D'Agata and Jim Fingal." *New York Times*, February 21, 2012. http://www.nytimes.com/2012/02/26/books/review/the-lifespan-of-a-fact-by-john-dagata-and-jim-fingal.html.

McGinniss, Joe. *Fatal Vision.* New York: Putnam, 1983.

——. "The 1989 Epilogue to Fatal Vision." http://www.joemcginniss.net/the-1989-epilogue .

"Memoir Week Collection." *Slate*, 2007. http://www.slate.com/articles/arts_and_life/memoir_week.html.

Morris, Errol. *A Wilderness of Error: The Trials of Jeffrey Macdonald*. New York: Penguin, 2012.

Nester, Daniel. "Notes on Frey." *Creative Nonfiction*, 2007.

Plimpton, George. "The Story Behind a Nonfiction Novel." *New York Times*, January 16, 1966. https://www.nytimes.com/books/97/12/28/home/capote-interview.html.

Reporters Committee for Freedom of the Press. "The Reporter's Privilege." http://www.rcfp.org/reporters-privilege.

Schulz, Kathryn. "Dead Certainty." *New Yorker*, January 25, 2016. http://www.newyorker.com/magazine/2016/01/25/dead-certainty.

Shafer, Jack. "Dismantling the Capote Myth." *Reuters*, March 14, 2012. http://blogs.reuters.com/jackshafer/2012/03/14/dismantling-the-capote-myth.

Shapiro, Dani. "Open Letter from Dani Shapiro: 'Dear Disillusioned Reader Who Contacted Me on Facebook.'" *Salon*, January 9, 2014. http://www.salon.com/2014/01/10/open_letter_from_dani_shapiro_dear_disillusioned_reader_who_contacted_me_on_facebook.

Silverman, Craig, and Kelly McBride. "How to Handle Plagiarism and Fabrication Allegations." *Poynter*, August 15, 2012. http://www.poynter.org/2012/how-to-handle-pla-giarism-and-fabrication-allegations/184895.

"'Serial' Collection." *Slate*. http://www.slate.com/topics/s/serial.html

"Solve This Crime." *Crime Watch Daily*. http://crimewatch-daily.com/solve-this--crime.

The Smoking Gun. "A Million Little Lies: Exposing James Frey's Fiction Addiction." *The Smoking Gun*, January 4, 2006. http://www.thesmokinggun.com/documents/celebrity/million-little-lies.

Uribarri, Adrian. "Ethics Case Studies: The *Times* and Jayson Blair." *Society for Professional Journalists*. http://www.spj.org/ecs13.asp.

Yagoda, Ben. "Fact Checking 'In Cold Blood." *Slate*, March 20, 2013. http://www.slate.com/articles/arts/culturebox/2013/03/fact_checking_in_cold_blood_what_the_new_yorker_s_fact_checker_missed.html.

# CHAPTER NINE

# Line By Line—Editing and Revision

Nobody knows everything—one of the pleasures of language is that there is always something new to learn—and everybody makes mistakes.

—**Mary Norris,** *Between You and Me: Confessions of a Comma Queen*

OR CLOSE TO eleven years—my tenure as editor of the *Reporter*—I went to sleep every Tuesday night with fear in my heart—the fear of a horrible stupid error that had snuck by me and would be out, for all to see, in the pages of the paper the following day. I would love to claim that thanks to my eagle eye and control-freak tendencies, more than a decade went by without so much as a misplaced modifier, but I'd be lying. And I'd be ridiculous. Mistakes happen. Given enough time, some of my most horrendous errors have become funny (or will, any minute now).

But mistakes add up. Grammar mistakes will almost always hurt your submissions, upset a copy editor, and possibly earn you scorn in the public comments section. Consistent factual errors will hurt your credibility with your editor, your sources, and your readers.

The best way to avoid mistakes ending up in print is to avoid making them in the first place. The best way to avoid making them in the first place is to be vigilant and methodical with your editing and proofreading processes. The checklist below may seem overwrought (see "control freak," above), but much of what I'm suggesting will soon become second nature if it is not already.

Before you send your work out, use this extended (or abbreviated, at the end of the chapter) checklist:

1. **Check your spelling.** Here is a confession: I'm not much of a speller. I realized this in the last few years when I was asked to serve as a judge for the Santa Fe Public Schools county spelling bee. At this event, I learned not only about my lack of innate spelling prowess, but also that compared to the average seventh grader, I wasn't particularly adept at pronouncing words or extrapolating their definitions based on their languages of origin (so much for high school Latin).

On the bright side, Microsoft Word has a function called Spell Check.[36] Use it! But use it thoughtfully. Spelling software—as anyone who has ever allowed AutoCorrect to do its evil deeds unchecked knows—will catch most typos; it can also create new ones by suggesting the wrong word, correcting proper names, and failing to distinguish which word is appropriate in which circumstance. For seemingly endless examples of the latter, read through the *New York Times* "When Spell-Check Can't Help"[37] series from its Newsroom Notes on Usage and Style, primarily an examination of Homonyms Gone Wrong. Examples cited in

---

36    In the interest of accuracy, I guess it's actually called "Spelling and Grammar." Moreover, I've just wasted more time than I am willing to admit searching for consensus on how to spell "Spell Check." I've decided randomly to go with Spell Check.

37    I don't understand why the *Times* has chosen to hyphenate Spell Check and am now tempted to change Spell Check to Spell-Check, except that its hyphenation doesn't jibe with my understanding of the purpose of hyphenation, so I'm standing firm.

this series include *cache* versus *cachet, horde* versus *hoard*, and one of my favorites—as I've had to correct this one myself approximately three million times—*council* versus *counsel*.

Misspelling names falls more into the category of accuracy, so perhaps I'll repeat this mantra there: Make people spell their names for you. Don't assume you know how to spell Jon or Jenniphr (yes, I know someone who spells her name that way; she's a lovely person). I have been that person who misspelled someone's name. As an intern in my early twenties, I was tasked with writing an obituary of approximately 300 words in which I spelled the deceased's name not just incorrectly but three different ways in one story (none right . . . which seems almost impossible). There's a word for this kind of mistake: inexcusably sloppy (I guess that's two words).

If you forget to ask someone how his or her name is spelled, don't check the Internet, particularly if by Internet, you mean Facebook. For reasons I will quietly file under the heading "psychological," some people use alternative spellings of their names on social media. Moreover, some organizations' websites spell their employees' names wrong. Ask the source—98 percent of the time, people know how to spell their own names.[38]

2. **Police grammar.** I was meeting with a very good student and reviewing with her a few small grammatical errors from one of her papers. I try to talk about grammar in an uncharacteristic, chipper, nonjudgmental way, since some people exhibit signs of trauma associated with their particular grammatical foibles. I tell them the truth: some of the best writers I know have grammatical blind spots. But, as with so many things in life, admitting the problem is the alleged first step toward active recovery. This particular student, however, remained stricken as I started gently reviewing the errors in her paper and asked me in a

---

[38]   I have actually encountered, more than once, exceptions to this rule, which seems statistically unlikely, but nonetheless is true.

trembling voice if I thought bad grammar might be contagious. She was worried that constant exposure to grammatical errors (on the Internet, in texts, etc.) might be rubbing off on her.

It's not a bad question, or certainly not an unprecedented one. The *Observer* associate editor, writer Robert McCrum, has pondered the topic more than once, for example in a May 2013 column, "George Orwell's Critique of Internet English," in which he writes:

"Twenty-first century civilisation has been transformed in a way without precedent since the invention of moveable type. English prose, so one argument runs, must adapt to the new lexicon with all its grammatical violations and banality. Language is normative; it has—some will say—no choice. The violence the Internet does to the English language is simply the cost of doing business in the digital age."

Perhaps. Certainly correcting/mocking folks' public grammar seems both obnoxious and Sisyphean. Writer Andrew Heisel posited in an April 2015 *Washington Post* column that the human brain may simply be hardwired to make such mistakes, regardless of how well one knows the rules.

George Orwell and neuroscience notwithstanding, one should at least *try* to produce clean copy as part of the editing process. I'm not going to attempt to review every conceivable grammar situation—I'm not an actual grammarian—but I will outline a few that in my experience are the most common errors. In the resource list at the end of this chapter, I've included some of the grammar resources by actual grammarians that I have found to be clear and helpful.

Again, everyone makes mistakes. The important goal is to become aware of the mistakes you are the most likely to make, and use the editing/proofing process to take a special look for those mistakes. And if certain grammar rules are fuzzy, I recommend bookmarking Mignon Fogarty, a.k.a. Grammar Girl, whose website is smart and funny (not to mention clear and helpful). Karen Elizabeth Gordon's book *The Transitive Vampire* also is a favorite of mine.

And, yes, sure: for every grammar rule out there, you likely can and will find an extraordinary writer—in the canon, writing today, not yet discovered—able to break the rules with breathtaking results. I'm not here to thwart genius, only to point out proper use of commas and such (which reminds me of a wonderful *Paris Review* interview with fiction writer Ann Beattie, in which she discusses her use of a comma in a story at length, saying, sans irony: "It was that comma that said everything to me." I love Ann Beattie).

### *Its* **vs.** *It's*

I have a close friend who, for more than a decade, has looked at me skeptically when I try to explain the difference between *it's* and *its*. I can't quite decipher the expression on his face, but it's something like, "Oh you and your crazy grammar talk!" As it happens, he is not the only person in my life who seems dubious about the distinction between a contracted form of the verb "to be" and the singular possessive pronoun. *Its* versus *it's* is the most common grammatical error I see online and in my students' papers. It's possible I have explained the difference more times than I have explained anything else—and, at times, it would seem to no end.

Still, here goes:

**It's = it + is**

**Correct**: It's nice to use grammar like a Boss.

**Incorrect**: Its sad to use grammar like a Bot.

**Its = singular possessive pronoun**

**Correct**: The heart has its reasons, which reason knows not.[39]

**Incorrect**: The mind has it's way of sabotaging it's best efforts.

---

39    This particular example is somewhat less trite in the original French version of Blaise Pascal's *Pensées*.

## Apostrophes

It was a dark and stormy night, and I was in the production area at the *Reporter* waiting for final pages to proof before signing off on that week's paper. A designer beckoned to me; she was working on making my corrected changes. She pointed to an apostrophe I'd indicated needed to be deleted. "What's that called?" she asked. "What?" I asked. She pointed again at the apostrophe. "That's an apostrophe," I said, wondering, as I often do, if secret cameras were recording the interaction. "I've always wondered," she said.

I think most people know the word *apostrophe*, and even what an apostrophe looks like, but it does seem to be one of the most commonly misused punctuation marks, often appearing almost as a decorative mark.

As the *it's* versus *its* example shows above, an apostrophe can be used in a contraction, taking the place of a missing character or word (it + is = it's; the apostrophe appears rather than the *i* in *is*).

Another example of this is:

*Your* vs. *You're*

**Your = a possessive pronoun**

**You're = you + are**, in which the apostrophe takes the place of *a* to form the contraction

**Correct:** "You're not going to believe how weird it was when I saw my mother lying motionless on the floor on Mother's Day."[40]

**Incorrect:** "Your not a bad person for not caring if she lived or died; it's a hard situation watching someone have all their limbs amputated."[41]

---

40  Verbatim quote from people sitting next to me in the coffee shop where I'm writing today.

41  Ibid.

Apostrophes also are used for possessives, singular and plural:

**Singular Possessive**

**Correct**: Julia's car has many dents because she tends to run into inanimate objects.

**Incorrect**: Julias' head hurts from listening to the people next to her complain about their children, parents, and all of their relatives/friends/co-workers.[42]

**Plural Possessive**

**Correct:** Both parents' complaints about their children seemed petty and nasty.

**Incorrect:** Both parent's seemed unaware of how loud and awful they were being.

## Some Other Common, Albeit Understandable, Errors

*There* **vs.** *Their* **vs.** *They're*

**There = location, as in a place**

**Correct:** When Gertrude Stein said, "There is no there there," she was talking about Oakland.

**Incorrect:** It may have been Confucius who said that wherever you go, their you are.[43]

**Their = plural possessive**

**Correct:** Republicans seem alarmed because their presidential candidate is bat-shit crazy.

**Incorrect:** Even die hard Republicans say their not voting for the nominee.

**They're = They + are**

**Correct**: They're coming to take me away.

**Incorrect:** You can't get they're from here.

---

42   One of the downsides to trying to write a book in a coffee shop, but seriously, if your children are that selfish, isn't it at least partially your fault?

43   It may also have been Pigkiller in *The Adventures of Buckaroo Banzai Across the Eighth Dimension.*

*Hear* **vs.** *Here*

**Hear** = to receive sound
**Here** = a place
**Correct:** I hear you loud and clear.
**Incorrect:** Can you here me now?

*That* **vs.** *Which*

If you are truly hot for learning the term *restrictive clause*, again check out Grammar Girl. But here is the basic gist of *that* versus *which*. **That** is used to characterize a subject and can't be eliminated without changing the sentence. **Which** is also used to characterize a subject, but it can be eliminated without changing the sentence's overall meaning.

An even easier way to remember this is that *which* requires a comma, due to its nonrestrictive qualities.

**Correct:** *Orphan Black* is a clone show that I love.
**Also Correct:** *Orphan Black,* which I love, is a show about clones.
**Incorrect:** *Orphan Black* is a clone show which I love.

I should point out, too, that not every publication handles *that* vs. *which* in this way. Mary Norris, a *New Yorker* copy editor (I think her actual title is query proofreader or possibly Page OKer; the *New Yorker*'s elaborate copy editing process isn't entirely clear to me) and author of *Between You and Me: Confessions of a Comma Queen,* describes that publication's approach to *that* vs. *which* as "interpretative, not mechanical." Her Comma Queen videos are an excellent resource.

*Who* **vs.** *Whom*

**Use *who* for subjects and *whom* for objects.**
In sentences, subjects perform actions:
**Julia** (subject) **writes** (action) **the book** (object).
I can also rewrite that sentence with pronouns:

**I** (pronoun subject) **write** (action) **it** (direct object pronoun).

So here is *who* versus *whom* in action:

**Correct:** He's the man whom I love.

In this sentence, *I* (subject) am performing the action (love) and *he* is the object of my love. Therefore, *whom* is the correct choice.

**Correct:** That's the guy who cut me off in traffic.

In this case, *the guy* is the subject who performed the action (cut) to me (object). So *who* is the correct choice because it refers to the subject.

3. **Restructure sentences.**

*There are some sentences that sound boring. They are about the same length. They are similar in rhythm. They are a mystery. They are unavoidable.*

The sentences above demonstrate a common but easily fixable sentence structure dilemma in which sentence after sentence begins with a vague pronoun construction, such as "There are." If you are actually riveted by how these constructions work grammatically, Grammar Girl has a better explanation than I can pull together, but the long and short of it is that such sentences can usually be rewritten to avoid their vagueness (and blandness). The above also functions to demonstrate why one should edit to vary sentence length for the sake of rhythm.

**Passive vs. Active Sentences**

Like sentences with vague pronouns and similar lengths, sentences with passive construction can often start to be dull to read when they dominate a text. Active sentences make better use of a wide variety of verbs and are often, as a result, more content-rich.

Active sentences are those in which the subject of the sentence performs the action. In passive sentences, the action is performed on the subject.

**Active:** Julia ate a piece of chocolate cake the size of her face.

**Passive:** The gigantic piece of cake was eaten by Julia.

You can count on passive sentences using some form of the verb "to be," which contributes to the dullness of having too many of them in a row.

## Conciseness

An important part of the editing process is eliminating dead language. Dead language is my pretentious way of referring to unnecessary words that don't add to the meaning or beauty in a sentence or are clichéd. Conciseness does not have to mean short sentences; it means sentences that make the best use of language through elimination of unnecessary and wordy phrasing. Many (most?) writers and writing teachers also rail against the proliferation of adjectives and adverbs in writing. I say: Don't overuse either, but they are both parts of speech, so no need to ban them outright. Below I have both fabricated and edited a paragraph to demonstrate what writing edited for conciseness might look like:

~~What~~ The owners of the coffee shop ~~failed to~~ didn't realize ~~is that~~ their Internet connection was ~~pretty~~ slow and ~~that~~ sometimes ~~it~~ failed entirely. ~~to work at all.~~ One ~~of the~~ customers ~~attempted to even~~ tried—unsuccessfully—to complain to the City Council about the south side's sluggish connection, ~~Internet was on the south side of town but she couldn't get through to anyone. It turned out that~~ In fact, the Council already had an Internet-improvement plan ~~it hoped would improve the Internet~~, but ~~before they could make that plan become a reality, they~~ had to hold ~~some~~ public hearings prior to implementing. The City Council's plan ~~of the City Council~~ was published in the newspaper and ~~a lot of the~~ numerous public comments ~~had to do with the fact that~~ indicated Santa Fe residents ~~of Santa Fe~~ were worried

~~that~~ the Internet was a government mind-control conspiracy. ~~designed to take control of their brains.~~

**Fragments and Run-ons**

Sentence fragments are ones in which the subject fails to perform an action. So, in other words, they are not actually sentences. Run-on sentences include more than one complete sentence without any punctuation.

**Fragment:** The caffeine overload.

**Run-on:** Julia drank too much coffee too much coffee makes her jittery.

In the first case, poetic though it may be, "the caffeine overload" is not a sentence because it lacks an action (verb). Some writers use some fragments to nice poetic effect, but deliberate poetic effect is different from an error (usually).

In the second case, two different sentences are happening without any punctuation, creating a run-on. This can be fixed in a variety of ways, such as:

**Julia drank too much coffee. Too much coffee makes her jittery.**

**Julia drank too much coffee; too much coffee makes her jittery.**

**Julia drank too much coffee, and too much coffee makes her jittery.**

4. **Vanquish verb tense inconsistency.** OK, so this could have either been filed under grammar or sentences, but it's a big enough deal that I'm listing it by itself (and with a little bit of alliteration!). You can write in present tense or past tense (or, I suppose, any tense you want), but the main issue here is to be consistent. If the main action of your piece is written in present tense, then keep it there or risk confusing your readers. If verb tenses confuse you, you're not alone. Years ago, I suffered from

Past Perfect Problem Disorder myself. I am quasi-sure plenty of writers consider discourse about transitive verbs and gerunds one of the levels of hell Dante forgot to mention. No worries: You don't need to become a contestant on Verb Wars to use them correctly.

> **Correct**: I walked down the street to check the mail, carried it home, and threw away the junk flyers.
>
> **Correct:** I walked down the street to check the mail and, while walking, remembered a time when I had looked forward to receiving letters from friends.
>
> **Incorrect:** I walk down the street to check the mail, walked home, throw out the junk, cried, and then sing "Hungry Like the Wolf" to myself before I cooked lunch. "This tastes good," I said to myself. The phone rings. "Hello?" I say, forgetting I have caller ID.[44]

5. **Double-check facts.** Many years ago, a fellow reporter wrote a story about a few suspects who had been arrested for something (stealing a car? escaping from jail?). At any rate, in the caption for the suspects' photos, the reporter wrote something along the lines of "Find names for these clowns." The copy editor—beleaguered as he was—missed the note. If memory serves, the story ran with the caption.[45]

The point of this story, and countless ones like it, is this: Don't send a story through unless you are 100 percent confident the information you've included is accurate. If you're waiting on confirmation of a name spelling or any other factoid, indicate this in the text. The common copy editing mark for such

---

44　In addition to verb tense irregularity, this example also is insane.

45　Perhaps using an anecdote that my best efforts have failed to verify in a section on verifying facts is ill-conceived, but I did actually witness this and my memory is not entirely shot. Yet.

situations is TK, which means "to come."[46] You can also write TBD (To Be Determined) or I HAVEN'T FACT-CHECKED THIS YET, but TK is the publishing standard. Just be sure not to put unverifiable information into writing without some indication you've done so.

6. **Test transitions.** Transitions refer to connectivity between sentences and paragraphs. Some types of creative nonfiction—lyric writing, for example—are often less driven by logical progression. Other types, particularly writing that follows a more linear trajectory, may need clearer connections between sentences and paragraphs. If you are in a true state of confusion and can't tell, try creating a reverse outline of your story. Pulling out each element into an outline form can help to review the story's structure. You might also try a "cut-up test" (as described in chapter 6). In a cut-up test, take actual scissors and cut apart each paragraph of the story. Can you (or someone else if you have a willing victim) put these back together in a way that makes sense? You can also try this sentence by sentence, but I wouldn't recommend it for long stories unless you are truly a masochist.

7. **Read out loud.** I am sure a fascinating neurological reason explains why we miss mistakes when we read silently but catch them when reading aloud. If I were a *Washington Post Magazine* writer, I would research this extensively and write an article titled "Silent Subterfuge."[47] But I have enough empirical evidence to confidently state that reading your work aloud will help you not just catch mistakes, but make improvements to the

---

46    I believe this is because copy editor marks generally are ones that are intentionally designed to look like errors and not be accidentally ignored.

47    This digression brought to you by a *Washington Post* article I just read titled "Fatal Distraction," in which science was employed to discover why people accidentally leave their children in hot cars.

text. You might also ask a friend to read your piece to you. This is excruciating as an exercise but can be helpful. If reading to yourself is uncomfortable, read to someone else.

8. **Don't plagiarize.** As mentioned in the ethics chapter of this book, you can avoid plagiarizing by crediting others for their work. I am only being mildly sarcastic. We live in an info-overload society, and sometimes we forget where we've heard information or even that we've heard it all. For example, you'll notice I mention the Grammar Girl website repeatedly in this chapter. I'm not using its examples here or any direct quotation, but I am well aware of how often I've consulted the site over the years. I have no doubt it's influenced my own understanding of grammar and, moreover, I think it's an excellent resource.

Direct quotation should always have attribution. Mistakes happen (accidental plagiarism), but in some editorial contexts, intent isn't treated the way it might be in a court of law. And repeated instances of lack of attribution or accidental plagiarism can have devastating effects. Make sure to account for any information you use in your work.

9. **Eliminate repetition/avoid redundancy.** Did you see what I did there? I'm funny, right? Hilarious! What I mean by avoiding repetition is to look for it at the micro and macro levels. Have you used the verb *absquatulate* seven times in one essay? If so, first step away from the thesaurus, and then mix it up. At the macro level, be sure you haven't stated a point, a quote, or a sentence repeatedly. Or, if you have, be sure it is intentional and effective.

10. **Check for clarity.** Because I am both reductive and simplistic, I believe two main culprits bear responsibility for confusion in writing: (1) explanation through jargon, and (2) lack of explanation.

Read through your work. Does it have sections in which you allowed an expert's words to explain a technical matter? Are there places where you've failed to explain something small (an acronym, for example) or something large (New Mexico's priority rights system for water use)? Have you quoted people making statements you yourself don't understand? If you don't understand what someone is saying, chances are your readers (and your editor) won't either.

# STYLE

AP. MLA. APA. Chicago. Yes, style guides abound, and these are actually just the four most common ones, not the only ones. Style guides dictate rules for various and extensive usage, from names to punctuation to citations and so on. Many publications use AP—the *Associated Press Stylebook*—but have small in-house style guides that dictate minor variations to AP's rules. The *MLA Handbook* (from the Modern Language Association) is a standard usage guide for scholarly writing. Mastering a style guide is no easy task. Sometimes I tell despondent students the story of how I had to reformat my graduate school thesis three times due to MLA errors (this is supposed to be an inspirational story; I fear it is not).

I have the most experience with AP style and a workable mastery of its rules, but even the most devoted of copy editors find themselves checking specific rules as issues arise, and these rules are as ever changing as the culture that uses them. If you plan to write for a publication, ascertaining which style guide it uses and working to turn in style-appropriate copy is a noble and smart goal. If you are working in the newspaper or magazine business, a subscription to AP's online stylebook is an affordable investment, and creates access to its Ask the Editor archives as well as AP's Media Law Guide (you can also purchase access to AP-style quizzes to test yourself, which sounds more fun in my head than it does in this parenthetical comment).

I also recommend following AP on Twitter (@APStylebook), as it posts entertaining and informative updates from the world of usage. Just the other day, @APStylebook tweeted that one should lowercase words that derive from proper nouns but no longer depend on that noun for meaning, like french fries. Who knew?

MLA has an online style center, which is useful particularly for students and others who need to properly format academic papers and citations. APA (American Psychological Association) and *The Chicago Manual of Style* are the other two most prominent style guides (APA tends to be used for more social science papers; *Chicago* is popular for books and has been the primary reference for this book). Both have print and online versions.

## THOUGHTS ON PEDANTRY

Today on my morning walk, I listened to a *Slate* magazine *Culture Gabfest* podcast in which the panelists, all writers, discussed a recent *New York* magazine article on the overuse of adverbs (never say I don't know how to party). The conversation was interesting, as was the article—neither was pedantic—but both spurred a small panic attack.

*Oh God*, I thought. *I bet my manuscript is littered with adverbs, teeming with adjectives. I know I rely on semicolons too much. I'm an em-dash whore.*

I calmed down eventually and returned to work. Striving to understand basic grammar rules, working to improve one's writing, caring about diction, avoiding clichés—all of these, and many other noble goals, are part of caring about writing. For some writers, clean, clear prose comes naturally. For others, excessive attention must be paid. Refusing to heed basic strictures strikes me as arrogant and self-defeating. Writing pedants make me think of Ralph Waldo Emerson's quote: "A foolish consistency is the hobgoblin of little minds."

And nobody likes that.

## CRITIQUE AND REVISION

My least favorite type of editor, before I was an editor, was someone who could tell me a piece wasn't working but couldn't pinpoint why. In writing workshops, I try to emphasize evaluation of individual elements of writing—the craft elements of creative nonfiction—rather than the subjective response of readers as a basis for revision work.

Learning to read one's work (and others') with an eye toward evaluating individual elements has the potential not just to allow a writer to improve the work—obviously the ultimate goal—but also provides multiple re-entry points into writing. Re-entry into writing is another way of saying "revision."

When you're not certain if a piece is finished, or if it's ready to be sent out, or when it's been rejected a few times for no stated reasons, the elements of critique can help you re-enter the writing from a different angle. For larger writing groups, such as workshops, written critique that evaluates not just the whole but the pieces can provide structured feedback for the writer.

In classes, I have found that structured critiques cut down on sloppy feedback of the "I loved this" variety. Writers should also be smart readers who understand why and where a piece of writing succeeds, and why and where it has failed. I am not trying to be reductive and suggest that writing never works for magical reasons or that rules can't be broken (wow, a triple negative. I'm leaving it; Strunk and White, be damned). On the other hand, magic and broken rules are probably not what you're after if you're using a craft book on writing or seeking formal critique.

What follows are four main critique sheets I have used for memoir, reported personal essays, journalistic writing, and lyric essays in a variety of courses I have taught. They obviously are not exhaustive (despite what some former students may think), and, in some cases, my choice to focus on some elements for one type of writing and not another is mostly a case of false taxonomies born out of pragmatism.[48] Feel free to modify and/or mix-and-match as suits your own writing and teaching needs.

Although I developed these critique sheets for specific courses, some of the thinking behind them grew out of reading and teaching from Janet Burroway's craft book *Writing Fiction*, as well as *Creative Nonfiction* Editor Lee Gutkind's essay "The Five R's of Creative Nonfiction."

---

48    i.e. I have to grade these and generally, in my classes, students will end up writing all four types of writing and using all four critique sheets, so I don't make any single critique sheet exhaustive for their sake. And mine.

# MEMOIR REVISION CRITIQUE

1. **Description and Detail:** Identify specific places in the piece in which the writer provides significant detail and description, such as visual description, sound or smell. Identify potential areas to expand this type of detail.

2. **Scene vs. Summary:** Does the piece include the immediate action of scene in real time? Are there places that could be more developed and use less exposition? Provide specific examples.

3. **Characterization/People:** Does the piece make use of direct and indirect characterization? Provide specific examples of where these are used successfully and suggestions for expansion. Be specific. Are there people without faces? Are all the conversations summarized?

4. **Voice:** How would you describe the voice of this piece in one word? Provide examples of places in the text that exemplify this voice. Provide examples of places where voice falters or could be enhanced. **Pro tip:** Please do not say "The voice sounds just like (fill in the name of the writer)." This is not helpful unless the writer is 100 percent clear on how you perceive his or her voice.

5. **Reflection/Interpretation:** How would you describe the point of the piece? Does it have thematic resonance? Are there places in the text that could be strengthened and expanded for these elements?

# REPORTED / PERSONAL
# ESSAY CRITIQUE

1. Discuss the relationship between the personal and reported elements of this essay, including any areas that require more development or information. In other words, how do the internal and external elements work together or not work together?

2. Which element of creative nonfiction technique is the most developed in this piece? Please provide at least two examples with specific citation from the text for each.

3. Which element of creative nonfiction technique is the least developed? Please provide at least two suggestions for how this element could be further developed.

4. What would you say is the theme of this essay, and how might the theme be further developed?

5. What reported information in this piece is either unclear or incomplete? If able, provide suggestions for the author to expand the reportage.

# JOURNALISTIC WRITING CRITIQUE

1. What type of lede does this story have? Provide one suggestion, based on the story, for an alternative beginning.

2. What is the point of this story—not just what happens, but what is its purpose?

3. Identify direct quotes that convey emotion and opinion. Identify those that would be better as summarized/paraphrased information.

4. Identify opportunities for greater physical description of people, places, or objects.

5. Identify any information that is incomplete or confusing.

6. Who are the important people in this story? Are they fully identified, and are there opportunities to develop their characters more?

7. How is this piece organized? Chronologically, or otherwise? Does the overall structure make sense? Are there places in which the transitions could be strengthened?

# LYRIC ESSAY CRITIQUE

1. What form is this lyric essay—flash, hermit, prose poem, other? How does the form of this work with the content? This portion of the critique should, in other words, consider and discuss structure specifically, both in and of itself, but also as it relates to the whole and the parts.

2. **Association:** What is this piece concerned with, and where in the text do you find these associations? In other words, what information, ideas, emotions, narratives exist?

3. **Lyricism:** Identify lyric elements in the writing, but also include any observations about the language of the piece.

4. **Response:** What other observations can you offer on this piece, either about its content, its device, its execution, or its use of creative nonfiction craft elements?

# EDITING CHECKLIST

1. Check spelling
2. Police grammar
3. Restructure sentences
4. Vanquish verb tense inconsistency
5. Double-check facts
6. Test transitions
7. Read out loud
8. Don't plagiarize
9. Eliminate repetition
10. Check for clarity

## READING AND RESOURCES
## FROM THIS CHAPTER

"After Deadline: Newsroom Notes on Usage and Style." *New York Times*. http://afterdeadline.blogs.nytimes.com.

Burroway, Janet, Elizabeth Stuckey-French, and Ned Stuckey-French. *Writing Fiction: A Guide to Narrative Craft*. New York: Pearson Longman, 2009.

*Chicago Manual of Style: 16th Edition*. Chicago: University of Chicago Press, 2010. http://www.chicagomanualofstyle.org.

Cox, Christopher. "Ann Beattie. The Art of Fiction." *Paris Review*, Spring 2011. http://www.theparisreview.org/interviews/6070/the-art-of-fiction-no-209-ann-beattie.

*Culture Gabfest*. Podcast. *Slate*, May 25, 2016. http://www.slate.com/articles/podcasts/culturegabfest/2016/05/slate_s_culture_gabfest_on_neighbors_2_amc_s_preacher_and_a_look_at_christian.html.

Emerson, Ralph Waldo. *Self-Reliance and Other Essays*. New York: Dover Publications, 2012.

Fogarty, Mignon. *Grammar Girl*. http://www.quickanddirtytips.com/grammar-girl.

Gordon, Karen E. *The Deluxe Transitive Vampire: The Ultimate Handbook of Grammar for the Innocent, the Eager, and the Doomed*. New York: Pantheon, 1993.

Gutkind, Lee. "The Five Rs of Creative Nonfiction." *Creative Nonfiction*, 1996. https://www.creativenonfiction.org/online-reading/whats-story-6.

Heisel, Andrew. "Stop Shaming People on the Internet for Grammar Mistakes. Its Not There Fault." *Washington Post*, April 17, 2015. https://www.washingtonpost.com/ posteverything/wp/2015/04/17/stop-shaming-people-on-the-internet-for-grammar-mistakes-its-not-there-fault.

Lorentzen, Christian. **"Could We Just Lose the Adverb (Already)?"** *Vulture*, May 18, 2006. http://www.vulture.com/2016/05/could-we-just-lose-the-adverb-already.html.

McCrum, Robert. "George Orwell's Critique of Internet English." *Guardian*, May 20, 2013. http://www.theguardian.com/books/booksblog/2013/ may/20/george-orwell-internet-english-robert-mccrum.

Minthorn, David, Sally Jacobsen, and Paula Froke. *Associated Press Stylebook 2015 and Briefing on Media Law*. New York: Basic Books, 2015. https://www.apstylebook.com.

*MLA Handbook for Writers of Research Papers*. New York: The Modern Language Association of America, 2015. https://style.mla.org.

Norris, Mary. *Between You and Me: Confessions of a Comma Queen*. New York: W. W. Norton, 2015. http://video.newyorker.com/series/comma-queen.

*Publication Manual of the American Psychological Association*. Washington, DC: American Psychological Association, 2010. http://www.apastyle.org/.

Strunk, William, and E. B. White. *The Elements of Style*. New York: Macmillan, 1959.

# CHAPTER TEN

# Future Casting

> Despite every advancement, language remains the defining nexus of our humanity; it is where our knowledge and hope lie.
>
> —**Andrew Solomon,** "The Middle of Things: Advice for Young Writers"

> From the beginnings of human civilization until 2003, five exabytes of data were created. We are now creating five exabytes every two days. In fact, in the minute it's taken you to read this far, 2.8 million pieces of content were shared on Facebook alone. 250,000 new photos were posted on Instagram.[49]
>
> —**Amy Webb,** "Novelty is the New Normal"

THERE COMES A time in every woman's life where she will find herself in New Delhi, India, standing at a podium at the front of a very long room, staring at a packed audience of Indian journalists and educators who appear to be listening as she speaks lengthily about . . . news games.

---

49   According to Google, an exabyte is "a unit of information equal to one quintillion (10$^{18}$) bytes, or one billion gigabytes." So, like, a lot.

OK, this is probably not a universal experience. It was, however, where I found myself in November 2014. I had traveled to New Delhi, through the international teaching program at my school, to run student journalism and online magazine workshops for one week. These workshops were, as they say, in my wheelhouse: I conducted interview training writing exercises, and then led the students through building blogs with WordPress.

It was my third international trip of this sort, but the extreme travel of visiting India for a week, and teaching for thirty hours, coupled with the jet lag, had cast the entire experience into a surreal haze (not to be confused with the actual haze, which was the air quality).

In addition to teaching classes every day, I had been scheduled to speak publicly as part of Pearl Academy's lecture series on "What's Next." Possibly because of the jet lag (or possibly because no one had actually told me what was going on), I ended up googling the event. From the Internet I learned: "The event will witness the esteemed presence of Julia Goldberg, Transmedia Journalist, who will be conducting a workshop on 'Media Convergence,'" and went on to explain that my talk would cover "the disruption of traditional media models, the convergence of old media with new technologies, the current challenges faced by media practitioners and educators, as well as some of the current and forecasted innovations and trends under consideration."[50]

This sounded like an alarming array of topics for one person to cover in forty-five minutes, but ever the people pleaser, I plunged into sweaty panicked preparation mode and, when the time came, stood at the head of that very long room, staring into an audience filled with the some of the best-dressed people I had ever seen, and started talking.

---

50    http://www.buzzintown.com/delhi/events/whats-next-session-transmedia-journalist-julia/id--951633.html

*This photo is mostly included to prove that,*
*as stated twice, the room was indeed freakishly long.*

What I had wanted was to emulate David Carr, whom I had
heard speak numerous times over the years at conferences held
by the national Association of Alternative Newsmedia (formerly known as the Association of Alternative Newsweeklies),
on whose board I had served. As I wrote in a piece after Carr's
death, "What I always took away from his talks was not a specific mandate for a particular approach to journalism, but rather
a sense of mission to do more and to do more better. This was
particularly needed during the strange early portion of the
'Here Comes Everybody' decade, when the call to convergence
journalism often felt less like a rallying cry to forge ahead and
more like a warning to go hide under the bed. No matter what
he was talking about, David Carr always seemed to be having
a good time, to prize journalism no matter what form, and his
unceasing good will toward the profession was contagious."

And so I plunged in, discussing news gaming (Why? Why was I so intent on discussing the gamification of news? I don't even play video games. Why?), other interactives, virtual reality, cross-platform collaborations, mobile technology, wearable technology, and on and on and on. One of my many theses in this ramble was that the future would be filled with #failure, as #failure is an inevitable outcome of our current media climate. I think I thought that was an uplifting notion—#failure at least being a sign of having tried—but I'm not sure I succeeded in conveying the message (#failure).

And then, when I had finally stopped, I took questions. And the only question that I remember—it may have been the first question—was:

"So, is print dead?"

I would argue that some variation of this question has been at the core of every word written or spoken about the future of journalism, the future of books, the future of every aspect of communication for now more than a decade. In 2006, I was part of a Pew Research Center roundtable of alternative newsweekly people on the "future of the news media."

One of the questions was, "How much confidence do you have that traditional mainstream media organizations will survive and thrive in the transition to the Internet?"

My answer, in part:

"The Internet is a platform; it's a technology, just as the printing press was a technology. There still need to be creative people with vision behind it."

I'm not sure my printing press / Internet comparison is holding up very well, but I obviously still believe "creative people with vision" are always going to be a key factor in any creative endeavor, regardless of medium.

Oh me and my rose-colored glasses!

Believing in the value of creative acts is all fine and well, but not quite on point when thinking about the business side of it all.

So, yes, print journalism has obviously suffered, and continues to suffer, substantial losses. Pew's State of the News Media 2015 report digs into these numbers extensively, but in short: circulations fell; revenues fell; workforce numbers fell (though not as much as they had in previous years). Perhaps more to the point, a May 26, 2016, report from Pew revealed 62 percent of Americans acquire their news from social media.

I was a newspaper editor during the print-to-digital era, and I saw firsthand the budget cuts, the layoffs, the "do more with less" mantra. The only *Jeopardy!* topic I ever answered correctly was one that required naming newspapers that had closed, and instead of feeling pleased with myself, I burst into tears (such a drama queen). Book publishing has changed dramatically as well, of course, although the news from this front is a bit less nihilistic (and less prolific; the news media seems to like reporting on its own demise more than that of other industries). In 2013, *Wired*'s article "Book Publishers Scramble to Rewrite Their Future" proclaimed that "after centuries in which books and the process of publishing them barely changed, the digital revolution has thrown the entire business up for grabs." But just two years later, the *New York Times*, looking at data from the Association of American Publishers (AAP), had a more optimistic viewpoint in its article "The Plot Twist: E-Book Sales Slip, and Print Is Far From Dead," which notes that despite the dire predictions:

"The digital apocalypse never arrived, or at least not on schedule. While analysts once predicted that e-books would overtake print by 2015, digital sales have instead slowed sharply."

There's no question that the barrier to entry into publishing has fundamentally changed. On the bright side, the diminished role of traditional gatekeepers means more diverse voices, more collaborative undertakings, more interactivity. The downsides of expanded opportunities for publishing, aside from the hemorrhaging of jobs and proliferation of unpaid and low-paying jobs, include political echo chambers, virulent trolling, and what my friend (and former *Santa Fe Reporter* staff writer) journalist Corey Pein describes in his *Baffler* article, "Amway Journalism," as "a toxic concoction of marketing-seminar bluff and hypnotic technobabble."

Pein's 2017 book with Metropolitan Books will be looking, in part, at the problematic bed-fellowship between journalism and technology companies, what he described to me as the "irreconcilable differences" between the sectors. In the major technology companies, he notes, "There's no culture of journalistic values at the tops of these organizations; it's a very ruthless capitalist ideology that does not really allow for concept of a civic good, which as bad as some of the old time newspaper proprietors could be, tended to be there."

Those possibly unholy partnerships, though, don't mean that the emerging and still-to-emerge tools for storytelling won't lead to exciting and interesting endeavors.

"I don't want to be discouraging to young people who are just starting out as writers or journalists," Pein says. "I see them doing a lot of creative things with the only tools they have available, which in some ways are greater than when I started out."

Pein is only thirty-four years old. And though I am a little bit older (ahem), he and I both share the experience of straddling the digital divide, of working in journalism as a print-only medium before the so-called digital revolution. Pein noted to me that in some ways, the experimentation of today is reminiscent of the way in which alternative newsweekly culture began in the 1970s, "completely unprofessional and completely unlucrative."

What will last? This chapter is called "Future Casting," which I'm pretty sure means determining what is going to happen based on what has happened or is happening now.

What has happened? The Internet has fundamentally changed the publishing environment across all sectors.

What is happening? Lots of stuff; some of it online, some of it not. Some of it awesome; some, not so much.

Awesome: Wandering around the Association of Writers and Writing Programs' Bookfair, where more than eight hundred exhibitors display literary print magazines, literary online magazines, small presses, independent presses, big presses.

Less awesome: I don't want to name names, so let's just say "clickbait" culture has proven mostly anathema to civilized discourse, not to mention presidential elections, and leave it at that.

For all that, I enjoy reading about and playing around with new technologies. When I was asked (ordered) in 2002 to "start blogging," I dutifully, if sulkily, futzed around with HTML and started blogging. Ditto when it came time to start making videos, then interactives. I went to Twitter workshops. We CoveritLived, we Storified (Spell Check doesn't think I am writing words anymore; it may be correct). Some of the rewards of this convergence work included awards for the paper—and awards for work created with scant know-how and scanter resources are particularly rewarding because they're acknowledgment for the ideas and talent the writers and reporters and designers I worked with brought to the projects, not just the technology itself.

What's happening now? At AWP's 2016 book fair, the *New York Times* had a virtual-reality demonstration, which allowed me to try out the Google Cardboard viewer (and really enjoy that it's made out of cardboard). "Immersion" storytelling may turn out to be a nonstarter, but the *NYT* version of it—I believe—is founded on the principles of storytelling, not gimmicks. "The Displaced" tells the stories of three of the thirty million worldwide child refugees. In a NiemanLab interview, *Times* editor Sam Dolnick said that while the *Times* has "written hundreds of stories about the refugee crisis," what we kept hearing from people was that they had become somewhat inured to it. But with this new medium, they were making eye contact with these kids, and it shocked them in a profound way. Less enticing, in my opinion, is the emergence of "chat bots," formula-driven interactive "conversations" via text messaging, with which a variety of news and other organizations have been experimenting. A Nieman report on the topic notes, "Looking to the future, you can imagine an AI-based chat bot that truly comprehends intention behind language, a bot that you can have long-term discussions with about the news the way you would with a well-informed friend."

Maybe I've seen *The Matrix* one too many times, but does this really sound like good news? (On a lighter note, writer Kyle Chayka took aim at chat bots in his interactive text piece for *Mel* magazine by creating an "essay bot," that interrogated the user with questions.)

Predictions abound. Every year, the NiemanLab rounds up journalism predictions for the next year. These are pretty entertaining. Some are actual predictions; some seem more like a wish-fulfillment strategy. They range topically from technology to staffing to revenue models. Obviously, only time will tell.

In a June 1, 2016, *Fast Company* interview about his new book, *But What If We're Wrong?: Thinking About the Present as If It Were the Past,* Chuck Klosterman discusses the book's interrogation of contemporary certitude and the futility of predicting anything.

Nonetheless, in the book's introduction, Klosterman writes that given the longevity of the term *book*, "It seems impossible that we'll ever stop using that term, even if the future equivalent of a 'book' becomes a packet of granulized data that is mechanically injected directly into the cerebral cortex." He goes on to write, "It's possible that no one will buy (or read) books in some remote future, but we can (tentatively) assume that people of that era will at least know what 'books' are: They are the collected units containing whatever writers write. So even though future writers might not be producing anything resembling present-day books, that's still how society will refer to whatever works they are producing."

Perhaps you noticed, as I did, that the one unquestioned premise in Klosterman's quote is that no matter what the future brings, writers will be writing.

Works for me.

# READING AND RESOURCES FROM THIS CHAPTER

Alter, Alexandra. "The Plot Twist: E-Book Sales Slip, and Print Is Far From Dead." *New York Times*, September 22, 2015. http://www.nytimes.com/2015/09/23/business/media/the-plot-twist-e-book-sales-slip-and-print-is-far-from-dead.html.

Bilton, Ricardo. "The New York Times is Trying to Make VR Films That Aren't One-Offs, and That Keep Readers Coming Back." *NiemanLab*, May 6, 2016. http://www.niemanlab.org/2016/05/the-new-york-times-is-trying-to-make-vr-films-that-arent-one-offs-and-that-keep-readers-coming-back.

Goldberg, Julia. "Back to the Future." *Santa Fe Reporter*, June 24, 2014. http://www.sfreporter.com/santafe/article-8838-back-to-the-future.html.

——. "The Cult of Carr: 'We Are Legion.'" *Santa Fe Reporter*, February 13, 2015. http://www.sfreporter.com/santafe/article-9948-the-cult-of-carr-we-are-legion.html.

Gottfried, Jeffrey, and Elisa Shearer. "News Use Across Social Media Platforms 2016." *Pew Research Center*, May 26, 2016. http://www.journalism.org/2016/05/26/news-use-across-social-media-platforms-2016.

Hughes, Evan. "Book Publishers Scramble to Rewrite Their Future." *Wired*, March 19, 2013. http://www.wired.com/2013/03/publishing-industry-next-chapter.

Jordan, Maya Baratz. "The Medium is The (Text) Message." *Nieman Reports*, April 13, 2016. http://niemanreports.org/articles/the-medium-is-the-text-message.

Pein, Corey. "Amway Journalism." *Baffler*, July 28, 2014. http://
    thebaffler.com/blog/amway-journalism.

——. coreypein.net.

Pew Research Center: Journalism & Media Staff. "Alternative
    Weeklies in Transition." *Pew Research Center*, August
    28, 2006. http://www.journalism.org/2006/08/28/
    alternative-weeklies-in-transistion.

——. "State of the News Media 2015." *Pew Research Center*,
    April 29, 2015. http://www.journalism.org/2015/04/29/
    state-of-the-news-media-2015.

"Predictions for Journalism 2016." *NiemanLab*. http://www.
    niemanlab.org/collection/predictions-2016.

Solomon, Andrew. "The Middle of Things: Advice
    for Young Writers." *New Yorker*, March 11, 2015.
    http://www.newyorker.com/books/page-turner/
    the-middle-of-things-advice-for-young-writers.

Wang, Shan. "'An Essay in Bot Form': Text with This Basic Bot
    to Read about (and Discuss) the Bot Boom." *NiemanLab*,
    May 13, 2016. http://www.niemanlab.org/2016/05/an-es-
    say-in-bot-form-text-with-this-basic-text-bot-to-read-about-
    and-discuss-the-bot-boom.

Webb, Amy. "Novelty is the New Normal." *NiemanLab*,
    2016. http://www.niemanlab.org/2015/12/
    novelty-is-the-new-normal.

# Acknowledgments

I FEAR I am bound to forget someone whose help was crucial in this book, so apologies ahead of time.

Thanks, indeed, to the many writers and journalists who took time to talk to me directly for this book and/or allowed me use of their work: Emily Rapp Black, Jimmy Boegle, Chelsey Clammer, Matt Donovan, Dan Frosch, Jon Frosch, Julie Ann Grimm, Billy Jensen, Enrique Limón, David Stuart MacLean, Rubén Martínez, Vanessa Martinez, Rani Molla, Laura Paskus, Corey Pein, James Reich, Jim Ruland, Mike Sager, Peter St. Cyr, Robert Wilder, Mark Zusman, and Anne Valente.

I am indebted (not literally, fortunately) to Mark Zusman and Richard Meeker, owners of the *Santa Fe Reporter*, for my close to fifteen years at the *Reporter*, nearly eleven as editor—a professional experience that shaped my entire adult life (so far) and for which I am grateful. I worked with many talented people over the years at the *Reporter*, some of whom are in this book and all of whom helped shape it in one way or another. Special thanks to Zane Fischer for help with this book and along the way.

Thanks as well to my many friends from the Association of Alternative Newsmedia (aan.org), and to AAN itself for allowing me to serve on its board and help with its programming.

Special shout-outs to Jason Zaragoza, Richard Karp, and Patricia Calhoun, who were especially generous with their time and friendship during my AAN days.

Thanks to Scott Hutton, Honey Harris, and Hutton Broadcasting for initiating my adventures in radio, and to the gazillion guests who came on for live interviews.

In memoriam, thanks to Bob Trapp, founder of the *Rio Grande Sun*, for providing me with basic journalism building blocks, and a whole lot of shoe-leather experience.

Andy Dudzik planted the idea for this book and was incredibly patient waiting for it. It would not exist without him and Sarah Stark at Leaf Storm Press.

I am extremely lucky to have amazing colleagues at Santa Fe University of Art and Design, whose own work inspires me and whose support at my own endeavors is fairly astonishing. Thank you Matt Donovan, Dana Levin, Tony O'Brien, James Reich, and Anne Valente.

Teaching, my second career, has been inspiring, challenging, and sometimes super weird. Thanks to Miriam Sagan for pulling me in, and thanks to so many students whose work and questions helped inform this book.

I have been inspired and taught by the writers I have the privilege to read and teach—too many to list, but if they are mentioned in this book, they have my gratitude as well.

My friends are awesomely supportive, especially Andy Primm, Cat Davis, Geet Jacobs, Mikey Baker, Samia van Hattum, and Sonya Hymer.

And thanks to my husband Mike, for all the dinners, patience, confidence, love, and a bunch of other stuff I'm probably forgetting. This book was created while listening to David Bowie in a facility including nuts, sugar, and occasional glasses of bourbon. No animals were harmed in its creation, although the cat seemed bored at times.

# Index